Thule and the Third Reich

Perry Pierik (red.)

Thule and the Third Reich
The genesis of National Socialism

Aspekt Publishers

Thule and the Third Reich

© 2023 ASPEKT Publishers
© Introduction Perry Pierik (red.)
© Translation: Evert van Leerdam

Amersfoortsestraat 27, 3769 AD Soesterberg, The Netherlands
info@uitgeverijaspekt.nl - http://www.uitgeverijaspekt.nl

Translation: Evert van Leerdam
Editor: Isabel Oomen

ISBN: 9789464870114
NUR: 680

All rights reserved. No part of this publication may be reproduced, stored in a retrieval system or transmitted in any form or by any means, electronic, mechanical, photocopying, recording or otherwise, without the prior permission of the publisher.

Table of contents:

Perry Pierik: Why this book   7

Perry Pierik: Introduction   12

Perry Pierik: On anti-Semitism in the work of   33
Von Sebottendorff

Documents from the early days of the   37
National Socialist movement.

Why this book?

In the historiography surrounding Hitler's Third Reich, the shadowy early period is often an underexposed theme. Not for nothing did historians from the former Soviet Union and the Eastern Bloc get annoyed that many Western historians present Hitler as a kind of 'business accident', a by-product of nationalism and imperialism. In turn, communist historians were blind in one eye and placed the rise of the Hitler movement in purely socio-economic frameworks. Hitler himself was quite selective in what he wanted to say about the origins of National Socialism and his own role in it. For that reason, the Allies, at the time, were very interested in what renegades from the Nazi camp had to say. For instance, in his Hitler Report: *The Mind of Adolf Hitler*, which he wrote for his OSS boss 'Wild Bill' Donovan, Walter C. Langer of the US intelligence agency OSS (*Office of Strategic Services*) paid a lot of attention to the testimonies of Otto Strasser, the brother of Gregor Strasser; the politician, fellow fighter and later rival of Hitler, who was assassinated in the 'Night of the Long Knives' in 1934. US intelligence was looking for the origin of the 'riddle' Hitler and for the '*film noir*' secrets from his past, which it could possibly use as a response to Joseph Goebbels' German propaganda machine. People were looking for '*inside*' information. However, historians were interested in the person behind the myth as well. The myth-making around Hitler, the successfully introduced *Führer cult*, has long supplanted the image of the human Hitler. Hitler himself was also careful not to have any precursors. Influential figures were often relegated to the background, gagged and sometimes even assasinated.

Bevor Hitler kam, the book that we bring here in full translation by Evert van Leerdam, shows what lay behind the stylised reality. It shows Hitler's role in the early days of the NSDAP, and even before that, when Hitler was still in military service and, as his commander described it, 'looked like a wet poodle looking for a boss'. It is the story of Hitler's discovery and a description of the forces that propelled Hitler into politics. Central to this is the role of the Thule Society, a secretive organisation that championed '*Deutschtum*' and ariosophy (the doctrine that assumed the Aryans had a special role to play as a creative force in history; a doctrine that soon evolved into the idea of the '*Übermensch*' versus the '*Untermensch*'). The leader of this Munich-based society was the equally mysterious and avuncular Rudolf von Sebottendorff.

The importance of this book can be summed up in a few key terms:

> It shows the environment in which someone like Hitler could become great: amid reactionary military and radical ariosophists, all unadulterated nationalists who dwelt on a mystical approach to '*Deutschtum*' and firmly believed in the pioneering role Germany should play in the world.

Bevor Hitler kam is a 'banned book'. Hitler, once he had made a career, wanted nothing to do with the exclusive Thule society that had produced him. Hitler styled himself as a curious mixture of worker ('I have stood among you') and leader sent directly by God (*Führer*). In this respect, the book offers a unique insight into the very beginning of the 'Hitler movement'.

Hitler's thoughts were already manifest within the Thule Society, including a deep-rooted anti-Semitism. These thoughts were mainly spread by a newspaper from which the *Völkischer Beobachter* would later emerge, the organ of the NSDAP. Members of the Thule Society founded the DAP (*Deutsche Arbeiter Partei*) to prevent German workers from sympathising with communism. The NSDAP emerged from this party. The swastika, the symbol of the Thule Society, was adopted by the Nazis. Prominent Thule members and guests became leading members of the Nazi movement, such as Hitler's deputy Rudolf Hess, party ideologue Alfred Rosenberg, and Dietrich Eckart, the man to whom Hitler would dedicate *Mein Kampf*.

Furthermore, the book shows how direct the contact was between the military and the Thule Society. In both camps, people were very frustrated regarding the lost World War and feared communist domination. The German army had been shortened to 100,000 men after the war as a result of the Treaty of Versailles. The Thule members found the policy of the Weimar government, which cooperated in this treaty (*Erfüllungspolitik),* extremely reprehensible. It was, after discovering his oratorical talents, at the request of the

Thule Society that Hitler was discharged from military service, so that he could make himself available for their political purposcs.

It was the military who agreed to it. In addition, the relationship between the Thule Society and the military leaders is further highlighted by the fact, that after the defeat of the Raden Republic, General Ritter Von Epp established his headquarters in the same premises as the Thule Society, namely at *the Hotel Vierjahreszeiten* in Munic.

Finally, the book is important because it shows that the rise of the Hitler movement had metahistorical roots. Anti-Semitism in these circles had a much more radical form than the 'bourgeois' anti-Semitism of the *belle époque*. The Thule Society was part of the world of Theodor Fritsch's *Germanenbund* and the Hammer or- ganisations, in which people believed in a Jewish world conspiracy as described in the *Protocols of Zion*. Moreover, they propagated this thought. By occupying themselves with pseudo-sciences such as runic science, ariosophy and racial science as well as a perverted folklorism - in short, with everything that is so concisely summarised with the term *Blut und Boden* - the monster had been created within the Thule Society that would provide the spiritual fuel for the later Holocaust. Theodor Fritsch (1852 - 1933) himself was honoured with a monument unveiled in Zehlendorf on 7 September 1935. It depicted the 'Aryan' Fritsch shattering a dragon-like figure meant to represent a 'Jew' with a hammer. This first, openly anti-Semitic monument was installed on the initiative of the very early NSDAP member Walter Helfenstein and crafted by sculptor Arthur Wellmann.

Some more details about the book that are of interest: Von Sebottendorff, like Julius Caesar, wrote his book in the third person. This sometimes feels a bit schizophrenic. The reader should not forget that the book was also conceived as a vindication of Von Sebottendorff's own role in history. Von Sebottendorff was not interested in objective historiography, but in establishing his own role in it. Yet in the latter regard, there was a certain reluctance on his part. The fact that no photographs of him exist also indicates that this man always operated from the wings.

As for the text, it is translated in full from German. The register added by Von Sebottendorff to his text is only partially reproduced. We have used and supplemented the persons and cases mentioned therein insofar as the facts mentioned were historically justified. Negative stereotypes have been omitted. Those who want to check the original time- and ideology- based descriptions as far as the register is concerned, we refer to the various websites that have the original German text of the book *Bevor Hitler kam* available. As the book has a detailed register, as well as an introduction outlining the political context, the editors have refrained from further annotation.

Perry Pierik

Introduction

For a long time, there has been a debate about how far Hitler was 'catapulted' into politics. Was Hitler a plaything of big business, as the communists often claimed, or was he the product of a long, unified political struggle in which chance and circumstance gave him a helping hand? In addition to these two views, there is a third vision, namely that Hitler and the NSDAP were not so much put forward by big business, although there were certainly money lenders, but by a secret society: the so-called Thule Society (*Thule Gesellschaft*), led by the mysterious leader with the equally mysterious name: Rudolf von Sebottendorff. This third vision regarding Hitler's career has long been neglected for various reasons. From the Marxist perspective, economic processes always took centre stage and there was little regard for occult- looking groups working from the wings. For others, there was simply a lack of understanding that the utterly irrati- onal ideas of the Thule Society and other affiliated groups would have had real political influence. After all, was Hitler, especially early in his career, not an extremely cool and calculating politician who was often too cunning for his opponents? The fact that Hitler intelligently operated and showed raison d'etre accordingly does not take away from the fact that behind all those rational decisions there were sinister and utterly amoral and irrational motives, which would confront the world with an endless series of campaigns and the extermination of European Jews. Another reason why the Thule Society was able to operate 'in silence' for a long time had to do directly with the Nazis themselves. Once established within politics, Hitler got rid of his teachers one by one: geopoliticologist Karl Haushofer (the man of *Lebensraum* and *Heim ins Reich*) disappeared in Dachau concentration camp, ariosopher Jörg Lanz von Liebenfels was banned from publication, runic cultist Guido von List was ignored, Father Bernhard Stempfle who was involved in the creation of *Mein Kampf* was murdered, Karl Maria Wiligut (Weisthor), 'specialist' in the field of *Ahnenerbe,* was sidetracked, grail scientist Otto Rahn committed suicide, First World War promoter and competitor Erich Ludendorff was gagged - his organisations (o.a. the *Tannenbergerbund*) were banned - and the journalist/poet and arch-antisemite Dietrich Eckart died 'in time'. And Sebottendorff? He was expelled from the party, muzzled and shown out. In any case, crossed out - 'erased' as Hitler used to say - from history. However, his book *Bevor Hitler kam* was his legacy to the world. A legacy which, incidentally, irked Hitler. Therefore, the book was banned. The idea behind this was as logical as it was morbid: someone as 'divine and genius' as the *Führer* could obviously not have predecessors. At its core, this was the message that was successfully repeated continuously by propaganda minister Joseph Goebbels until no one asked any more questions.

On the question of the relevance of the third vision, it is important to underline that the influence of ariosophy, which the Thule Society advocated, namely the belief in a leading and active role of the 'Aryan' (*Tatmensch*), provided fertile ground for the ideas of Hitler and the Nazis. Furthermore, there were very concrete influences that rightly claim a place for the Thule Society in the historiography. After all, it was the Society that, in the stormy days after the collapse of the Wilhelminian empire in November 1918, wanted to 'save' German workers from communism; and it was also the Thule Society that founded the DAP, the *Deutsche Arbeiter* Partei, from which the NSDAP would later emerge. It was the reactionary military and among them, who oversaw and made it possible for Hitler to be discharged from military service after they discovered him as an orator. This cleared the way for Hitler to begin his political career. The party's organ, the *Völkischer Beobachter*, was originally owned by the Thule Society. Sebottendorff himself had added this newspaper to the Thule Society out of political conviction. These facts are harsher than anything communist historians have ever been able to assemble around the 'big money theory'. All the more reason, therefore, to dwell on this mysterious organisation and its leader and to publish a translation of his book *Bevor Hitler kam*. However, this book does not take a stand on the question whether this third vision - if one should call it that - was indeed a co-determining factor in the successful start of the Hitler movement. Nor is it an attempt to unravel the history of the mysterious Thule Society in detail, nor to write a biography of Rudolf von Sebottendorff. It does, however, call attention to this mostly forgotten facet of the important early period of National Socialism, the Genesis.

By way of introduction, we would like to dwell on a few issues:
Where did the Thule Society come from, and what did the thinking consist of?
Who was Rudolf von Sebottendorff?
What was the political influence of the Thule Society?

The origins of the Thule Society are anchored in a widely held and prevailing cultural pessimism in the 19th century that went hand in hand with the glorification and perversion of romanticism. This cultural pessimism was sceptical of the emerging modernism with its urbanisation, emancipation movements of women and minorities (Jews), socialism, communism and anarchism, and opposed western capitalism, democracy and imperialism which was considered a 'plutocracy'. Nowadays, the best- known exponent of cultural pessimism is often cited as the German historian and cultural historian Oswald Spengler (1880 - 1936), who openly predicted the 'Downfall of the Occident'. However, he was certainly not the only one. Both the books of Paul de La Garde and Julius Langbehn - deeply rooted in a *völkisch* tradition that pursued a romantic 'natural life', in 'harmony' with the 'rhythm' of nature and seasons, with the highest goal of the 'Adam-like ideal man' - as the more aesthetic antimodernism of the poet Stefan George. The many youth movements (the *Artamanes, Freischar Schill, Bund der Lichtfreunde, Kyffhäuserbund, Jungdeutscherorden* and others) emerged from the mixture of antimodernism and perverted romanticism and were catalysed by the lost First World War and social uprooting. The same was true of the many veterans' associations, such as *Stahlhelm*, and the *Frei- corps* whose former soldiers were highly frustrated with regard to the run-off of the First World War. Yet, there were also deeper, more occult forces at work, which used a Masonic like method to propagate their ideas through 'initiates' and shared their agenda with the electorate through public channels.

It is not easy to pinpoint the 'beginning' of such a process, but most historians who have dealt with this theme, such as Nicolas Goodrick-Clarke, David Luhrssen, Detlev Rose, Peter Viereck, Claudia Bart and Wilfried Daim, Leon Poliakov, Hardy Rupp and George L. Mosse, put forward two individuals: Guido von List and Jörg Lanz von Liebenfels.

Guido von List (Guido Karl Anton List, 1848 - 1919) emerged from the rising tide of folklorism, which in turn was a reaction to the modern state and urbanisation, a process that took off in central Europe in the 1990s. For a long time, it looked as if Von List, who had added the 'von' to his name single-handedly in 1907, would remain a complete outsider. Von List had already become intrigued at a young age by 'Wodanism', a kind of worship of what he saw as the pre-Christian primal culture of 'Nordic man'. Within this ideology, a worship of the '*nordic pantheon*', as David Luhrssen called it, played an important role, along with occult sciences such as e.g. runic science.

Von List got wind of this when folklorism became popular in Europe under the influence of Sir James Frazer's *The Golden Bough* (1890). Moreover, modernism caused a decline in the influence of traditional religions, making room for new, metaphysical world views. Theosophy and anthroposophy played an important role in this. We will see that men like List and Lanz von Liebenfels regularly 'borrowed' from the new ideas about God of Helena Petrovna Blavatsky (founder of Theosophy) and Rudolf Steiner (founder of Anthroposophy). Von List filled the gap left by traditional religions with his rich imagination, in which, seeking a 'harmony with the cosmos', he embraced self-knowledge, *gnosis*. The rural Eastern kingdom played a leading role in this. From an early age, he wandered past castles and other special places like Kahlenberg, Leopold's Mountain, St.Stefans Cathedral and *Carnuntum* near Vienna, believing these to be ancient sacred sites from pre-Christian times. After the death of his father, a leather merchant, Von List decided to devote himself entirely to journalism. His articles and books proved successful, and supported by the zeitgeist that opposed modernism, he created a furore. In 1888, he published his mystical novel about the fortress of *Carnuntum*, in which he gave a mythical dimension to the battle between Germanic and Roman tribes. Publisher and Reichstag member Karl Wolf gave him a regular column in the *Ostdeutsche Rundschau* magazine. List became the focal point in literary circles and the foreman of anti- modernism. All this led to the foundation of the so-called *Guido-von-List-Gesellschaft* in 1908, which advocated esoteric research. In the same year, almost the entire theosophical movement in Vienna merged into the *Guido- von-List-Gesellschaft*.

This development was not insignificant, because with the advent of the Theosophists, the idea of (root) races assumed an important place in 'Wodanism', which was already characterised by a radical nationalism. Much has been written about theosophy. Basically, the theosophists believed in the incarnation of man and that each epoch was part of a larger esoteric process. Theosophy had emerged in 1875 with the founding of the *Theosophical Society*. Its main exponent was the lady Helena Petrovna Blavatksy, of Russian origin, who was born in 1831 in what is now Dniepropetrowsk (then Ekaterinoslav).

Blavatsky claimed that she had the sight and that, on her adventurous travels, she had come into contact with the 'forces of the mystery places' of this world, such as Egypt, India, the Himalayas, and with the 'teachers' living there. The Himalayas in particular played an important role in her teachings. There, the 'true princes' lived on the 'roof of the world', in Sanskrit the *mahatmas* - the great souls. They were 'the adepts of the highest wisdom' and escaped the spinning wheel of death and rebirth. As a result, they were no longer slaves to their body; they were able to manifest as a cloud of atoms and could rule as Greek Gods. All this time, 'this wisdom' had remained hidden, until Blavatsky 'discovered' it. From this emerged an alternative creation story that spoke of a sequence of seven root races, bound to seven continents. According to her, the first, non-physically existing race lived at the North Pole. The territory of the second race extended over a wide area, from Greenland to Kamchatka, and she called this race the 'Hyperboreans'. These creatures tried to assume a human form. The third root race emerged in 'Lemuria' and formed the beginning of humanity. After this empire perished, the survivors settled in 'Atlantis'. When that too perished, the survivors fled to northern and central Europe and from there moved eastwards via central Asia. There, the fifth root race arose: the Aryans, with whom, according to Blavatsky, we had arrived in the present time.

The idea that the Aryan race fulfilled a pioneering role was adopted by the most radical part of the anti-modernists. French historian Leon Poliakov called it the 'Aryan myth'. Identity needs territory and history, and people were looking for glorious front runners. Since the

German-speakers were late to nation-building, a fundamental historical base was missing.

Moreover, historically, 'German borders' (*Deutschland, wo liegt es?*) were in fact missing, and the German empire did not really come into being until 1871. This was the reason why the temptation of the esoteric root races was great. How the Germans struggled with their history was shown, for example, by their image of Charlemagne, who was first seen as a 'French man', then as a 'Saxon butcher' (following the massacres of the rebellious Saxons near the town of Verden), and finally as the precursor of Hitler's '*Grosswirtschaftraum Europa*'. The Aryan idea was thus adopted and perverted. Fully in line with secret societ tradition, where there was a general circle and an initiate circle, there was also an *inner circle* within Von List's society, the so-called *Hoher Armanen-Orden*, the HAO, which came into being in the summer of 1911 and whose initiates engaged in pilgrimages to the '*Nordic*' homeland. Thule, Ostara, Atlantis were the lands sought. They were said to be in the Arctic zone and were of mythical origin.

Here the other exponent, Jörg Lanz von Liebenfels (1874 - 1954) enters the picture. Whereas Von List still used a certain ethics, Von Liebenfels adopted a much cruder tone. In fact, he deployed ariosophy as a political weapon, no longer classifying people by nation and religion, but by ethnicity. Von Liebenfels, like Von List, had been deeply interested in the new discoveries of his time from an early age, especially the excavations in Assyria and Mesopotamia. Additionally, it was the time when the German archaeologist Heinrich Schliemann caused a furore, showing everywhere the *swastikas* that had been excavated. Von Liebenfels, who saw history as a permanent struggle, effortlessly adopted the ideas of the *Guido-von-List- Gesellschaft* into his own perverted worldview. As a modern Templar - he was the founder of the *Ordo Novi Templi* (ONT) - Aryan man had to arm himself under the *swastika*. He rewrote the *Bible* according to his 'original' racial interpretation. In his book *Theozoologie oder die Kunde von den Sodom Äfflingen und die Götter Elektron* (1905), he claimed that non-Aryans - and above all Jews - were 'half-humans'. The latter should be deported, suggesting that Madagascar would be a good destination. If we consider that Hitler introduced the Aryan Declaration and that deportation to Madagascar was indeed worked out in detail (Theodor Dannecker did this on behalf of the SS), we can already see here that Von Liebenfels' words had not fallen on unfertile ground. He further believed that the Jews could serve as a 'burnt offering'; the literal translation of the word *Holocaust*. The non-Aryans he called *Urmenschen* or *Tschandalen*, here too the relationship with the word *Untermensch* is immediately striking. Moreover, it is noteworthy that Jörg Lanz von Liebenfels established a relationship between Judaism and Bolshevism; one of Hitler's later hobbyhorses. In his magazine *Ostara*, which Hitler read, he wrote, among other things, an article entitled *Der zoologische und talmudische Ursprung des Bolschewismus*. *Ostara* was full of articles on the 'dangers' of non-Aryans to the German people, whom he described as *Übervolk* (with Hitler: *Übermensch*).

Through these two proponents, the poison of their world-view entered European history. The *Guido-von-*

List-Gesellschaft was supported by an 'influential minority', as Luhrssen put it, and - not unimportantly - there were backers such as e.g. the Austrian industrialist Friedrich Wannieck. Young enthusiastic followers, who were themselves successful, propagated the ideas further, such as writer, philosopher and art historian Ernst von Wolzogen (1855 - 1934), who introduced the cabaret in Germany and founded the *Munich Freie Literarische Gesellschaft*. In 1923, the same year Hitler committed the *Feldherrnhalle-putsch* in Munich, he published his anti-Semitic autobiography in which he proved to be a strong supporter of Von List's theories. The popular writer, comedian and *globetrotter* Hanns Heinz Ewers (1871 - 1943) followed his example. Among other things, he wrote a novel about Horst Wessel, the SA man revered by the Nazis who was murdered by the communists. The links in the chain between the *List-Gesellschaft* and the Nazis were slowly but surely riveted. The List group developed contacts with the so-called *Germanic orders*, which in turn were linked to the *Edda Society*, founded by Wolf John Gorsleben, who in turn was a member of the *Thule Society* and the *Ordo Novi Templi* of Lanz von Liebenfels as well. Publisher and publicist Theodor Fritsch (1852 - 1933) played an important role in the *Germanic orders*. One of the major disseminators of anti-Semitic thought, he collaborated with American anti-Semite and car manufacturer Henry Ford. The latter businessman was one of the major disseminators of *The Protocols of Zion,* which claimed that the Jews had staged a conspiracy to obtain world power. Fritsch was clearly inspired by Von List and he operated similarly. In 1912, he founded the *Reichshammerbund* around the anti-Semitic magazine *Hammer*, which later merged into the *Schutz und Trutzbund*. It was from these circles that the Thule Society arose.

Often, contacts ran back and forth, and many members were in multiple organisations. However, they had one thing in common: they all came from the same political-radical background. It was like a kind of *al-Qaeda avant la lettre*. Not all the lines ran from Osama Bin laden, Ayman al- Zawahiri or Mokthar Belmokhtar or other leading figures. The ideology was simply adaptable and malleable to others.

It was in this context that Rudolf von Sebottendorff surfaced, born on 9 November 1875 under the name Adam Alfred Rudolf Glauer in Hoyerswerda, not far from the town of Görlitz in Saxony. Anyone taking note of the life of this adventurer is involuntarily reminded of the life of Aleister Crowley, the British occultist, writer and mountaineer, who combined adventures with occultism, in a perpetual struggle for money and a life off the beaten track. Glauer seemed destined to become an engineer, following in the footsteps of his father, who worked as such with the German railways. However, he did not complete his education, as the sea lured, but the navy turned him down. As the private tutor of two children of a beautiful and wealthy widow, he ended up on the French and Italian Riviera. However, adventure kept drawing him and eventually he could not resist the lure of the sea. In 1898, he sailed on the S.S. *H.H. Meier* from Bremerhaven in the direction of New York. New voyages and destinations followed on several other ships. For example, he sailed from Italy to Australia where he tried his hand as a gold prospector in the Great Victoria Dessert. In the summer of 1900, he arrived in Egypt where Turkish influence was strong at the time. Here, he fell under the spell of the Levant and Eastern mysticism, especially that of the Sufis. Glauer learnt Turkish and Arabic and, through business contacts, eventually ended up in Turkey. Here he befriended a Jewish silk merchant who initiated him into the Jewish mysticism of the *Kabbalah* and introduced him to the Masonic lodge of Bursa. It is interesting to see how these precursors of Nazism influenced the modus operandi of their (later) opponents. Hitler would later ban all references between his person and occultism. This also included the works of Von Sebottendorff who, apart from *Bevor Hitler kam*, had written a dozen books on astrology and occultism. The predecessors had their own 'justifications'. The SS later believed that kabbalistism was actually an 'Aryan invention', which 'the Jews had appropriated'.

Influenced by the Levant, Glauer returned to Germany. A marriage in 1905 to farmer's daughter Klara Voss from Bischofswerda was dissolved after only a year. In 1907, he settled in Berlin, where he was initiated into astrology by Dr Richard Hummel - a dentist, occultist and publisher. Possibly because of financial or judicial problems, Glauer again emigrated to Turkey. There he hoped to find work with the *Anatolian Railroad Company,* but again ended up as a private tutor, this time in Alemdag, the Jewish quarter of Constantinople. Here he witnessed the successful revolt of the Young Turks led by Kemal Pasha (Atatürk), and saw how the Freemasonry supported the Young Turks and how it made its temples available to the revolution. Historian David Luhrssen has given an interesting insight into how this Turkish period influenced Glauer. At some point, he returned to Germany equipped with a new name. In fact, he had met in Constantinople a certain Heinrich von Sebottendorff, an American of German descent, who had accepted him as a stepson, which Rudolf had recorded by Turkish law in 1908.

Apart from this new name, Rudolf von Sebottendorff also brought new ideas to Germany. The Young Turks had not only seized power, they had used this power to rewrite history. They had diligently searched for the pre-Islamic roots of Turkish culture, just as the Thule Society in Germany advocated: the search for the Germanic primal roots. Additionally, he had seen how the new forces in Turkey warmed to the great-Turkish (pan-Turkish) thought. Here, Turkish variants of the 'German by choice' Houston Stewart Chamberlain, the British Germany-adept, had emerged in the person of the French hisoric David Leon Cahun and the Polish historian with the Oriental name Mustafa Celaleddin. They propagated a renewed vision of history, adding, for example, the renowned conqueror Dzhengis Kahn to the Turkish inheritance, just as Ataturk claimed Troy and Homer for Turkey. With Dzhengis Kahn, the pan-Turks had created their copy of the '*völkisch*' Charlemagne. Moreover, there was open writing in Jongturk circles about the geopolitical conflict of interest between Turkey and Germany. Neither country would be safe as long as the Moscow-led pan-Slavism would exist. It was Jewish Young Turk author Moiz Cohen (aka Tekin Alp/Munis Tekinalp) who called for securing the common interests of Turkey and

Germany with regard to this pan-Slavic movement. Von Sebottendorff may not have been unsympathetic to this, even though he considered the Turks 'impervious to communism'.

Once back in Germany, von Sebottendorff, following what he had seen in Turkey, conceived the idea from the wings (i.e. the Masonic lodges of Alemdag) to seize the momentum of history. As a result, we constantly see individuals with Turkish connections in Von Sebottendorff's environment popping up. This has been a hitherto under-reported fact. Rudolf Gorsleben, for example, who had served as a German officer in Turkey, was a member of all the organisations, such as the *Guido-von-List-Gesellschaft*, the *Ordo Novi Templi*, the *Edda Society* and the Thule Society, which allowed him to work as a liaison. Käthe Bierbaumer, one of his main backers, had lived in Turkey for years. It was rumoured that she was Von Sebottendorff's mistress. More important, however, was the fact that she financed the purchase of the *Münchener Beobachter und Sportblatt*, which gave the Thule Society the chance to go public and, as Von Sebottendorff had seen in Turkey, to provide ideological and political nourishment to the revolution. Later, the newspaper's name was changed to *Völkischer Beobachter*.

The newspaper was first published in 1887 and had been owned by publisher Franz Eher since 1900. When the owner died in June 1918, Von Sebottendorff, through Eher's notary, a Thule member, saw his chance to use the newspaper as a mouthpiece of the Thule Society. The political message would be wrapped up in innocent sports reports to reach the 'right target group', because

'Jews did not like sports', Von Sebottendorff argued the newspaper's purchase. The newspaper became a binding medium between Thule members and later foremen of the Nazi movement, such as Dietrich Eckart, to whom Hitler would dedicate *Mein Kampf*, and Nazi ideologue Alfred Rosenberg. The editorial office was based at the posh Hotel *Vierjahreszeiten* in Munich and was headed by Hans Georg Grassinger. Käthe Bierbaumer's shares later passed into the hands of Sebotttendorff's sister, Dora Kunze. They were then sold on again to Gottfried Feder, another important foreman and economist from the early period of National Socialism and, of course, a Thule member.

By paying attention to the Turkish connection, we have made a small leap. An important precursor lies in Von Sebottendorff's time with the *Germanic orders*. He had joined this in 1916. The order had come into being four years earlier, in May 1912, at a meeting in Leipzig at Theodor Fritsch's home. There, entirely in List style and in the presence of many List followers and other pan- Germanic people, after initial overt political ambitions (through the *Deutsche Sozialistische Partei* and the *Deutschsoziale Reformpartei*), they had decided to go underground as well, and to create a secret lodge within the *Hammer group* in an *Armanenschaft*-like manner. Chosen for this purpose was the so-called *Wodan lodge* of the Magdeburger *Hammer* club, which was renamed *Germanenorden*.

This order had to stay below the surface and guard 'German interests'. The *Reichshammerbund* was the overt shield under the more or less hidden supervision of a 12- member '*Armanen Council*'. Even the *Hammer* magazine barely mentioned the *Germanic Order*. Yet it did exist and had lodges in several cities. Their foreman was Hermann Pohl who sought a workable relationship with church and national circles through underground and above-ground channels. In doing so, the *Hammerbund* and the *Germanic orders* followed the same path that Hitler would later take. Through agricultural ideologue and minister R. Walther Darré, especially in the early years, the *Bauerntum* played an important and rich role within the ideology and politics of the NSDAP. Furthermore, concordat with the Pope was a high priority after Hitler's rise to power in 1933. Remarkably, the Germanic lodges already spoke of 'deportation of Jews' from Germany as early as 1912, i.e. before World War I.

World War I had a dual effect on the *Teutonic Order*. Many members volunteered and died; on the other hand, the order radicalised even further. Within the lodge, a power struggle broke out in late 1916 between Hermann Pohl and Philipp Stauff, a member and journalist who published books on Jews and their position in Germany. Stauff committed suicide in July 1923, but the split was a fact. Pohl continued under the name *Germanenorden Walvater*. At that time, Von Sebottendorff, who had settled in Bad Aibling, Bavaria, was in regular contact with him. Sebottendorff became increasingly active in the order's Bavarian circles and on 21 December 1917, they named him 'Master of the Province'. With this, Von Sebotttendorff had arrived at the political destination he so coveted. Meanwhile, he had married Bertha Anna Iffland, a wealthy woman who did not otherwise care about his esoteric and political ambitions. At the time, Von Sebottendorff's anti-Semitism was fuelled by a business dispute with Jewish lawyer Max Alsberg. Von Sebottendorff seemed to have been 'floating' for some time with regard to his position towards Jews, as he was rather 'indebted' to them in occult matters.

After the Russian Tsarist Empire had already collapsed in 1917 - with German support no less, because the German government had allowed Lenin and his comrades to travel to Russia from Switzerland - the Bavarian house of Wittelsbach fell in November 1918. On that day, Rudolf von Sebottendorff gave an emotional *speech* that was full of ariosophy and occultism. Then the Habsburg Empire (Austria-Hungary) and the Wilhelminian Empire (Germany) collapsed as well. All this was followed by a period of great political instability and revolutionary actions by the left. For the Thule Society, as the Munich branch of the *Germanic orders* had been christened by Von Sebottendorff, the fall of the monarchy meant a spectre come true. In the Jewish Kurt Eisner, who established a Raden Republic and - with French support - pursued the separation of Bavaria from the German Empire, the Thule members saw their fears realised. A number of Thule members paid with their lives for their membership and were shot dead without trial by the council communists in the courtyard of the *Luitpold Gymnasium* in Munich. Von Sebottendorff himself was also briefly detained, but he hid behind his Turkish nationality and managed to break free. From the circles around the Thule Society, the first vigilante group was now organised against the revolt: the *Thule Kampfbund*, which has gone down in history as the first *Freikorps* of nationally-minded paramilitaries. As is well known, the *Freikorps* (including Brigade Ehrhardt from which the assassins of *Erfüllungspolitiker* Walther

Rathenau emerged) played a crucial role in the power building of the NSDAP. They later provided training for the SA and were also involved in Hitler's two coup attempts: the *Kapp-putsch* and the *Feldherrnhalle-putsch*.

Arms for the *Thule Kampfbund* were provided by Julius Lehmann, bookseller and publisher of many pan-Germanic books. The council communists were eventually overthrown by the *Freikorps* and troops loyal to the government. When the new commander of the *Reichswehr*, Ritter von Epp, entered Munich, he established his headquarters at the Hotel *Vierjahreszeiten*, where the headquarters of the Thule Society was located too. The military and the ideologues were now closer than ever. Hitler, who had remained in German military service after World War I, meanwhile served in a political spy service. In practice, this meant attending and reporting on political meetings for his boss, Captain Mayer. Through Mayer, who clearly had far-right sympathies, Hitler had already come into contact with Thule member and *Hammer* publicist Dietrich Eckart in September 1919. This would have a great influence on Hitler and he, like Von Sebottendorff, would write a book about it. This book, like Sebottendorff's book *Bevor Hitler kam*, would be banned. It was the book *Von Mozes bis Lenin* in which the Jewish-Bolshevik *link* already put forward by Liebenfels had been developed into a dividing line that ran through the whole of history. On his deathbed, Dietrich Eckart is said to have said: 'It was Hitler who danced, but we determined the melody'. Through Eckart, the Baltic-German Alfred Rosenberg came into the picture, who would later, when the great German writer Thomans Mann was awarded the Nobel prize, elevate

Hitler to his 'literary' equal. Rosenberg's books, of which *Der Mythos des 20. Jahrhunderts* (inspired by Houston Stewart Chamberlain) was the most important work, were to be full of theosophical and List-Lanz-like theories that eventually found their way to Hitler and the NSDAP via *Hammer*, *Germanenorden* and Thule Society. In December 1919, Hitler joined the *Deutsche Arbeiter Partei* (DAP). After previously stranded attempts, a party had once again been formed from the *Germanic orders*, behind which the ideals of the Thule Society and the *Germanic orders* were hidden. Its aim was to promote the workers from communism and preserve them for the national cause. During one of his 'spying activities', Hitler had ended up at the DAP and had interfered in the political discussion there, against the very purpose of his arrival. He made such an impression that by the second meeting, he was already known as 'the Austrian with the big mouth'. Anton Drexler, Thule member and one of the founders of the DAP, approached Hitler for party membership. Captain Mayer, Hitler's commander, then reported personally to Erich Ludendorff. This 'hero of World War I' had great authority within the reactionary camp and was in a position to dismiss Hitler from military service. This paved the way for Hitler to pursue a career in German politics. And so it happened.

At about the same time, Sebottendorff's career with the Thule Society was falling apart. He was accused of being careless with the membership list during the Raden Republic, which led to the arrest and execution of several Thule members. In addition, the press took him to task and the question of whether he might have used his

Turkish citizenship to get out of military service during World War I resurfaced. Meanwhile, Jewish companies filed lawsuits against him for his anti-Semitism. This was still possible then, as Hitler's political career had just begun and it would be until 1933 before the Nazis came to power. Membership of the Thule Society declined rapidly. According to Von Sebottendorff's own report, there were only 25 active members in 1925. In 1930, the organisation was officially dissolved. The last chairman was a certain Max Sesselman. Von Sebottendorff retired to Bad Sachsa where he wrote for the *Astrologische Rundschau*. In 1923, he again left for Turkey to, as he himself claimed, gain 'occult knowledge'. This trip too was accompanied by many adventures and again, in 1928, he got divorced.

When Hitler came to power in 1933, Von Sebottendorff returned to Germany and joined the NSDAP. He published his book *Bevor Hitler kam* which received an initial print run of 3,000 copies, followed by a second printing of 5,000 copies. The publisher was former Thule member Hans Georg Grassinger, who had worked at the *Völkischer Beobachter* as well. However, the Nazi authorities soon turned against him. At the end of 1933, Von Sebottendorff was expelled from the party and his publisher suddenly believed that his book would be 'against Hitler'. In September 1933, the Gestapo even started an investigation against the then no longer existing Thule Society. They started looking for documents that were not in Hitler's interest. Miraculously, the commander of the police team was a certain Captain Kraus, himself a former Thule member. Thus, the revolution ate its own children.

Sebottendorff's arrest followed in February 1934. A large number of copies of the second edition of his book were withdrawn from circulation and destroyed. One copy, according to Luhrssen, went to the NSDAP archives and was given the red stamp *Volkswidrig* (against the people). After the Night of the Long Knives, the 1934 reckoning with the SA, publisher Grassinger was arrested as well, as was Bernhard Stempfle, a veteran of the ariosophist camp. It was suspected that Stempfle too had contributed to the confessions in Von Sebottendorff's book *Bevor Hitler kam*; he was murdered.

As so often in Von Sebottendorff's life, the trail became unclear. Grassinger claimed that the Gestapo had killed him, but it was more likely that he was allowed to escape to Turkey. That Sebottendorff was still alive was confirmed by Herbert Rittlinger, the chief of German intelligence in Istanbul, who would soon make use of his services. He described Von Sebottendorff as an amiable man who 'talked more about Tibet than Nazi Germany'. However, he did not consider him a good spy and even feared that he might also be working for the Allies. Despite this, Von Sebottendorff was on the payroll for a not inconsiderable amount. When the German embassy closed, Rittlinger took leave of the ariosopher. One gave him some extra money to pass the time. Rittlinger later learned that Von Sebottendorff had drowned himself in the Bosphorus on 9 May 1945, four days after the capitulation of the Third Reich.

Perry Pierik

On anti-Semitism in von Sebottendorff's work

Besides the above life sketch of Von Sebottendorff and the insight into the origins of the Thule Society, this is also the place to dwell on the anti-Semitism in his book *Bevor Hitler kam*. We see in his work how the old, smouldering anti-Semitism took on a new and brisk form under the influence of the events of November 1918 (the catastrophic end of World War I and the subsequent revolutions for Germany). Without wishing to be exhaustive, we can distinguish the following, stereotypical characterisations in Sebottendorff's work:

the eternal Jew
the Jew as usurer
the Jewish world conspiracy / the Jewish revolutionary
the Jew as traitor
the Jew as capitalist
the Jew as communist.
the Jew as 'stay-at-home'.

The 'eternal Jew' took root as a myth in Germany as early as the 17th century with the publication of the *Volksbuch* containing the history of Ahasverus (1602). With Sebottendorff, the Jew appears as a 'kind of blood-sucking vampire' (incidentally also a myth about Jews) who 'sucks out' the host people until they 'disappear from history.' Then the 'wandering' or 'walking' Jew goes in search of a new host people.

The success of the Jews, according to Von Sebottendorff and his followers, came from the fact that they controlled altar and throne, divided the people through democracy and then made them politically and economically dependent. The myth of the 'Jew as usurer' played a role in this. They were the 'inventors' of the joint-stock company in which workers and employers were separated, making exploitation easier.

The myth of the 'Jew as traitor' refers to the fact that people saw the Jew as a 'traitor to the people', as a 'profiteur' who had placed himself outside the people and as such had betrayed the 'people'. The myth of the 'Jew as communist and as capitalist' followed naturally from this. The contradiction inherent in both ideologies was simply dismissed by Von Sebottendorff and his anti-Semitic contemporaries by pointing to the role of the 'secret societies' (note the irony here) in which the Jews were united. Freemasonry was thereby pointed to as vehicels 'in the service of the Jews', after all, through Freemasonry, the Jews, according to Von Sebottendorff and his ilk, obtained high positions in important organisations. These 'high Jewish brothers' would again be united in a strictly Jewish freemasonry, the *B'nai B'rith*, from where the strategy was determined.

Here, Von Sebottendorff cites Walter Rathenau (foreign minister in 1922) as a typical example of this 'secret Jewish leadership', because Rathenau himself is said to have belonged to this organisation.

Furthermore, we find the myth of Jewish bodily 'otherness', known from the cartoons in which Jews were depicted with an off proportioned nose, in Von Sebottendorff's case, who used a 'sports newspaper' to inform his supporters for a reason (Jews and sport 'of nature did not go together).

According to Von Sebottendorff, physical imposing behaviour was not a strong point with Jews, whom he attributed the role of 'stay-at-home' during World War I (the myth of 'Jewish stay-at-home'), while Thule supporters flocked to the front to make the 'blood sacrifice' for the fatherland. It is noteworthy that Von Sebottendorff himself was among the stay-at-home Jews at the time.

Finally, for a complete overview of the various characterisations encountered with Von Sebottendorff and their historical explanation and development, we must refer to the standard work by Julius H. Schoeps and Joachim Schlör: *Antisemitismus, Vorurteile und Mythen*, published by *Piper Verlag*, Munich, in 1995.

Perry Pierik

Before Hitler Came

Documents from the beginning of the National Socialist Movement by Rudolf von Sebottendorff

Assignment

This book is dedicated to the memory of the seven Thule members who were raised in the *Luitpold Gymnasium*; in memory of the Thule members and the members of the *Kampfbund* belonging to the *Freikorps*, who lost their lives for the sake of the liberation of Munich, and to all the eployees in the difficult years of preparation for the revolution.

It describes the years from the modest beginnings of the national socialist movement in the middle of the World War until the appearance of *Führer* Adolf Hitler. That is why this book bears the title: 'Before Hitler came'.

Now at last it can be said, what hitherto could not be said so as not to arouse the hatred of 'the system' towards the pioneers. Now, there is no more need to make it a secret that the said seven Thule members did not die as hostages, no, they were murdered, because they were anti-Semites. They died for the swastika, they were victimised by the Jews, they were murdered because people wanted to nip the national revolution in the bud.

Now that which the seven and the entire Thule Society (*Thule Gesellschaft*) longed for, for which they fought passionately and determinedly, for which they were prepared to die and died, has been fulfilled.

We recognise the merits, greatness and power of Adolf Hitler. He achieved what we aspired to; we prepared, what he implemented.

When we started speaking of the German national character and socialism more than 15 years ago, we were laughed at. It was Hitler who instilled in the German the unity of these two concepts.

Whenever we spoke of blood purity, we were mocked. It was Hitler who awakened this thought in millions of Germans.

When we dreamed of the old German law and said that Roman law should be replaced by German law, we were met with incomprehension. This thought finally became commonplace among the German people because of Hitler. However, our work at the time was not in vain, it was the seed, forging the tools with which Hitler could work and had to work towards his destiny.

This book shows what it was like before the *Führer* joined the movement. It shows the sources, which then merged into the stream that was to wash away everything un-German.

It was the people of Thule, where Hitler came first, and Thule members were the first to rally behind Hitler!

The combat resources of the coming *Führer* consisted besides Thule itself from the *Deutscher Arbeiterverein* which emerged from the Thule Society and was created by brother Karl Harrer, and from the

Deutsch-Sozialistische Partei, led by Hans Georg Grassinger, of which the *Münhener*, later the *Völkischer Beobachter* was the organ. These were the three sources, from which Hitler created the *Nationalsozialistische Deutsche Arbeiterpartei.*

We salute our *Führer* Adolf Hitler with a *Sieg Heil!*

9 November 1933 The author

In memory

As the first martyrs of awakening Germany, the following Thule members fell at the *Luitpold Gymnasium* in Munich on 30 April 1919 from the bullets of Bolshevik assassins:

Heila Countess Von Westarp, secretary of the Thule Society Gustav Franz Maria Prince Von Thurn und Taxis Franz Karl Baron von Teuchert, first lieutenant Friedrich Wilhelm Baron von Seidlitz, painter Anton Daumenlang, railway official Walter Deike, craft designer Walter Nauhaus, sculptor

Table of contents

I	General political considerations	47
II	Sources of the movement	65
III	Germanic orders and the Thule Society	69
IV	The Thule Society and the Munich Beobachter until the 1918 revolution	79
V	Thule society, Kampfbund and the circles around Thule	103
VI	Thule's political activities until Eisner's death	119
VII	Thule during the rule of the Council government	131
VIII	Thule's Kampfbund and the counter-revolution of 1919	155
IX	Entry of the Freikorps Oberland in Munich	177
X	The victims of Thule - murder of Thule members	189
XI	The Thule Society after the murder of the hostages	227
XII	From the Thule Society emerged organisations	237
XIII	Origin and growth of the Völkischer Beobachter	257
XIV	Thule without a founder and the resurgence	263

Register of persons and cases 267

Literature 333

I
General political considerations

One can lament the World War and its consequences, lament the collapse of the First German Empire and the existence of the Second German Reich, one can pity the German people who had to live through these terrible years, but one thing is certain: without these tides of distress, Germany would never have become united. For the German people, the lost war, the Second Reich and the mismanagement of the system were indeed necessary.

The Ice Age brought forth the Aryan, the white, wise man from the north, who would bring culture to the world. His sign of recognition, the victorious sun path, can be found everywhere he went. However, the wandering Aryan did gift other peoples with its culture, even if it was so degraded by inferior races that hardly anything can be found of it.

The disasters of war, the subsequent difficult years made the Germans! Once again the sun sign, the swastika of the past raised itself; the ancient symbol of salvation of the Aryans became the identifying sign of the new Germany! Now the German will never forget that every fellow citizen is blood of his blood, that all Germans are brothers and sisters; a great, holy family!

One wonders why these terrible times had to come first, why the goal was not achieved before, after all, hundreds and thousands of German men worked on this goal.

The greatest evil of the Germans had to be overcome and conquered first and this greatest evil is: disfavour, listening to strange whispers, the lack of community spirit.

A battle was already lost earlier because the Alemanni leaders did not know that they had to lead by example. 'Come off the horses,' shouted the followers and the Romans prevailed - such is the envy and one must be careful not to arouse envy and avoid anything that might arouse jealousy.

Listening to foreign influences is the German's second born evil. Never before and during the war did foreign powers mock anything more than the Great German Movement. Instead of thinking that what my enemy taunts must be good for me, the German agreed with the taunts. It was exactly like that at the beginning of the Hitler movement.

The third evil, however, is the lack of community spirit and thus the habit of beating each other's brains out because of trifles. 'German problems', the French say when they want to refer to such quarrels because of trifles.

The German never looks at the common goal, he only looks at the road! He wants everyone to follow the road he believes to be the right one, the only one that is blissful; he forgets that all roads lead to the goal only when this goal is so grand that it encompasses everything.

The German needs a leader who compels him. Who forces him to focus his gaze solely on the goal and not on the road. The leader must have the power to compel! This power can be obtained in two ways. It can be given to the leader by heredity, i.e. from outside, or it can be given to him by the people of their own free will, i.e. from within. What comes from outside can also be changed, distorted and destroyed from outside. What developed harmoniously from within, what came into being, will be permanent! The former is something of a materialistic nature, it wants to work from outside and has to, because after all, the material cannot create itself. It is something perishable out of which the imperishable spirit, the eternal, forms something new. Materialism wants to make good people from this situation. How wrong this position is, the last years before the war show.

Never did a nation fare better than the German one at the time. Under Kaiser Wilhelm II, Germany meant something in the world. The German flag flew on all seas, trade flourished, industry was second to none. For the worker, well-paid work was plentiful; if he did not like it, he quit and went somewhere else. Since every worker was dutiful and honoured his work, he soon found a new, well-paid job. People claim that wages were low back then. That is not true, they were geared to the low prices of means of subsistence and rents, low taxes and social charges back then. Never again did the savings banks, cooperative consumer associations, trade unions and political parties dispose of such large sums of money as they did then, and if these bodies still exist today, they owe it only to the pre-war years in which they laid a sound foundation. Money was always available and for every purpose; everyone had money. The possibility of making money again gave rise to the materialistic view of life and attitude. The worship of the material increased greatly. The worker looked after himself, did not care about his comrades. It was enough that he was a member of a trade union, paid his contribution, read the party paper and went on strike when the union prescribed it; other than that, he went about his business. At work, he did his best; that was his duty; he did not know anything else. However, he had learned to see the enemy in the citizen, the civil servant, in the state itself.

The citizen who was liberal, national-liberal at best, lived entirely his own life. He was not distinctly hostile to the worker, on the contrary, but neither was it his best friend, because he felt the enmity and because it disturbed his peace of mind. Anything that disturbed him in this comfortable tranquillity could limit his gain, but making money he wanted and could. He did not care about the worker, he hated the official.

Civil servants' salaries were low; at the time, the view was that the small salary was compensated by the prospect of pension. The civil servant had to look after the little ones. He could not join in when citizens celebrated; in this way, civil servants closed themselves off and formed a caste in themselves.

While this was the condition in which the people in general turned, under Kaiser Wilhelm II there was something more special. The increasing affluence of the entrepreneurs, the businessmen provided new investments of capital. A class arose among the citizens who had no roots in the people's nature and, due to the increased affluence, forgot this rootlessness. The nobility, the officials wanted to go along in this opulence and were forced to do so by Kaiser Wilhelm II's court. Thus began a process of decay from above that went hand in hand with the same process from below.

Contradictions between religions did not play a major role in Germany at the turn of the century. The two confessions were busy surviving. Belief in God was considered old-fashioned and outdated. Those who did not leave the church were at least indifferent to it. The worker on the one hand with defamation and scorn, the scientist on the other with the weapons of his scholarship, attacked the church. It was the time when Büchner's *Kraft und Stoff*, in which Haeckel's *Welträtsel*, the bible of materialism, was distributed by a hundred thousand copies at a time.

That was the time when Judaism conquered the position it had held until recently. The position for which it had fought relentlessly and doggedly for centuries.

However, it was a gross tactical error on Judaism's part to venture so far into the foreground, because now people became alert. What was proclaimed by only a few penetrated the people who, after all, had always been purely instinctively anti-Semitic.

Mommsen who surely cannot be considered an anti-Semite had said that Judaism is a source of destruction. Retcliffe's novels of the 1970s became topical; what the well-informed *Hofrat* Schneider of the *Kreuzzeitung* wrote and why he was laughed at took on colour, shape and form. One should read again that fantastic scene in the Jewish cemetery in Prague, or the history of the Frankfurt banker.

One read with amazement Dr Walter Rathenau's statement in the *Wiener Neuen Freien Presse*, in which he put his money where his mouth was: 'Three hundred men, who all know each other, determine the history of the continent and choose their successors from among themselves '(25 December 1909).

The anti-Semitic movement of the last years of the century grew and became increasingly powerful. Antisemitism has always existed, the word meaning nothing more than attacking or defending against a foreign race, a foreign people. Antisemitism is actually as old as the Jewish race. Pressure will always create counter-pressure. As the pressure of Judaism grew, so did the national resistance of the host people, and one day it had to erupt. If the host nation was still strong enough, then the Jews had to leave, otherwise the host nation went to ruin. In that case, too, the Jews moved on and thus the legend of the century-old Jew was born. The exodus of the Jews from Egypt, which we had to learn in school as an example of God's concern, is in reality such an expulsion. Historically, the exodus of the children of Israel is the expulsion of the Hyksos, the Bedouin tribe that had invaded Egypt and ruled there for a hundred years. And we read with dismay in the Bible, in the second book of Moses 5 verse 21, how the God of the Jews tempted his children to steal so they did not leave empty-handed. Egypt had thus lost its Jews for the time being. Cyrus, who wanted to return the praised land to the Jews for services rendered, did not get rid of them; they remained on the banks of Babylon's waters and trudged on. Only about a thousand men followed Ezra to Jerusalem where they rebuilt the city. That the captive Jews sat by Babylon's waters and wept, as we should learn from the Bible, is not true; they were doing well there, they had so much power that they could slaughter 30,000 Aryans and still today celebrate this event festively. At the time when Ezra returned to Jerusalem, around 300 BCE, that enormous deception from which Christianity still suffers today began: the Bible was edited from back to front, the genealogical registers were compiled according to a numerical mysticism and Aryan knowledge gained in Babylon was incorporated into the Bible. At that time, the Hebrew script originated from the runic script, which was spread from Mycenae among the 'eastern' peoples.

The Jew has always been a businessman, a trader; on the voyages of Alexander the Great, the Jew came everywhere and we find him around 200 BC already in all the trading cities of the Mediterranean, especially in Rome.

It was under his influence that a democracy emerged there, exactly as he wanted it. One more time, the great Sulla managed to save the Roman people, but its downfall could no longer be stopped. The wealth amassed in Rome and the many peoples prepared an amalgamation of races, which was crowned by Christianity; after all, which taught: everyone who is baptised is your brother. At the time of the migration of peoples, when the young Germans overthrew the decaying Empire, all of southern Europe was Christian.

How difficult it was to convert the Germanic people to Christianity is shown by the battles fought over half a century. Charlemagne, the emperor of the Franks, still had to kill thousands of Saxons to convince the survivors how people-friendly Christianity was. Germanic people only succeeded in converting to Christianity when the church adapted Germanic mores and traditions and turned Germanic festivals into Christian ones.

At the time when Islam was on the rise, we find Jew worship among Arabs. In the Qur'an, whole passages deal with the reprobation of the children of Israel.

With the monks and the incipient formation of cities in Germany came the Jews. Soon they were in the cities along the Rhine and penetrated eastwards from here.

Persecutions of Jews took place throughout the Middle Ages, but because Germany disintegrated into many small and large states, such persecution could never be grandiose; the Jew crawled into his shell until the storm passed and then just as shamelessly began to continue his rampant practices. Protection the Jews found mainly from the church. Even if the church managed to cover medieval anti-Semitism with a Christian cloak, it was basically always the intercession and protection of the Jews because the Jews had influence on the church. Baptised Jews could get the highest positions in the church, once a baptised Jew stood even higher than the pope.

This changed when Protestantism became the state church in the north. Luther himself was a formidable anti-Semite, but he was it only from a religious point of view. To gain influence over Protestants too, Jews invented Freemasonry. At the time, the old Freemasonry was the guardian of a secret taught at the medieval workplaces (*Bauhütten*) where Gothic cathedrals were built. We find a tremendous amount of Aryan wisdom in the teachings of the alchemists and Rosicrucians, who had joined the building guild. With the demise of Gothic architecture, the workshops also disappeared, and Aryan wisdom remained the secret of the few who kept it. When the thirty-year religious war was over, and Protestants and Catholics no longer beat each other to death for having the right sense of religion, the time had come for the Jews to revive the Masonic orders. They founded the first lodges towards the end of the 17th century, which united into a Grand Lodge in York in 1717. The secret of the old Freemasonry was to be taught, that every person had to work on himself to become good, then he would radiate goodness outwards like a sun. Everyone should become such a sun. Then, ancient Aryan wisdom taught, if the individual, the leader is perfect, from him his surroundings will also become perfect. The new teaching of the Freemasons turned the matter around, saying: first we create good conditions, then people will also become good. In accordance with the three degrees in true masonry- apprentice, journeyman and master - three degrees with equal names were created in the Masonic Row; the symbolism was a custom borrowed from the Old Testament. The work in the lodges was symbolic of the construction on the temple of Zion. Slowly, higher degrees emerged from the last and third degrees, and around 1780 the system of higher degree Freemasonry was complete. Invariably, however, Jews were the driving force in the lodges. The stupid Germans allowed themselves to be lulled to sleep by the talk of world brotherhood, equality and freedom. Lessing's *Nathan der Weise* was based on ideas of the Freemasons. Frederick the Great, who was admitted to a lodge in Brunswick, founded the Grand Lodge *Royal York* in Prussia when he became king. In France, the lodges prepared the revolution. After the end of the wars of liberation, Freemasonry had gained a foothold throughout the world. On freemasonry contra Aryan worldview, an article that can be found in *Runen* No. 7 of 21 July 1918 provides clarification. In it, Sebottendorff replies to an article against him that appeared on the part of the lodges in the *Munich-Augsburger Abendzeiting* and in the *Bayerischer Kurier*.

'What separates us (Germanic lodges) from Freemasonry is our worldview. We regard the world - the environment - as a product of man. Freemasons claim that man is the product of circumstances.

We do not know international brotherhood, but national interests, we do not know the brotherhood of men, but only blood brotherhood.

We want freedom, not the freedom of the herdsman, but freedom in the face of duty.

We hate the slogan of equality. Struggle is the father of all things, equality is death.

We want to live, live long and live happily. Our conception of equality is equality in relation to duty. We want to make everyone as bright and capable as possible, so that he feels duty not as a burden, but as a piece of himself. Then we will also hold our own in the battle that will come, must come, the battle between Aryans and Jews. A recognised enemy is no longer an enemy; we will open our people's eyes, and show them where their enemy is, fighting us until we are destroyed.

We dispute Freemasonry's theories that circumstances shape man; that is a thesis that Marxism has adopted and with which people bake sweet rolls, because if that is so, then man, the leader, is free from any responsibility.

Such a materialistic view leads to decay.

We have nothing in common with Freemasonry in terms of traditions either. They were clever enough to blame everything on the law of Moses. With 'the sword in one hand, the wooden hammer in the other', the freemason must build the temple of Zion.

We carried the iron sword and the iron hammer and built on the German Halgadom.

We no longer want to be the anvil, but the hammer. We do not pray: 'Grant that the world may be united, that the human race may fraternise', because we know that this is impossible, sand in the eyes of the stupid who will always be there.

We work for our people and know that we do far more for the progress of humanity than all the lodges in the world. We know from history that the Aryan builds, but the Jew tears down.

The character of the Jews is rigid and inflexible, the Jews cannot change themselves, from time immemorial they have sucked the guest peoples who trusted them until the guest peoples disappeared from history. Freemasonry too is rigid and inflexible, every Freemason will have to affirm that it cannot change in terms of its nature and structure. It will therefore likewise disappear, for only that which develops organically remains, that which is alive.

We are not democrats, we absolutely reject democracy. Democracy is Jewish, the whole revolution of democracy is Jewish. 'The revolution is the darling of the Jews', Grätz says as a *motto* in his history of Judaism.

We are aristocrats, we want to make every German aware of his national character a nobleman, then we are equal. That is what we mean by equality.

We call every Germanic a nobleman, aware of his duty to wield the sword and hammer.

We do not engage in feeble humanitarianism, we support the weak when it is weak by nature, but we do not turn one cheek to the one who slapped us on the other, we strike back and use all our pride to strike back vigorously, to strike so that the enemy is totally defeated. After all, that was also our Saviour's view: he had come to bring the sword.

We fight to the blood the spirit that is swirling around in the appeal of the Milanese lodge, the spirit of mammonism that aims to establish the republic everywhere because it can rule there. It is true that this spirit will create an era without throne and altar, but it is not true that this era will mean the happiness of the peoples, nay, where the masses rule, there the Jews rule, and their tyranny will be terrible.'

According to the articles of association, any free man of impeccable conduct can become a member of the Masonic lodge; in reality, he must also be well-off, because the contributions are high; the Masonic fraternity includes entrepreneurs, merchants, scholars, civil servants and military personnel. This was enough for the Jews to lead the nations until around the middle of the last century. Around that time, new classes developed: the class of low and senior civil servants and office workers and the class of factory workers.

For the first group, the commoners, they quickly found a means of controlling them. A special order for the rank was created, one that matched the customs of the freemasons, the *Odd Fellow order*. The lodges of this order were more focused on supporting its members, than those of the Freemasons. However, to better control Freemasonry too, the order *B'nai B'rith* was created. *B'nai B'rith* means: sons of faith. Only Jews could become members. *B'nai B'rith brethren*, however, had to sit in all the lodges of Europe and were promoted as quickly as possible, so that almost all the leaders of the individual lodges, the 'masters of the chair', sat in the *B'nai B'rith* at the same time and got their information from there.

In this way, Freemasonry, which was still run internationally by an institute in Geneva, was only subject to the orders of the *B'nai B'rith*. Now as for the fourth class, the class of workers, they could not join the lodges, but for them they invented international social democracy. It has already been said above that Freemasonry and Social Democracy adhere to the same principles and are perpendicular to Aryan doctrines.

In the Germanic countries and in the eastern part of Europe, relations were essentially different from those in France and England. These two countries already had a strong democracy and a social-democracy, albeit one with a national orientation. Industrialisation was more advanced in these two countries as well. In Germany, a patriarchal relationship between employee and employer still prevailed until the end of the last century. This had to disappear. Workers were worked by the organisations of social democracy - the three Jews Marx, Engels and Lasalle; employers became addicted to capitalism. The aim of the struggle was to pit the separate classes against each other. Conforming to the German orientation, the Social Democratic doctrine for the German worker was presented as world brotherhood. 'Proletarians of all countries unite,' was the slogan. In France, social-democracy initially aimed at uniting the Romani races; later, the major part became nationalist, the left wing communist. The *Commune* uprising in 1871 served as an example. In England, social democracy played no role, and where it did, it was always nationalist. Nor did it matter much there; business was in Jewish hands, power only had to be secured and not exaggerated as in Germany. Therefore, all powers were used here. Here, all means were employed, because there was a danger that the German tribes would cooperate in a German state. Prussia in particular was an enemy of Judaism; it was known as reactionary. The 'Prussian squire' became a household word. One drove a wedge between the nobility and the king. One won the nobility, after it had been ruined by mixing with Jews; one spoke to the king. Finally, one arrived at a character as unstable as Kaiser Wilhelm II's and was able to win him over by tightening the circle around him.

Jews drove a second wedge between workers and employers. On the one hand, international capitalism stepped in and turned private enterprises into joint-stock companies. Now the entrepreneur lost interest in his staff. After all, he was no longer the owner of the business, it was no longer necessary for him to treat his people with caution, to keep them through good pay and good treatment; on the contrary, the more he could squeeze out of them, the bigger the profit. Both were hostile to each other.

In the late 1990s, around the begin of our century, the organisation of trade unions was completed; every worker was forced to join a trade union; those who started as apprentices had to join the workers' youth.

Exactly like the Social Democrats, the Catholics acted wherever they held power. From the cradle to the grave, the clergy guided and patronised German Catholics and influenced their political thinking.

Bismarck had recognised the danger; he tried to fight both directions. This had to fail because he did not know the common source of the centre and social democracy: the Jews. That he did not realise this, he owed to his court Jew Maximilian Harden.

Thus, we see that at the beginning of the century, all German parties were under Jewish influence and Jewish leadership. At court, they simply ruled. Wilhelm had become so dependent that he had made Ballin, Rathenau, and Friedländer-Fuld his advisers. If he wanted to gauge the mood of the people, he would go to Katzenstein's leather goods shop *Unter den Linden* in Berlin and ask his loyal Katzi what the people thought. Katzi was the only citizen in Germany who was allowed to present His Majesty with a present on his birthday.

During the last years of the 19th century, there were two men who acted against the Jews. Both were vilified and had to step down. Ahlwardt, the rector of the Germans as the Jewish press mockingly called him, was accused of a disgraceful crime and thus eliminated; Count Pückler-

Muskau who kicked up anti-Semitic riots was declared insane. It was already becoming difficult to sideline court preacher Stöcker; he had the Christian Socialists behind him. When the Prussian government dropped Stöcker, he had to resign.

II
Sources of the movement

At the turn of the century, a man appeared who the Jews could not eliminate because he was independent. When he was imprisoned, it was already too late; the prison sentence no longer affected his honour; on the contrary, people had more respect for Theodor Fritsch. Fritsch published a monthly magazine entitled the *Hammer*; the readers formed a community, the *Hammerbund*. He was the first to tackle the problem scientifically and his books still belong to the classic library of the anti-Semitic movement today.

Fritsch was fortunate to experience the dawn of the new age, the growth of the movement. Only recently he died at an advanced age. Fighting to his last breath, he died in harness.

Against the International, Hugenberg made a front, founding the Great German Confederation *(Alldeutscher Verband)* with the lawyer Claß. Unfortunately, the workers did not get their hands on the very well-run monthly; it did not get beyond the upper echelons of the population. Before, during and after the World War, the Great Germans belonged to the most hated and blackened section of the population. Great-German was synonymous with squire.

The current century had three Austrians on the battlefront against Judaism at the beginning. The first was Guido von List. Lists books on ariogermanic wisdom today still form a valuable resource and should not be forgotten, even if they go a little too far in terms of mysticism. Philipp Stauff, known for his book on half-timbered houses (*Runenhäuser*), united List's supporters in the *Guido-von List-Bund*. Von List died in Berlin shortly after the war.

The second was Lanz von Liebenfels, who still lives in the Rhineland today. He published a series of brochures, which he called *Ostara*, the Books of the Blind. Liebenfels had tried to reconstruct the primal text of the New Testament from the writings of the Church Fathers. His books were confiscated and destroyed.

The third was Baron Wittgenberg, the author of the *Semi-Gotha*, the *Semi-Alliancen* and of the *Semi-Kürschner*, which Philipp Stauff published. In these three standard works, he demonstrated the Jewish slant in German nobility, art and science. In 1920, Baron Wittgenberg preferred self-murder to the shame of knowing his wife and daughter were in the hands of a Jewish banker. That is why it is currently impossible to republish his books, all but a small number of which were bought up by Jews.

It is no coincidence that it was precisely Austrians who stepped into the breach at the time. They had seen the Jewish influence in Austria first hand; they saw the coming doom earlier than the Reich Germans who were still too well off at the time.

Among the German scientists who fought for enlightenment in the German sense, Wilser, Much, Penka should be mentioned. They provided the weapons that ensured the legends were refuted and spread about the origin of all cultures from the east. They proved that all culture came from the north and came exclusively from Aryans.

From the *Hammerbund* had emerged the *Deutschvölkischer Schutz- und Trutzbund*, which fought the Jews mainly in the economic field. Besides these groups and unions, there was a large number of small associations, such as an anti-Semitic lodge in Magdeburg, an association to combat the arrogance of the Jews in Berlin, and many others.

From all these associations, the *Teutonic Order* emerged in 1912. The first thing the Germanic *orders* did was to bring together the *völkische* alliances in a Pentecost meeting in Thale (Harz) in May 1914. The most active members in the Germanic *orders* formed the first anti-Semitic lodge, a secret alliance that was deliberately meant to act as a secret alliance against the Jewish secret alliance. The directives that were worked out were as follows:

Only Germans who could prove that their blood was pure to the third degree could become members of the *Teutonic Order*. This was to prevent descendants of Jews and halve Jews from infiltrating the order. Furthermore - because women could also become members of the order as 'friends' under the same condition - the circle of acquaintances of purebred Germans had to be expanded to promote marriage mediation.

Great value was to be placed on the propaganda of racial science. Knowledge gained in the animal and plant realms had to be applied to humans.

It had to be shown that the root cause of all diseases and all misery lies in the mixing of races.

The principles of the Great Germans had to be spread throughout the Germanic race. The aim was to unite all peoples with Germanic blood.

The fight against everything un-German, the fight against the International, Judaism in Germany, had to be vigorously promoted.

The leadership of the order was based in Berlin. Sections were founded in the states and it soon managed to gain a foothold in all major cities. When war broke out, the order had thousands of members and more than a hundred lodges. The board was composed of the leaders of the individual groups. To the outside world, the Order acted only in the person of Philipp Stauff (Großlichterfelde) and Pohl (Magdeburg).

III
Germanic orders and the Thule Society

When war broke out, 95 per cent of all members rushed to the front, the lodges ceased to function, the Confederation disintegrated, its members had scattered to all winds. The purpose of the order, to create unity, also seemed to have been achieved; never had Germany been so united as in the days before the outbreak of war in 1914. While the Germans were dreaming and fighting of a bright future, the Jews were working. The first blow was that they took advantage of the enthusiasm and persuaded the government to declare the armistice. In doing so, they put a stop to all the work, every announcement and all the propaganda of the Greater Germans and thus opened the door for Jewish propaganda.

Slowly, the men who could not take up arms because they were too old or unfit for military service for other reasons realised that they had been cheated. The social democracy that had emerged during the early days and was led by German leaders had again become dependent on Jews. Rathenau had become the dictator of Economic Affairs, Jews were present at all military parties, Jews were constantly pouring in from the east across the Polish border into Germany and settling here.

As a flaming signal, the mutiny of the sailors in 1917, staged by the unions, worked. It showed the enemies where to deploy the propaganda and the signal was promptly heeded. Then followed the stab-in-the-back myth, the munitions workers' strike of January 1918. Now the enemy could be relieved, now he knew that one German was stabbing another in the back, as had so often happened in the past. Instead of immediately putting the ringleaders against the wall, they were sentenced to a few months' imprisonment, then let them walk again. Treason remained unpunished; was even rewarded. On 20 October 1918, *Vorwärts* wrote: 'Germany must, that is our firm will, lower its war flag forever, without having brought him home victorious for the last time.' What else is needed to prove the enormous popular deception that the black-red-gold International has devised and consistently implemented. All of Germany has suffered for the last 14 years. At the time, however, people were not allowed to talk about it, they were not allowed to say anything, because then it was called being against the people. Nevertheless, towards the end of the war, from 1917 onwards, people vigorously opposed the International.

To show how the Jews slowly achieved the stated goal, an article from the *Beobachter* is printed here, which is still relevant today.

Jewish economy in Belgium

The history of the political department of the German governorate general of Belgium is classic proof of what happens as soon as a Jew joins the board.

The administrators in Belgium (insofar as they were not directly under the supreme command) were the military governor-general: Baron von der Goltz, then Bissing and finally von Falkenhausen. As departments, they fell under:

1. The civilian leadership (Excellency von Sandt). Later, this department was split into the group administration for Flanders in Brussels, and into that for Wallonia in Namur.

2. The political section with the press office, the Flemish section, the political service.

3. The new ministries that ran Belgium.

Baron von der Goltz was already derailing things. It was not enough that he allowed a dozen French newspapers, he also appointed Baron von der Lanken-Wackenitz as chief of the political department, who was married in Darmstadt to Mrs von Günthershof, the Jewess Renate Friedenthal, daughter of Karl Rudolf Friedenthal and Lea Rosenberg. At the same time as this baron, his brother-in-law Friedenthal appeared and allowed himself to be called exclusively Baron von Falkenhausen. For one von Falkenhausen married the Jewess Elsbeth Friedenthal in 1887 and called himself and his children 'von Falkenhausen-Friedenthal'. Although Friedenthal had become a lieutenant, he never spent a moment at the front throughout the war. He lived with his sister's husband, baron von der Lanken, over whom he always had much influence.

Lanken and Friedenthal appointed the co-owner of the *Frankfurter Zeitung* as leader of the press centre, the Jew and lawyer Simon. While envoy Kempf remained officially the chairman, Simon ran the business. When the *Deutsche Tageszeitung* criticised this situation at the time, it was said Simon would resign. However, he was gone for only eight days, after which he returned and joined Von der Lanken's diplomatic department. This had only increased Simon's influence. Via Friedenthal and Lanken, the Jew Ulrich Rauscher, *März*'s socialist collaborator, further joined the diplomatic department as a confidant. He immediately wrote a brochure on Belgium.

In charge of censorship on behalf of Belgian newspapers was the Jew Dr Ebstein; he managed to suppress any mention of scandalous events. Besides Ebstein, the Jew Schotthöfer, the former correspondent of the Paris *Figaro,* was appointed. His wife, who was of course Jewish as well and lived in Brussels, was a French spy. She was therefore at the source.

Alongside this couple, another Jewess, Mrs Ebstadt whose husband was active at the front, worked as an official at the press office, as in fact almost all lower-level officials came from un-German circles.

Mrs Ebstadt became involved with the Aryan baron von S... and became pregnant. She therefore had to leave Brussels. Baron S... went to the front where he was soon killed. (Sam. 2 ch. 11, 15) The Jews avenged every degradation of their women, while they themselves violated German women and girls with impunity.

For Belgian propaganda, the Jew Dr Oswaldt was appointed. He was first in Antwerp, where he quarreled with his military chief and was soon after transferred to Brussels. The 'quarrelsome' Aryan officer had to go to the front and was killed soon after. (Sam. 2 ch. 11, 15).

Dr Oswaldt's activities consisted of sabotaging German-minded Flemings. His right-hand man was the Jewish shorthand typist Bloch.

When the *Wolffbüro*, the official news service, established a branch in Brussels, the Jew Julius Wertheimer of the *Vossische Zeitung* was put in charge there. Leader of the *Wolffbüro* in Antwerp, and at the same time leader of the police department there, was the Jew Schiff, appointed by Lanken.

As general legal secretary, Baron Lanken imported the Jew Dr Schauer from Frankfurt. Schauer had previously worked as a lawyer in Paris. Mrs Schauer, again a French Jewess, was in the Flemish department, although she did not speak a word of German. One can imagine how useful she was there.

As a confidant, they appointed the commercial traveller Rosenbaum, who had previously sold fashion magazines on a commission basis. Rosenbaum got the magazine *Bruxellois* set up by the German authorities for free - he, who did not own a penny at the time, became a multiple millionaire in four years thanks to the German government's money.

Lanken further appointed the Jew Hausenstein, who had already been active in French service in the spring of 1914 as a divisive figure between Bavaria and Prussia; he was given the newspaper *Belfried*.

Every German office in Belgium was teeming with Jews; all the typists, all the junior civil servants were Jews.

Of the senior officials, the following should still be mentioned: Dr Markus Hübner who sat in the Flemish department alongside Dr Oswaldt, the Brussels Jew Driessen and the Jewish riding master Behrens.

The entire occupation of the political section was, of course, given the Iron Cross, which is also worn a lot by Hebrews: by Hebrews who were never in the trenches.

Helpers of the Jews were Baron von Strempel, who served as a senior government official and then became a captain. Today, he is a major and adjutant to the govenor general, Mr von Falkenhausen.

Furthermore, the head of the pascentral knight is von Marx, who can be recognised from afar as a true Jew. Marx has a palace on the hill in Bad Homburg and has been allowed to serve the emperor at breakfast on several occasions. He is an important link in the string of Jews that surrounds the emperor and will be his downfall.

Lawyer Stocky is a baptised Jew and served as a Jew in the administration of Belgium.

The private secretary of Mr von Sandt and his successor Schaible - these are both Aryan - was and is the Jew Kempner, son of the well-known Jewish lawyer and leader of the Liberals in Berlin.

Due to the ubiquitous Jewish court clique, the actions of the excellent Mr von Bissing were crippled and things were very much to Germany's detriment. It was simply impossible for Bissing to act. Bissing died in time, to the great joy of the Jews, and his successor became von Falkenhausen who brought with him his Jewish body physician Fürstenberg. It was impossible to get to Falkenhausen without Fürstenberg. This is the same tactic followed by Ballin, Rathenau, Friedländer- Fuld, Koppel, Jules Simon, Goldschmidt. They form a circle around the emperor and the latter hears only what the gentlemen want.

As it is described here using an example from the west, so it was in the east. One need only think of Kühlmann's scandalous peace. He married Friedländer-Fuld. As Germany's plenipotentiary, Kühlmann made the peace with Romania and, in the process, placed German interests so far behind Jewish interests that he squandered Bulgaria and turned the Bulgarian people, who were still German-minded during the war, against Germany.

In the north, too, Jews were in splendid postions, not to mention Turkey. There the Jews were in their element, for the Young Turks (Dschavid, Talaat etc.) were, after all, Jews converted to Islam.

All these facts led the men who had to stay behind in the fatherland to unite and form the *Germanen orders revived*. During the Christmas Congress in 1917, the new venues could be inaugurated.

At this Christmas congress, it was decided to improve propaganda. Sebottendorff declared that he would take over and finance the running of the *Allgemeine Ordens-Nachrichten* for the benefit of the initiates and the *Runen* for the benefit of the friends. He got the province of Bavaria under his control. This choice became important, as it made Bavaria the cradle of the social-national movement. The southern German tribes, the Baywars and the Swavs, are more mobile and join more easily than the northern German ones. They are not as critical, not as individualistic. The lords who joined in central and northern Germany had a more difficult time. While a large following soon emerged in the south, the order grew slowly in the north.

Sebottendorff had received the address of a couple of gentlemen who had applied through an advertisement; these he visited first. It was very convenient for him that he met a brother of the *Teutonic Order* in Munich, Walter Nauhaus, who worked as an apprentice with Professor Wackerle. The two decided to go out separately and strike together. Nauhaus would approach the youth and Sebottendorff wanted to form the backbone of the movement with older gentlemen. The first members of the circle were Mr Georg Gaubatz, who had put himself at the disposal of the *Red Cross* and was legal adviser to the Bavarian avian protection organisation, the teacher Rohmeder, president of the German School Association, and Johannes Hering, who had made a name for himself in the *Hammerbund*; he was the disseminator of the theories of Much, Penka and Wilser.

Just as a stone thrown into the water makes bigger and bigger circles, more members soon joined this first group. They toyed with the idea of renting a house in the Zweigstrasse to hold meetings there. Sebottendorff himself moved into a house in Bad Aibling with his wife and servants.

As propaganda, Sebottendorff placed advertisements in various magazines inviting readers to join a national lodge. These ads had also been the reason for the clash with Freemasonry. A freemason declared in the *Munich-Augsburger Abendzeitung* that this could only be a seedy lodge, as it was not customary among Freemasons to recruit members openly.

Propaganda sheet 1 was sent to those who signed up, briefly referring to the race problem. It was pointed out that an order was needed to propagate this idea, a secret league, and that those who wanted to join this secret league must first make a blood confession through an enclosed sheet. This one read:

'The undersigned declares to the best of his knowledge and conscience that no Jewish or coloured blood flows in his veins or those of his wife, nor are there any members of coloured races among his ancestors.'

Had the candidate signed this blood confession, he received propaganda sheet 2 with the swastika and the image of Wodan. He then had to fill in a form and send his photograph. This photo was printed on racially pure heity, an enquiry was held and if the conditions were met, the candidate was invited to appear at the meeting. After a certain trial time, he was admitted as a friend. Initiation consisted of a solemn pledge in which the candidate had to swear absolute loyalty to the master. The return of the lost Aryan to German Halgadom was symbolically depicted. Women and girls could also be admitted to this first degree.

IV
The Thule Society and the *Munich Beobachter* until the 1918 revolution

It was soon clear to Sebottendorff that he could not achieve great success in the small flat in Zweigstrasse. He got the chance to rent the space of the sports club in hotel *Vierjahreszeiten*, which could accommodate 300 people. Here, meetings could be held and more members could be won over to the ideas of the *Germano-orden*. Public meetings were impossible at the time. They were forbidden because of disturbances or, if allowed, one would undoubtedly be booed. It was the time when the youth that later unleashed the revolution was brought in, when the individual classes were most badly incited against each other; the time when Erzberger, Scheidemann sowed what would ripen on 9 November 1918; when no military dared to act forcefully against social democracy and the centre any more. If anything was to be achieved, ideas first had to take root in large circles; the field had to be ploughed first. Since the spoken word had no effect, it had to be replaced by the printed word. A new newspaper could not be published because the paper shortage was already very high and the government did not allow the publication of new newspapers. The opportunity then presented itself to take over an existing newspaper, the *Münchener Beobachter*, which had been published since 2 January 1887. Franz Eher, the publisher of the *Beobachter* and a client of the lawyer Mr Gaubatz, had died. From the widow of Franz Eher, Sebottendorff obtained publication rights for 5,000 marks. The magazine had no subscribers and was sold on the street. As owner of the *Münchener Beobachter Verlag Franz Eher Nachf.*, Käthe Bierbaumer, a sister of the *Germanic orders,* was registered. Miss Bierbaumer came from a farming family from Burgenland; one of the families that set out to rebuild the country in the east that was destroyed during the war with the Turks. Sebottendorff signed on as editor of the *Beobachter*. The *Beobachter* was set up as a sports magazine, putting it in the hands of young people. Another thing about this format was very favourable. Jews were only interested in sports if it paid off. Jews would therefore neither buy the *Beobachter* nor read it, because after all, they had no interest in sport per se. So a sports magazine could carry out propaganda unnoticed.

How correct this calculation was later became clear when the Jews became angry at 'the editor of a sports newspaper', as Sebottendorff was always called. This came up again and again, a sign of how much the Jews were annoyed that they had thought this sports newspaper so unimportant.

A few articles by Sebottendorff are printed here from the first issues of the *Münchener Beobachter*.

Keep your blood pure

In the middle of the last century, the English minister Disraeli-Beaconsfield wrote in his novel *Endymion*: 'The race issue is the key to world history, and that alone is why history is often so confusing, because it was written by people who knew neither the race issue nor the events associated with it.'

Beaconsfield was right in his remark. After all, he had to know too, because he was a Jew himself. One only has to look at the meaning given to the world war in terms of its nature and origin, and one has to agree with him. Side effects, pretexts are usually regarded as the root causes of this world tragedy. Most have not yet found the key. It also lies here in the race issue.

Actually, it is about the struggle between two opposing worldviews, two opposing races. The Germanic, creative race on the one hand, and the parasitic, big-capitalist race on the other.

It will be objected that surely the English and Ameri- canes are also Germanic in origin. True, but that is not important; what matters is who rules these peoples, who leads them. The secret ruler of our enemy is undoubtedly international big business, which aspires to world domination. The representatives of this big business are the outspoken enemies of our people and our nationhood. They are the Jews.

They fight our national character and have done so through the centuries under various masks and forms. Unfortunately, they all too often find their greatest allies among our own people themselves. The Germanic has the character of someone like Faust. Possession alone cannot satisfy him. Often purely as a 'fool' he grasps at apparent values and images (ideals), which his mortal enemies talk up as higher civilisation, as higher cultural values. However, these delusions are nothing but poisons and anaesthetics to bring the Germans all the more surely under the yoke as slaves.

Our ancestors often had a natural feeling against their enemies. They knew the racial issue and the value of blood brotherhood, the value of the pure blood. They knew that they could trust only their tribesman, that only he could be loyal. A half-breed, someone from another race, was false, was strange.

Unfortunately, in many areas, the healthy instinct was muddied or completely uprooted. Walvater was dethroned and in place of our faith in the fathers came a new faith and in a form that does not correspond to our German and religious nature. One can fully and completely recognise the value of Christianity, but that does not exclude that one can differ greatly in opinion about the way it was brought to the Germanic people. Above all, we must now reject and fight against those who, under the guise of religion, quietly and resolutely strive to weaken our national character.

However, the suppression of our religion was not over. Our wisdom was wasted, our law nullified and broken by Roman law. Even our language was ridiculed and tried to be eradicated, reduced to the language of the common people.

That the decline of our nation was accompanied by complete political destruction is obvious. Yet time and time again, the people's nature proves strong enough to undo the enemy's plans. Invariably, men and leaders rose up, bringing the people out of the valley, and it was the will of God that the people always regained the way up.

The entire German people had to be struck with blindness if the enemies were now to achieve their goal.

An ideal of humanity alien to him provided the means to put Parzival, the fool in *optima forma*, in chains. Backed by Christianity, they spread the doctrine of the equality of men. Gypsies, Hottentots, Botokuds, and Germanic people were supposed to be perfectly equal.

It is just a pity that the great teacher, nature, teaches otherwise. Who teaches us that this equality is absurd! It is the biggest lie ever foisted on mankind, to destroy us Germans. There are higher and lower races! If one equates the mixture of races, the Chandalis with the Aryans, the noblemen, then one commits a crime against humanity. This needs leaders, including leading peoples, for their development to a higher level.

Among the races on earth, the Germanic race is called to occupy this position as leader by virtue of its disposition. As far back as we can look in history, people with Germanic blood in their veins have always also been the bearers, the creators of culture.

It is true that people have tried to talk us into believing - and the world still believes - that the origin of the peoples is the East Asian highland or Two-streamland. From the east, light is said to have come.

The latest research has shown that this assumption is wrong. Northern Europe, northern Germany is where the culture bearers come from, from here streams of inspiring German blood have poured out since grey antiquity to the present day, wave after wave of people have gone out to bring culture to the whole world.

The so highly praised Greek culture is a derivative of the German spirit. The Hittites, the Sumerians and whatever those peoples are all called, were of Aryan origin.

When the French and Spanish and Italians boast of their culture, they should not forget that they owe this culture to Germanic blood. The more the purity of the blood deteriorated, the thinner the Aryan blood became and the more obvious the cultural barrenness became. Greece and Rome did not perish because of moral decay and not because devotion declined; these were merely consequences. Rome and Greece succumbed to racial confusion, to the borderless ruination of the race.

The same fate also threatens us, threatens the Germanic race; on the one hand by the gospel of the equality of all men, on the other by the rule of international big capitalism, which demands racial mixing.

The weapon of the lower races, the Chandals, is money.

With this weapon, they seek to destroy the noble race. The danger is urgent, because on the one hand, the instinct has been weakened by the gospel of racial equality; on the other, racial mixing is highly favoured, because travelling in the world has become so easy.

That our government did not completely miss the danger before the war is shown by a law it introduced. Marriage between Germans and coloureds was to be banned. Who voted against this law? Germans, I show you your enemies: the centre, the Social Democrats, the Christian Socialists and the Liberals voted against it.

Racial purity means public health. When all members of the nation are imbued with the value of pure blood, then the social issue is also resolved, then it has lost its sharpness, then everyone sees in his compatriot a brother, a sister, then one supports the other, then the old Germanic religion, the knowing and wisdom of the 'you' is reawakened.

This was a language that had not been heard in Munich until now. The first edition of the *Beobachter*, which came out in 5,000 copies, was sold in its entirety, and later the circulation increased from issue to issue. Besides the big problems, the small ones were not forgotten either; there was sharp criticism. A few examples of this, too, concerning the Reichstag elections in which the *'Unabhängige'* (*Unabhängige Sozialdemokratische Partei - USDP*) had nominated the Jew Eisner. The *Beobachter* posted the following note:

A Russian Jew as a candidate in the Reichstag

We are told that the *Unabhängige Sozialdemokratische Partei,* Munich, is nominating the writer Kurt Eisner as its candidate in the Munich II constituency by-elections.

Eisner may not be elected, but the fact that a party even dares to nominate a Russian Jew, who was convicted of treason, should put the worker to shame!

Four months later, Eisner was prime minister in Beieren; he had unleashed the revolution.

In the summer of 1918, all sorts of rumours were circulating among the people. Milk was said to be sold on the black market from Bavaria to Prussia, the king was called milkman (*Millibauer*) and it was claimed that he was the protagonist. On the other hand, it was claimed in northern Germany that from there flour and vegetables went to Bavaria. Anyone who experienced the distress will understand the role this small, natural exchange of products played in the incitement of the individual tribes.

Only the *Beobachter* No 18 of 5 October 1918 dared to bring the truth:

Leutstetten and the Prussia pamphlet

We all have no idea by what means our enemies are working to sow discord, to reinforce the unsatisfaction. It has already reached the point where one is no longer allowed to utter the word victory. Milions of pamphlets are falling daily on and behind our front - a party press in Germany that knew what it wanted, hindered by no government, has scattered the seed, on which the rain of pamphlets successfully fell down. Now we can reap.

Dissension between north and south sought to establish the pamphlet, which was very insidiously printed in full by the *Berliner Tageblatt*. We did not learn that anything happened to the *Berliner Tageblatt* - they simply accepted the slap in the face.

With us, people try another way: in Bavaria, people always ask about the stomach. There, it is whispered that the king sends milk to Berlin, it is told that at night wagons full of calves go to northern Germany. It does not help when it is pointed out that milk from Leutstetten is delivered to the maternity homes for barely cost price. People simply do not believe that our king charges 28 *Pfennig* per litre, when he could get 80 *Pfennig*!

Here, however, it should be expressly noted once again that milk from Leutstetten has never been delivered outside Bavaria and that all milk from there goes to Munich, Nürnberg, Würzburg and Fürth, where it is used in hospitals and maternity institutions.

What is concealed

The following report appeared in all newspapers: 'In Nauheim, following the dismantling of a secret slaughterhouse, numerous rich leading citizens were arrested, including a religion teacher and a well-known hotel owner. The latter offered to pay 50,000 marks for his immediate release. The slaughterhouse was located in a barn close to the railway line. The addresses of the recipients were affixed to the numerous crates, so that people knew exactly who the buyers of the meat were. One of the best-known doctors in Nauheim was also involved in the case.'

As long as no names are mentioned, we do not trust the matter. However, the *Beobachter* established that the arrested religious teacher was the very pious Jewish butcher Oppenheimer, who secretly slaughtered the cattle whose meat was served in the kosher *Hotel Adler* according to Jewish ritual. The buyers included the Jewish doctor, professor and *Geheimrat* Dr Grödel, who operated a first-class sanatorium in Nauheim. This doctor - he is the Empress' physician and the King of Bulgaria's body physician - is the well-known doctor in Nauheim who was so shamefully hushed up. The other customers are Jews in Frankfurt and Berlin, the same ones conducting a smear campaign against Bavaria because of foodstuffs.

Mr Goldstein from Essen representing the Alliance of Bavarian Municipalities is the latest. A friend of our magazine sends us from Essen the following advertisement from the *Kölnische Zeitung*:

'Bavarian municipalities demand all kinds of vegetables for sale. R. Goldstein, Essen, Wiesenstraße 83.'

These are strange municipalities that want to buy vegetables for Bavaria in the Prussian industrial area of all places. Whether Mr Goldstein is concerned about more than just costs and commission? We absolutely cannot imagine that precisely the densely populated industrial area can do without vegetables. Or is it part of the tactic to create friction between north and south? Is it perhaps the intention in Prussia to repeat the trick played in Bavaria? 'Well, now you will have it, now the Bavarians are buying away our vegetables as well.'

These are enough examples to indicate the way the *Beobachter* fought.

The editorial office was still officially in Pfarrstraße 5, but in reality it was in *Vier Jahreszeiten*.

The society itself had now grown so large that it was possible to think of a change. As a pseudonym for the society, Nauhaus suggested the name Thule. This was accepted by Sebottendorff, because the name sounded secretive enough and immediately told the connoisseur what it was about. The inauguration of the site took place on the 17th of the harvest month (August). The ceremonies were attended by both presidents of the order from Berlin. They appointed Sebottendorff as their representative and master, appointed the head of the lodge and held the first proper lodge. On the following Sunday, 30 brothers and sisters were solemnly admitted to the first degree. Among them were members from all over Bavaria who had come to Munich for this. On the following Saturday another ordination could already take place, in which the lodge Nauhaus was consecrated. Now it was decided that an ordination would take place every third Saturday of the month, while lectures were held on the other Saturdays.

Master Griehl was in charge of the decoration of the lodge room, and he applied the symbol of the Thule company, the victorious sun path, in all rooms. Mrs Riemann- Bucherer had taken charge of the choir. Baron Seidlitz and Hering turned out to be artists on the keyboard or harmonium, Miss Karl sang her songs.

Each member wore the bronze eagle made at the Ecklöh firm in Lüdenscheid, which shows a swastika on its shield, crossed by two spears. The archetype of the symbol was a swastika applied to a Germanic axe found in Silesia. The sisters of the society wore a simple gold swastika.

On 1 November 1918, the *Teutonic Order* had around 1,500 members throughout Beieren, in Munich around 250. Entrance fees went to Berlin for propaganda purposes. Every member received the *Runes* and the *Beobachter*. The two sections of the order had made good progress in the rest of Germany too, but they still could not be compared to the success in Bavaria.

The revolution caused great losses. In Bavaria, almost all members lost the society. Apparently, one is only sure of its existence there, where the leader remains in constant contact with his supporters. The last issue of the *Beobachter* of 9 November 1918 carried the following article:

Germany's distress

Every day we receive letters asking: what should we do? Did Germany, did we, deserve this? Daily, our supporters are asking what to do to turn the tide of doom.

We can do nothing but wait and see and get on with our work!

We must work quietly and resolutely for the renewal of Germany. Joining forces, descending the half-way ladder that leads to the rich and deep well of the Germanic humanities. You all have no idea how great the knowledge, how high the culture of the Germanic people was, which spread everywhere inspiringly.

Six thousand years ago, when India and Egypt, the Mesopotamia, were still shrouded in deep night, our ancestors counted the stars on the stone circles at Sto- nehenge and Udry, set the year and the holidays. They carved runes that became the basis for the letters.

We find Aryan culture in Ur in Chaldea too, German tribes in Palestine even before the Jews fell in there, the Trojan, the Mycenaean culture is Germanic, the Greek is blood of our blood! India and Persia bear the stamp of German culture and what we later got back from the East, the East received from us.

The entire Middle Ages were flourished by German blood, France was revived by the blood of the Normans, Italy experienced its *Renaissance* by German blood and German spirit.

We will use our pride because what awaits us will be an iron life of work.

We do not yet know what fate will bring us; we know, however, that when it takes us through the valley of suffering, we will be sure of the way up.

Only through struggle does all culture exist, all culture emerge. And struggle will be abundant for us in the future.

Fight for existence, fight for life!

This should not make us narrow-minded, not despondent. We must stand straight, one must support the other. As sworn comrades, the Germans must stand side by side. We must wait and see, for time will come again for the Germans too. We must wait and work, always thinking about it, yearning for it and forgetting nothing.

We must all defend ourselves as one against what is foreign, what does not belong to our race. We need German judges, German lawyers, German doctors, German teachers of the people.

We have suffered enough from foreign blood.

From Bethmann-Hollweg to Erzberger, it is the Semitic slant that has ruled us to death. That will stop, that must stop.

We know that there is a large current among the Social Democrats pointing to *völkisch* waters. Read Erhard Auers' speech at the Bavarian Party Day. Our task is to make use of this current, we want a *völkisch* movement that keeps the German gouwen free of foreign races. The Germans in Austria are now free, and a long-cherished dream, the union of all Germans, comes true. The German's distress has always been the birth of a new boom period.

We are in the greatest need and that is precisely why fate will make us tough, it will give us the toughness we lacked.

Therefore: high the hearts and free the gaze. Only he is lost who thinks himself lost.

We, however, want to live, want to live long and happy lives. Everything that lives must perish to make way for the new life. We will die, but our children and children's children will live. The distress of the Germanic people is the threshold to the new life.

Lord, give us need, that we may become Germans.

And a second article in the same issue 23 of 9 November 1918:

To the emperor!

A new victim claims the raging storm! Wilhelm II abdicates the throne. And it is astonishing how many people who were otherwise happy in their slavish subservience when they received a Prussian bird (an award in the shape of an eagle - vert.) from the Kaiser, are nowadays walking around with the *Munich Post* in their hands asking: 'Is he not stepping down yet?'

A little independent thought is out of the question these days, everyone is competing for the favour of the new men. Backbone?

God, gone are the days when men still had a backbone. They lean forward, they wag backwards. We used to be different. Once, people spoke of German loyalty! But that was long ago. Loyalty and promise are no longer worth anything in the marketplace of life.

The emperor's problem is not a personal one. It shakes the foundations of the empire and of the people. Nor is the Kaiser the problem, but the 1914 war started and waged by international Jewry, international Freemasonry, international plutocracy with the sole aim of destroying the German Kaiser! One knows exactly that with him the and other monarchs in Germany were cast off.

Looking at the Kaiser's problem objectively, we must emphatically point out that Wilhelm II never wanted the war, that he delayed the start for so long - always hoping that a miracle would happen - until it was already too late for Germany.

We blame him for missing a lot of opportunities when he should have drawn the sword.

We reproach him for surrounding himself with foreign races, placing value on foreign influences and thereby putting his people in a precarious position.

But these problems do not matter these days, it is not about the person, it is about the principle.

Germany needs the monarchy, the leader! Without the leader, everything falls apart!

Our enemy knows this very well, but we do not.

Nor are we surprised that the centre, which has been so monarchist all along, was so committed to the fuss. The threads of international Jewry, the enemy of every monarchy, reach upwards, to the highest peak of the church.

Yet many people value their wallet more than their honour. Precisely those people should know that French presidential elections cost as much as the three-year budget of the German empire.

It was on 7 November 1918, when Kurt Eisner of the *Unabhängige Sozialdemokratische Partei* and the Social Democrat Ehrhard Auer agreed to stage a joint revolutionary action. The collaboration was announced at a meeting on Theresienwiese in the afternoon. Eisner, Auer, Unterleitner and Simon gave speeches demanding the abdication of Kaiser Wilhel II and the German crown prince. At 4 o'clock, the meeting was over and now the revolution was set in motion. At the blind Gandorfer's side, Eisner and his supporters hurriedly marched through the city. The soldiers in the barracks were soon won over to the revolution; the commander of the 2nd Bavarian Army Corps, General Kraft von Dellmensingen, was imprisoned in the Hotel *Bayerischer Hof*.

King Ludwig III left his residence and embarked on a terrifying and arduous flight with Queen Therese and the princesses. The publishers of the daily papers, the central railway station, the main post office, in short, all public buildings were occupied by Eisner's supporters. In the *Mathäserbräu* hall, the workers and soldiers positioned themselves, but moved overnight to the Landdag building in Prannerstraße and elected Eisner president here. In Bavaria, the republic was declared and the House of Wittelsbach (the Bavarian royal house - vert.) was deposed.

When Munich awoke on Friday 8 November, the republic was a fact. The various civil service offices were buzzing with activity; anyone who could show a Marxist participation booklet was given a job without regard to race. The only difference was that the *Unabhängige* got the best jobs.

In his appeal, Eisner promised to convene a *Nationalversammlung*, which should meet as soon as possible on the basis of a new and freer suffrage. He further promised peace and complete freedom soon. On the same day, he issued a second summons, promising the peasants that things would be better for them from now on. Peace had been secured; nothing would be destroyed but built up,

The revolution spread. Berlin followed on 9 November, and during those days the first sailors also appeared in Munich, the vultures of the 1918 revolution.

On Saturday 9 November, Thule had a meeting at which Sebottendorff made the following speech:

'Brothers and sisters!

Yesterday, we experienced the collapse of all that was familiar, dear and precious to us.

In place of our blood-related ruler reigns our mortal enemy: the Jews. What will come out of the chaos, we do not yet know. We can surmise.

There will come a time of struggle, of bitter distress, a time of danger!

We warriors are all in danger because the enemy hates us with the boundless hatred of the Jewish race; it is now an eye for an eye, tooth for a tooth!

Those who will not assist us in this struggle must go unchallenged and their names will not be mentioned. Nor shall we reproach him for having gone. He who does not know it yet will know it today: we do not have to count on being spared in this battle. Nor do I wish to be spared, nor will I spare anyone!

As long as I hold the iron hammer here, I am ready to engage Thule in this battle!

He who cannot follow me, who promised me loyalty and cannot keep her in his heart with joy, he can go; I will not blame him!

However, whoever wants to stay with me will know that there will be no back, but only forward!

Whoever wants to stay I will remind of his promise of faithfulness, even if it is in death!

I, however - I assure you and swear it by the sign sacred to us, may the victorious sun hear it - will be equally faithful to you. Trust me, as you have trusted me so far!

Our fight will be tough on both fronts. On the inner front, because we must become tough and tough! On the outer front, because everything un-German must be fought!

Our order is a Germanic order. Germanic is loyalty. Our god is Walvater, his rune is the rune of the eagle. And the trinity: Wodan, Wili, We is the unity of the trinity.

Never will the mind of anyone of a lower race understand this unity in the trinity. Wili, like We, is the polarisation of the Walvater and Wodan the divine immanent law.

The eagle rune means Aryan, primal fire, sun, eagle. And the eagle is the symbol of the Aryan.

To indicate the eagle's ability to burn itself, it was executed in red, then called the hawk.

Friends, from now on the red eagle is our symbol. He will remind us that we must pass through death to live.

The Jews know only too well that they should fear the eagle. After all, in their scriptures, Deuteronomy 28 verse 49 says: 'The Lord will raise up against you a people from afar, from the end of the earth, like as an eagle flies; a people whose speech you will not understand.'

What could be further apart than German and Jewish thinking, what is more incomprehensible than when a German speaks to a Jew?

Beware, friends, they will also abolish our German eagle! However, we want to see the eagle again and again as a symbol, as a symbol of decisiveness. Our firm faith is the hope of the poet:

Fly, then fly up Loudering world fire, Then rise victoriously high Imperial eagle of the German land.

Heine who spewed venom and bile at everything Aryan says somewhere:

You ugly bird, you will repent:
If I ever catch you, I'll pull all your feathers out of your body And chop off your claws!

Yesterday's revolution, unleashed by the low race to bring about the downfall of the Germanic people, is the beginning of purification. It will depend on us alone, how long or how short this purification will last. We must be aware of this, we must work on ourselves, so that each of us becomes the flame that gives light and warmth and consumes the enemy!

However, let us not forget the work, the outward struggle! Now, brothers and sisters, there is no more time for contemplative speeches and discussions and celebrations! Now we must fight and I will and I will fight! Fight until the swastika rises victoriously from the fim- bul winter!

People say the revolution brings freedom. Yes, it brings back our freedom, which was taken away from us four years ago! Now we will talk about the German Empire, now we will say that the Jew is our mortal enemy. From today we will act.

I wanted to give you, brothers and sisters, eight days time, eight days time for reflection. No friends, tomorrow the decision must be made. Those who are not here tomorrow will be deleted from our lists, they have thereby said: I am afraid and do not want to join you!

Let no one speak of compromise and wait patiently. Cursed be anyone who would tempt me to do so.
    Tomorrow is November 10, the birthday of Luther, Schiller and Scharnhorst!

Tomorrow at 8 p.m. there will be an ordination lodge. Those who do not come, those who stay away without notice, they no longer exist for us.

After leaving the dining room, do not let anyone come to me with 'let's be merry together' without asking and without advising. Everyone has to come to terms with themselves.

And so I close this meeting:

> I know, God, that I belong to you
> And you me through all times.
> Only one wish fills my mind,
> To fight tirelessly for You as a warrior. Give Your blessing! That we the brazen brood from the lowlands,
> That ruined us, subdued with courage and strength,
> And let in our Germanic blood
> The song of the solar eagle echoed again!

V
Thule society, *Kampfbund* and the circles around Thule

With Philipp Stauff's beautiful words, Sebottendorff had closed the lodge on 9 November 1918; the sun-eagle had come alive, no one was missing from the meeting on 10 November 1918. The master, who had been in bed with a high fever as late as Friday due to a pervasive, dangerous flu, suffered a relapse and had to be returned to his dwelling in boarding house *Döring*. Meanwhile, the fate that Germany had brought upon itself was striking. The individual Länder were almost interdependent and each pursued their own politics. Eisner, who with the blind Gandorfer had unleashed the revolution on 8 November 1918, was prime minister; a makeshift National Council had been convened in Munich. Here, Jews were already speaking. Toller, Levien, Axelrod, Dr Lipp, who declared war on Switzerland, Dr Wadler, who had once gone through life as a Great-German, now a fierce communist, appeared on the scene with many other Jews. New elections to the German *Nationalversammlung* and to the Bavarian parliament were called before the start of the new year. At Spa, the extension of the armistice was under discussion. Germany was blockaded on land and sea; the food shortage was increasing day by day.

At the meeting on 10 November, important decisions had been taken. The Thule Society would continue, but not actively participate in the expected battle; it was to work on itself.

Outwardly, there was to be a *Kampfbund*, whose leadership was reserved for Sebottendorff. This *Kampf- bund* soon had an unexpected success. The revolution had left almost all *völkische* associations homeless. The pub and hotel owners had cancelled rents. Sebottendorff opened his door wide and within a short time all important *völkische* meetings took place in the *Vier Jahreszeiten*. The advantage was that, for the first time, the individual groups came into close contact with each other, as it often happened that two, three meetings took place at the same time. In the Thule Society, things went on like a pigeon coop. Here again the National Liberal Party under Hanns Dahn was founded, here the Great Germans met under bookseller and publisher Lehmann, the German School Association under Rohmeder, the *Fahrende Gesellen*, the *Hammerbund* of which Dannehl was the most active member. In short, there was not an association in Munich with any national importance that did not find shelter at Thule. It was here that ir. Gottfried Feder first went public with his ideas on breaking the slavish obligation to pay interest.

The most active and stimulating member of the entire circle was the bookseller and publisher Lehmann, who constantly came up with new ideas and plans. Lehmann was known as a Great German in Munich and was accordingly hated by all parties. He had procured cautionary half-arms and was a main depot in the Thule Society.

These weapons were the cause of a minor incident that should not be hushed up. Sebottendorff was with his wife and Miss Bierbaumer for lunch and when coffee - a scarce item at the time - was to be served, he was seized by a sudden agitation that forced him to get up, leave and make his way to the office in Marstallstraße. There everything was quiet, only secretary Anni Molz was there. Sebottendorff began collecting the weapons hidden under the stages with her and wrapped them in writing paper. The packages were then stacked in the office, where they disappeared from sight behind the opened door.

They had hardly finished the work when the doorbell rang and the owner of the bookstore *Stiegeler* appeared, asking for a pair of *Mauser pistols*. Stiegeler is well known in the *völkische* movement because of his book *Deutschlands Werdegang* and his association *Urda*. Sebottendorff put two pistols and the necessary ammunition in the briefcase, he himself took two pistols, let Miss Molz go and locked the door of the Thule Society. As the two gentlemen turned from Marstallstraße into Maximilianstraße, a truck carrying the *Republikanische Schutzwehr* rounded the corner and stopped in front of the entrance to the Thule Society.

'They must have me,' Sebottendorff said, 'take my briefcase, Mr Stiegeler, I have to go back and see what's going on.'

'Surely you are not so crazy as to venture into the lion's den!'

'Yes, Mr Stiegeler, I need to know what is going on. Please take my bag, and I will see you at Paulaner today at 10 o'clock. If I am not there at 10 o'clock, you will then go to lawyer Dahn or Mr Gaubatz and tell him so that people know where I am!'

So said, so done.

Just as Sebottendorff came up the stairs, he heard people trying to open his door with keys. He asked: 'What are you doing there?'

'Yes, what do you want here then?' was the counter question. 'Excuse me, I am the owner of this property here.'
'Oh yes, we have orders to search for weapons.' 'Please come in.'

Sebottendorff opened the door and a thorough examination began. Everything, even the heating, the grand piano, the harmonium were opened, the stages in the lodge lifted. Sebottendorff was only too glad that he had hidden the weapons somewhere else in the afternoon! When they found nothing, Sebottendorff asked for an explanation for the search; he got this too. Nevertheless, they took him to the police station. There they asked him about the activities of the Thule Society. He said it was a sports club, and since he could identify himself as a Turkish citizen, they soon let him go. At Paulaner's he met Stiegeler and Dahn, whom Stiegeler had already informed. Another incident in which they wanted to catch Eisner was also unsuccessful. It was 4 December 1918, and Sebottendorff was on his way to Bad Aibling to visit his wife.

At the station, he was met by Lieutenant Sedlmeier, the son of the owner of the famous *Theresienbad* in Bad Aibling, who informed him that Eisner would give a speech at the *Kurhaus*. He would bring Auer and Timm with him. Surely that was an opportunity to seize him and declare Auer president. The matter seemed possible to them. A strong opposition against Eisner was already noticeable at the time. The *Mehrheitssozialists* in particular had resented Eisner for wanting to get friendly with the *Entente* in Geneva and blaming Germany for the war. The *Mehrheitssozialists* had almost nothing to say in the government itself; Eisner, Fechenbach, Unterleitner were the regents who had influence. The plan could succeed if Auer was present and if there were enough peasants to cover the raid. Sedlmeier himself had gathered around him about 15 youngsters who were willing to participate. Calls were drawn up and printed in the printing office of the *Miesbacher Anzeiger*, which at the time was still run by Klaus Eck.

The call was to be issued at the last minute, as soon as Eisner had spoken. Sedlmeier was to stand by the stage and would provoke Eisner after his speech. Sebottendorff would come to his aid from the other side of the stage and capture Eisner. A car would take the prisoner to the mountains, where he was to be held until a new government was formed. Anyone with a bicycle was sent out to get as many peasants from the villages as possible. They had to tell them that 'something was going to happen'.

Two things foiled the plan. Eisner did not bring Auer, but Culture Minister Hoffmann and Grandorfer of the Farmers' Council. Then had come workers from Kolbermoor - almost all of them pure communists and the people of the Rosenheimer Urban Renewal, who crowded around the stage in large crowds. It was impossible for Sebottendorff and his people to reach the stage. But that had not been so bad; the danger lay in the fact that people had underestimated Eisner's speech talent. One had not counted on Gandorfer winning over the peasants. Eisner's speech was a masterpiece of Jewish art of distortion. He began by accusing himself of having three flaws. First, he was a Jew and belonged to that unfortunate people who had lived in slavery for centuries, who were not allowed to practice any profession and who were hated. For this very reason, the Jews had always stood up for true freedom, true equality, because, after all, they had experienced first-hand the untold defamation and the misery. Secondly, he was a Prussian, a rotten Prussian, as they say in southern Germany. But he was an enemy of the way of thinking of the Prussians, an enemy of the 'junckers' ruling there, which is why he had lived in Bavaria for many years, and his first excursion had been here, to the beloved mountain country. Third, he was a social democrat. Now came the familiar talk of international social democracy that would help build a new Germany in beauty and dignity.

When Eisner finished, wild cheers rang through the hall and Sedlmeier could forget about his action. After Gandorfer had spoken and promised the farmers all sorts of things, it was no longer possible to carry out the planned action.

When Gandorfer had finished and the discussion was opened, Sedlmeier jumped on stage and began his speech: 'Salomon Kosmanowsky - in ordinary life Kurt Eisner - has spoken...', he got no further, a wild uproar broke out, the two guards pounced on the little lieutenant, Fechenbach pushed forward - then Aibling's blacksmith appeared in the background, stretched out his mace, grabbed the petite Sedlmeier in his collar and lifted him out of the crowd to put him back down behind him. This allowed him to escape.

Later, on Eisner's death, revenge was taken against him. Lawyer Eller, once a pillar of the *Vaterlandspartei*, then communist, led the procession. One pulled Sedlmeier out of his bed, put him on a wagon and at gunpoint with 25 ready-to-shoot rifles he had to repeat the words, which Ir. Herbst read to him: 'I ask forgiveness for having offended the prime minister, I am sorry that a member of the officers' clique killed him.'

Mayor Ruf was deposed and Eller took over his office. A third event, also without consequences, would become significant for the *Kampfbund* of Thule.

Dr Buttmann, formerly a deputy, had received permission from Auer, Timm and Haller to form a vigilante group. The three ministers were members of the *Mehrheits sozialisten* and wanted the vigilante group as a security service in the upcoming elections. Dr Buttmann probably had other intentions, but he was clever enough to keep them hidden under the guise of vigilante. Through First Lieutenant Kurz who was a member of the Thule Society, he was made aware of the Society and so he came to Sebottendorff and requested the main hall for the meeting to be held in the evening. This was granted; the meeting took place in the evening. One had, in order to keep the secret from the individual participants, not sufficiently controlled the visitors and so one Lieutenant Kranold had sneaked in, who worked at the War Ministry and had heard of the establishment. Lieutenant Colonel Haak explained on that evening, how Munich could be defended against a *coup* from within. He told what security measures had to be taken and where to set up guard posts. It was then decided to meet again at Thule the following afternoon to form the groups. As all those present were needed for this, Sebottendorff made himself available to receive the first notifications at the Kühbogen recruiting office already rented by Dr Buttmann.

On this morning, based on the posters already put up, more than 300 men came forward and pledged by handshake to act against any coup, be it from the left or right. The names and addresses were put on a list. At noon, Sebottendorff closed the recruiting office and made his way to the *Vier Jahreszeiten,* where he was told by Sell, the reliable doorman, that the *Republikanische Schutzwehr* had just picked up 35 men and taken them to the police station. People from the *Beobachter* had not been there.

Sebottendorff managed to be admitted to Eisner's office in the afternoon and to get the written order from him to start interrogations immediately. At the police station, he showed his recruitment lists and said that these people had commited to act in any coup, whether it be from the left or right.

By 9 am, 33 men had been interrogated and were able to await their release with sausages, beer and cigarettes, which Sebottendorff had sent for. Bookseller and publisher Lehmann, from whom weapons had been found, and Lieutenant-Colonel Haak, who had given the said speech, were detained. There were false statements against them, which had come from Kranold. Lehmann and Haak were taken to Stadelheim and remanded there for several weeks. Dr Buttmann had managed to leave the Thule building via a second exit. The 33 young people who had been arrested, including Kurz, Woerner, Lieutenant Parcus, Ahrens and Schwabe, joined the *Kampfbund*.

About the traitor Kranold, the *Beobachter* carried the following report a few weeks later:

From Bavaria and the Empire

The *Bayerische Kurier* published the following decision of 17 November 1918 by War Minister Roßhaupter:

'During the last days of the revolution, a series of sacrificial individuals volunteered their services to the good cause. Selfless and not afraid of danger, they have worked independently and with enormous dedication to build the new state. I consider it my duty to offer an honourable reward to all those who have worked faithfully here at the ministry. First Lieutenant Streit 200 marks, Lieutenant Schöpf 200 marks, Lieutenant Kranold 300 marks, lieutenant Rosenbeck 300 marks, lieutenant Edelmann 1000 marks etc.'

The lieutenant Kranold mentioned here had ensured the arrest of the vigilante through a false report. This arrest played a major role in the Provisional *Nationalversammlung* well into the new year. Timm, Auer and Haller were fiercely attacked by the *Unabhängige* and the communists. They were accused of planning to overthrow the government.

Besides the *Kampfbund*, which grew steadily, the Thule Society also expanded. Due to the revolution, it had lost the entire province land? Or countryside? But in Munich it was constantly gaining a firmer foothold. The *Beobachter* grew as well. Passing the magazine from hand to hand prevented the newspaper from being confiscated. The paper had never, even during the hard times of council rule, been subject to censorship, nor did it ever carry government press releases.

A few articles from this period are printed here; they are of interest because of their topicality.

Peace, freedom, bread

These were three things that were promised on 8 November 1918, when we woke up on the morning of the revolution.

In a speech Mr Eisner made when he introduced himself as a candidate, he promised peace within 24 hours from the moment he was supposed to be in power. Now he has been in power for almost two months.

Mr Erzberger assured that it took him and Lloyd George only half an hour to pocket the peace. That was two months ago.

Now you may take stock; the balance of two months.

Peace! That is still a long way off; and if the rulers in Berlin continue like this, we will have another war. After all, Radek-Sobelsohn has stated that the Russian army will fight together with the German Bolsheviks against big businesses on the Rhine. And the concluded armistice based on Wilson's 14 points? Has it been watered down? No, they unilaterally tightened the provisions. The Baltic Sea has been blocked, the Rhineland hermetically closed.

Our brothers who are still prisoners of war are suffering immensely; no hand is extended to help them. The government has something else, something more important to do.

In those two months of Republic Germany, we did not move one step closer to peace.

Freedom! We have freedom according to the saying: 'If you do not want to be my brother, I'll beat your brains in.' We do not have freedom, we have distrust.

The worker does not trust the citizen, the soldier does not trust the worker, the sailors distrust the soldiers. The ministery's do not trust each other, despite all the fine words of unity. Distrust reigns between city and countryside, between the individual states. One lurks at the other, telephone calls are tapped, letters opened, quotes taken out of context and speeches distorted. The occupation of the Austrian embassy, the arrest of vigilantes, the speeches of Mühsam and Sontheimer show how much freedom there is.

Bread! We have no coal because the workers have not been working since 9 November, but have been on strike. Our supplies are running out. We hope we will still have some on 1 March, but we do not believe it. We are living like children of the hand in the tooth. Bread! Still we have to eat. The supplies that could have stretched up to 1 July 1919 if we had handled them wisely have been wasted, stolen, squandered.

Peace, freedom, bread! - was promised, but nobody kept theirs. Unemployment keeps rising, productivity is at a standstill, our industry is on the verge of collapse. Read the touching letter to the workers published by the government a short while ago. And it helps nothing, because the wheels of fate turn inexorably. We are not prepared to intervene! We let things run their course!

As children, we hope for the big miracle, like a player hopes to win the top prize.

Germans! Workers! Citizens! Fellow citizens! Awake! Repent!

There is still time, start with yourself! Learn to think logically! Then, but only then, when Germany awakens, then you can get:

Peace, freedom, bread!

Where the money comes from and where it goes!

When we read in the papers recently the report that Bleichröder had spent two million marks for a Bolshevik newspaper, many shook their heads; they could not believe it. They had forgotten that the revolution had always been the darling of the Jews. When the communists' revolt raged in Paris in 1871, it was only Rothschild who remained unaffected, as he supported both parties and paid gold to both government troops and communists.

Russian government money rolls through our country to lead us to the blissful fields of Bolshevism. It is touching to see how freely Radek-Sobelsohn can move around Berlin and what a paper protest the government issues, this government that does not dare to have the man arrested and brought to trial. In Munich, they don't bother so much. One simply takes prominent men into preventive custody. For Sobelsohn, Sontheimer, Toller, Mühsam, who openly propagate the Council government, there seems to be no such thing.

However, Mr Radek-Sobelsohn was the one who came home with even more millions. People welcomed him with a laugh and a tear. What those millions are being used for? New newspapers are published and funded. The old newspapers must therefore give up 50% of their required paper. But that is the law in the new Germany. Everything belongs to all - at least on paper and because of the paper.

Party members are being recruited. 15 marks a day is very decent pay, especially since there are serving side jobs on top of that. Then comes the maintenance of the party heads and their families. They live it up, money does not matter, they have everything and it is not like with the poor people, the proletarians, the dismissed civil servants, the soldiers, the officers.

Delegates sent to Berlin are staying in first-class hotels - after all, one can do that on 30 marks travel and accommodation expenses.

This is how the money is used.

Gottfried Feder's lectures allowed a plan to mature that had long preoccupied Sebottendorff. He wanted to win over the workers. In the Thule fraternity, Brother Karl Harrer was chosen to form a workers' circle. Ir. Gottfried Feder offered to give lectures.

Another circle formed Anton Daumenlang; he dealt with heraldry and genealogy.

Nauhaus had further expanded his circle for Nordic culture. Johannes Hering had formed a circle dealing with ancient German law. Later, Frank, who studied law, expanded this circle further. The *Kampfbund* made propaganda through the *Beobachter*, one distributed overprints and pamphlets, most of which were written by Dannehl. Drawing began as well, at which Halbritter was particularly good.

Shortly before Christmas 1918, Sebottendorff went to the lodge's mid-winter meeting in Berlin and brought with him a draft of an appeal 'To the German people'. The appeal and programme of the *Deutsch-Sozialistische Partei* are printed at the beginning of Chapter XII.

VI
Thule's political activities until Eisner's death

Christmas itself was celebrated with great interest and so was the turn of the year. Both these feasts would be the last joyous gatherings for the time being.

The new year began gloomily enough: in Munich ten people had been killed and several wounded on New Year's Eve, street fighting raged in Berlin, a communist coup d'état took place in Düsseldorf, and now the British were about to occupy the city. The riots in Berlin lasted until mid-January and ended after the government, with the help of *Freikorps*, regained control of the city. 200 people were killed and 1,000 wounded. Karl Liebknecht and Rosa Luxemburg were shot. The Bavarian state elections were fixed on 12 January, the national elections on 19 January. For the first time, women participated in the elections.

On 7 January 1919, there was a demonstration by unemployed people in Munich, in which two people were killed by machine-gun fire and four seriously injured. A few days later, a coup attempt was made in Tal (street in Munich - vert.), again killing and wounding.

The election brought a devastating defeat for Eisner. Barely 2% of voters in Bavaria backed him. Munich expected

Eisner, Jaffé and Unterleitner - the three elected *Unabhängige* - would withdraw from the government.

The Land Day that was to be held was postponed to 21 February 1919 under various pretexts. Eisner and Jaffé went to the constitutional negotiations in Berlin.

Erzberger was able to secure an extension of the armistice on harsh new terms, which Germany had to pay for with outrageous supplies.

In February 1919, the *Nationalversammlung* would meet in Weimar; a constitution had to be made.

In Munich, the craziest rumours were circulating about what would happen at the Land Day, now definitively set for 21 February. The Communists wanted to prevent the Land Day, Eisner did not want to come, etc.

A couple of events took place at the *Völkische Bewegung*. The Greater German Confederation had invited friendly organisations to its meeting in Bamberg, and it had been decided to make all preparations to expand the *Schutz- und Trutzbund* into a means of battle. Since the alliance had to be active in its breadth, a blood confession was abandoned altogether. Now the open struggle against the Jews had to be opened throughout the empire. Such unions had already been formed in Lusatia and Thuringia.

Two books on Freemasonry were published at the time, which should be mentioned. Karl Heise: *Die Entente Fre-*

imaurerei and Wichtl: *Die Weltfreimaurerei*. Both books caused quite a stir. Here, for the first time, facts were given rather than vague conjectures and allusions.

At that time, the anthroposical Steiner, the prophet of Dornach, who was particularly well-known in Munich, started to make his presence felt again as well. Steiner wanted to become finance minister in Württemberg and promoted his system of tripartite representation.

This disastrous man's influence did not extend far. He worked with the later psychic Liesbeth Seidler in Berlin, Körnerstraße, before the war. Both Seidler and Steiner always had access to General Moltke and together prevented the deployment of fresh men on the Marne in time for this battle to be lost. (Schwarz-Bostunnitsch: *Doktor Steiner - ein Schwindler, wie keiner*, ['Doktor Steiner - a swindler like no other'] published by publisher *Böpple*, Munich).

Sebottendorff had previously acted against Seidler and Steiner. Additionally Seidler was in the police and had retaliated against Sebottendorff by filing a report. Now Sebottendorff was continuing the fight against the two in the *Beobachter*.

Apart from the *Beobachter*, it was the aforementioned *Miesbacher Anzeiger* that raged vigorously against the Jews.

Yet another magazine should be mentioned: Dietrich Eckart's periodical, which first appeared on 7 December

1918 and which he had named *Auf gut Deutsch*. This magazine was the trigger for the animosity between Eckart and Sebottendorff. Eckart, through Thule brother Kneil, had asked Sebottendorff to finance the magazine. Since Sebottendorff already had to finance the entire Thule Society and the *Beobachter*, he refused. The owner of the *Münchener Zeitung* then donated the required 10,000 marks. Of the magazine's issues, the headlines from the *Juden-Nummer* and the issue *Rätezeit in Ungarn* (The Time of the Councils in Hungary) were particularly significant. The main contributor to *Auf gut Deutsch* was Alfred Rosenberg. How Dietrich Eckart followed the Thule Society's activities in the political struggle is shown, among other things, by a report in No 42 of his magazine Auf gut *Deutsch*:

The downfall of the Empire

With us, Berlin is much frowned upon, and Prussia altogether. At a meeting of the *Deutsche Bund* - founded by a Mr Ballerstedt - the line of those who signed the appeal began with the Jewess Annita Augspurg; other names of Jews followed, including Franz Carl Endres and Mr Held, leader of the *Unabhängige* here on the spot, in short, a real 'German' union, and at this meeting, during Ballerstedt's speech, there was even a stormy shout for a declaration of war against Prussia. Thank God Franz Dannehl was able to jump in and still open the crowd's eyes in time.

From the *Beobachter,* a few more articles from that time are printed here:

The Jew

When one tries to clarify to someone about the Jews as a race, one often gets the reply: 'But I do not understand you, I know so many Jews, they are all very neat people.'

However, when we speak of Jews as a race, we do not mean the individual, but the whole of Judaism. Let us see what Theodor Fritsch says in his book *Der falsche Gott* (Leipzig, *Hammerverlag*, 1916): 'It is precisely this cue- rity that is one of their special stratagems. Were they to openly display their deeply felt hatred of us everywhere, how could they even exist socially or in business? They need us to exploit us, and the more they manage to deceive us with regard to their true thinking and knowledge, the more surely they reach their goal.'

'For would they know, what we say about them,' said a Jewish newspaper published in Lemberg years ago, 'would they not beat us all to death?' Hiding his true disposition is a necessity of life for the Hebrew, and by constantly practising this art he has now become a master of hypocrisy. The *Talmud* reads: 'The Jew is able to knock the teeth out of someone's mouth and pretend to caress his cheek.'

These Jewish distortion tricks simply have a hypnotic effect on weakly gifted people. They let the Jew tell them what to feel and think. There are cases, for example, where Hebrews are well-conceived, lovable people through usury and deceit down to the shirt and yet were still considered benefactors by them. The Hebrew manages to give all his shenanigans the appearance of a pure intention and every time he harms his victim, he pretends that it is done against his will and under duress of circumstances, as if he himself deeply regrets it. Wilhelm von Polenz has masterfully described such scenes in *Der Büttnerbauer*.

Indeed, the Jew often has a hypnotic influence, a spell, on people who are somewhat less gifted and not so strong-willed. It is as if he possesses demonic powers. The question to what extent the sexual motive plays a role here will not be discussed. Suffice it to point out that a being who lacks any concept of shame and morality also expresses his sensual desires in a way that must be blinding and confusing to a sensitive soul. Here one could use descriptions to reveal repulsive incidents, which would horrify many an unsuspecting soul. Women and girls who have been in Jewish service or otherwise have closer contact with Jews can absolutely no longer think and feel normally, so that they experience the humiliation they experience there almost as a boon and grace. They cannot praise the Jews enough.

They have been told that Jews belong to a privileged class in every respect, above all people. They faithfully imitate this and feel honoured to deal with Jews. Jews know how to explain away the concepts of shame and morality and dismiss them as foolish prejudices.

Deceiving people with weak minds is among the Hebrew's special talents. Thus, he has developed the art of getting in his good graces to perfection. His dishonest profession forces him to use smooth, engaging manners. If Goethe claims that the German is insincere when he is not rude, in this too the Hebrew is the distinct opposite.

Naturally, his cleverness repels strong, healthy and internally pure characters. The Hebrew fearfully avoids such people. The saying: every nation has the Jews it deserves is not unjustified! Only where talk and vanity and all other evil lusts meet, where the sense of moral purity is lost, there the Jew feels good, like a louse in the fur. Individuals, families, societies, peoples judge themselves by the relationship they have with Judaism. Where there is carrion, the vultures gather!

We want to leave it at that and continue the report.

On 18 January 1919, the *National-Sozialistische Deutsche Arbeiterverein* was founded in the premises of the Thule company. Writer Karl Harrer became first chairman, metal turner Anton Drexler second chairman. At the weekly meetings, attendance varied between 10 and 30 people.

As a result of Eisner's conflicts with the state authorities, the formation of armies had been rejected, even banned, on the Bavarian side. General von Epp therefore assembled troops outside Bavaria at Camp Ohrdruf in Thuringia. Sebottendorff had a large number of members of the *Kampfbund* and others who had signed up to go there.

The opening of the Land Day had been announced for 21 February. All of Munich was full of expectation as to what would happen.

On 16 February, Eisner held a meeting on Theresienwiese at which he promoted the ideas of the Council government. The demonstrative procession that had to be held at the conclusion of the meeting, if necessary, was led by Eisner himself in a truck. The procession carried posters propagating the Raden government. About 10,000 people took part in the procession and were particularly displeased with the press, because Eisner had clashed with it in a bad way a day before. Munich newspapers subsequently ceased coverage.

While on the Communist side people were roused by deeds, the moderate Social Democrats fought with words. Auer attacked the peasant leader Gandorfer, accusing him of being corrupt and chasing jobs.

On 20 February 1919, the councils vacated the Landdag building and moved to the *Deutsche Theater*. During this, it came to a clash between Eisner and Max Levien. Levien had announced a lecture for the next day under the title: 'Spartakus, the slave liberator'. It did not come to that, however, because on Friday 21 February, at quarter to ten, Eisner was shot dead by Count Anton Arco auf Valley on his way to the Land Day on the corner of Promenadestraße.

Count Anton Arco auf Valley had Jewish blood in his veins on his maternal side (born Oppenheim). A half-Jew, he was therefore neither a member of the Thule Society nor the *Kampfbund*. He wanted to show that even a half-Jew is capable of deeds.

Instead of Eisner, Auer opened the Land Day an hour later with a warm commemorative speech. He had hardly finished his address, or there the door opened and butcher Lindner, a convinced communist, fired several shots at Auer. Auer was badly wounded. At the same time, shots were also fired from the stands, where the workers' and soldiers' council had taken their seats. These shots killed delegate Osel and Major von Jahreiß, who was present as a visitor. In wild flight, the Landdag flew apart.

The second revolution was declared. The rabble gained power across the board.

The *Revolutionäre Zentralrat* announced the following:

The liberator of the proletariat, the prime minister of the People's State of Bavaria, Kurt Eisner, was treacherously murdered at ten o'clock this morning by a representative of the bourgeoisie, Count Arco-Zinneberg (must be Count Anton Arco auf Valley, the author). The spiritual instigator of this murder was the smear campaign of the press.

To secure the revolution in view of this crime, the proletariat has a duty to take over the press. All workers are requested to go on strike immediately and meet at 4 o'clock on the Theresienwiese.

Long live the memory of Kurt Eisner!
Long live the second revolution!
Long live the Raden Republic!

Munich, 21 February 1919.

The first thing they did was to call a general strike. All shops closed their doors, traffic jammed, posters appeared, calling for retaliatory measures against the ruling class. At 1 p.m., the bells sounded from all towers. The priests were forced to ring the bells themselves.

By 4pm, newspapers were stormed, rolls of paper dragged into the streets and set on fire. Looting and looting were everywhere, gunshots sounded everywhere.

At the spot where Eisner was shot, they had placed his portrait decorated with flowers, two sentry posts ensured that every passer-by saluted.

However, this fuss did not last long, as an old hunter's trick was employed. One had strewn a bag of flour with the sweat of two bitches in heat in front of the portrait and soon all the dogs in the area left their calling cards at the effigy, upon which the sentries disappeared.

Arco's mad act had thrown all plans into disarray. Eisner, who had already been half off, was given the halo of a martyr by this act. The deep hatred of the 'junckers' erupted again, for it was, after all, a 'juncker' who had shot Kurt Eisner.

That in the battle that has now erupted, the Thule Society's *Kampfbund* and the Society itself were left unmolested for the time being is due to the fact that the Society's premises were in the quiet Marstallstraße, in close proximity to the Army Museum, where the Supreme Command is located.

The entrance to Thule's meeting room was a side entrance to Hotel *Vier Jahreszeiten*, which was mainly used by the hotel's staff. It was therefore not very noticeable that this entrance was also often used by Thule's people.

A new issue of the *Beobachter* was due on 22 February 1919, on a Saturday. To avoid pouring oil on the fire, the issue was postponed for a few days.

VII
Thule during the rule of the Council government

From February to April 1919, things were fairly quiet in the Reich. Several communist uprisings of the Spartakus Union had been put down; only in Braunschweig did the councils remain in power. Things looked dangerous in Oppersilezia, where the communists took advantage of the looming danger from Poland to organise an uprising. In Hungary, Bela Kun had established the Council government.

In Weimar, the *Nationalversammlung* had convened. It was concerned with drawing up the 'system'.

In Munich, however, it was chaos. For the time being, a *Zentralrat* had been formed, consisting of the following: Gandorfer, Hoffmann, Utzendorfer, Sauber, Simon, Goldschmidt, Niekisch, Kröpelin, Eisenhut, Levien and Hagemeister.

All newspapers were banned and instead the *Zentralrat*'s newspaper appeared. *Arbeiterrat* Jakobi and *Soldatenrat* Ehrhardt were responsible for its publication.

The aforementioned 11-member college (i.e. the *Zentralrat*) had declared three days of general mourning because of Eisner. Furthermore, it had decided to close all civil amusements, abolish the nobility and abolish all feudal possessions.

On 24 February 1919, the general strike was over; on Wednesday, the twenty-sixth, Eisner's cremation took place.

Niekisch had convened the councils at the *Deutsche Theater* for 25 February. At this meeting, Kröpelin in particular urged those present to take hostages. 'People have to be taken hostage and if one revolutionary is now liquidated by a reactionary criminal, ten Kreß von Kressenstein will be executed.' Book dealer and publisher Lehmann, the already mentioned Kreß von Kressenstein and many prominent people were taken hostage and brought to Stadelheim. Landauer made a proposal at this meeting to declare the workers' rallies a *Nationalrat*. Levien informed that the *Revolutionäre Arbeiterrat* had declared itself permanent at the *Wagnerbräu*. He demanded that the Landdag should no longer meet; all power should lie with the councils.

On 6 March 1919, talks took place between the parties - the Communists, the *Unabhängige* and the moderate Socialists. It came to a compromise to which, however, they did not adhere. The Bavarian government prepared its move to Bamberg, but still dawdled in the hope of reaching an amicable agreement with the Spartakists. Instead of acting, it decided to take half-measures. At the time, they had behind the still unrepressed soldiers of the garrisons in northern Bavaria. The Third Army Corps had thrown off the following announcement over Munich:

To all soldiers and workers!

The situation created by the reckless murder of Eisner was exploited by a small group of Munich aggressors to seize control. Very decidedly opposed to this are the workers and soldiers of Amberg, Bayreuth, Sulzbach, Regensburg, Straubing, Erlangen, Ingolstadt, Grafenwöhr, Nuremberg and Fürth. They all condemn the tyranny of a small group leading Bavaria to ruin. Apart from a socialist government, they demand that the Landdag be convened soon. They all want democracy and reject dictatorship. Comrades and party members of Munich! You have shown the will to reject the tyranny of Dr Levien and his armed supporters. In this endeavour you are supported by all the soldiers of the Third Army Corps, if nothing else, by force of arms.

From 17 to 19 March, the Landdag met in Munich, but it had no power, which remained in the hands of the Russian plenipotentiary Axelrod and the councils Levien and Leviné-Niessen. The official government was composed of Hoffmann, Prime Minister, Endres, Internal affairs, Segitz, Finance and Frauendorfer, Transport. This was only a provisional government that was tolerated for so long, until the Council Government took its place. After all, the world revolution was on its way, as the example of Hungary showed. To move them forward, the prime minister appointed the Austrian Jew Dr Neurath as state commissioner. Neurath was to socialise all Bavarian companies; he became head and chairman of the *Zentralwirt- schaftsamt* (Economic Affairs).

When the Landdag was due to reconvene, the *Zentralrat* stated that such a meeting would be prevented, but on 4 April 1919, in Hoffmann's absence and under Minister of War Schneppenhorst, a meeting nevertheless took place, in which all socialist partners took part. Here, Leviné-Niessen again proposed the proclamation of the Council Government; however, this meeting ended without result.

On 6 April 1919, Klingelhöfer convened the workers' and soldiers' Councils in the Hofbräuhaus. On the same day, the Raden Republic was proclaimed in Munich. Typically, the communists led by Leviné did not participate; they formed their own group. Niekisch assumed all the power, Dr Lipp became People's Commissioner for Foreign Affairs, Dr Neurath remained chairman of the *Zentralwirtschaftsamt*, and the Jew Ret Marut became leader of press socialisation. Silvio Gesell was given Finance.

The public notice read as follows:

To the people of Bavaria!

The decision has been made, Bavaria is a Raden Republic. The working people are masters of their destiny. The joint revolutionary workers and peasants in Bavaria, including all brothers who are soldiers and no longer separated by any political oppositions, agree that from now on all exploitation and oppression must end. The dictatorship of the proletariat, which has now become a fact, aims to realise a true socialist community, in which every working individual must participate in the public life of a socialist-communist cconomy. The Landdag, that barren product of an obsolete bourgeois-capitalist era, has been dissloved, its appointed ministry resigned.

The fiduciaries appointed by the councils of the working people, who are accountable to the people, will receive extraordinary proxies in certain areas as people's commissioners. Their assistants will be experienced men of all directions in revolutionary socialism and communism. The many hard-working civil servants, especially those of the low and middle level, will be called upon to cooperate decisively in the new Bavaria. However, the system of bureaucracy is immediately overturned.

The press is being socialised.

To protect the Bavarian Raden Republic against reactionary actions from outside and inside, a red army will be formed immediately. A revolutionary court will immediately punish any attack on the Raden Republic.

The Bavarian Council government follows the example of the Russian and Hungarian peoples and makes direct contact with them. In contrast, it rejects any contact with the despicable Ebert, Scheideman, Noske, Erzberger government, because it continues, under the banner of a socialist republic, the imperialist-capitalist-militarist business of the German, sacked imperialism.

It calls on all German fraternal peoples to go the same way. The republic salutes all proletarians wherever they fight for freedom and justice, for revolutionary socialism, in Württemberg, in the Ruhr and throughout the world.

In the sign of the hope of a happy future for all mankind, 7 April is hereby declared a national holiday. As a sign of the impending farewell to damned capitalism, work will rest throughout Bavaria on Monday 7 April 1919, insofar as it is not necessary for the life of the working people. Further provisions will be announced in good time.

Long live free Bavaria! Long live the Raden Republic! Long live the world revolution!

Munich, 6 April 1919. Bavaria's revolutionary *Zentralrat*.

In Augsburg, the rule of the councils had already been proclaimed on Saturday. Rosenheim, Starnberg and the immediate Munich area followed on Monday. The Social- Democratic Party and the Hoffmann government protested and were able to precipitate the attempts to declare the Raden Republic that had begun in northern Bavaria. The Hoffmann government's decision read:

> 'The government of the Free State of Bavaria has not resigned. It has moved its seat elsewhere. The government is and remains in possession of supreme power in Bavaria and has the exclusive right to promulgate legally valid measures and issue orders. Further publications will follow'.
>
> Nuremberg, 7 April 1919
> Prime Minister Hoffmann

The plan of the council republic aimed to drag along all of Bavaria and to then take Austria, which was between two fires since the council system was already in place in Hungary. Furthermore, it was hoped that the movement in Württemberg would be successful. The plan failed due to the reluctance of the North Bavarian population and because the revolt in Württemberg was quickly put down.

Munich formed an island in early April 1919, whose borders ran from Dachau through Schleißheim to Rosenheim and the Oberland; to the west, the border ran between the lakes back to Dachau. This place was very important to the republic. Not only were there large munition supplies, but there was paper there to print paper money. Finance Minister Maenner made the classic statement: 'If we have the Dachau paper mill in our hands, the financial situation will be secured for four or five weeks.'

In Munich itself, a red army had been formed, of which Toller was the commander. 24,000 rifles had been distributed, to which were added the weapons in the barracks and depots.

Such was the general situation.

During the coming days of horror, the Thule Society took on greater political significance. The latest ordination had taken place on 21 March. During the wheel time, meetings were temporarily suspended.

In order to give Thule a permanent form so that the society could also act externally, it was decided to have the partnership be legally registered as an association. This required statutes, waiving the '*Führer*' principle. The registration office only registered associations with an elected board.

The financial commitments Sebottendorff had taken on had exhausted his carrying capacity and he had to ask members to pay a contribution by 1 March 1919. Kneil became treasurer. Associations wishing to hold meetings also had to start paying hall rent.

During that time, two events took place with which the Thule Society had to deal. The first was the visit of police chief Pallabene. He came to search for anti-Semitic pamphlets. Baron von Wittgenberg had warned Sebottendorff beforehand. Wittgenberg already knew Pallabene from when he was still an officer in Austria and had met him in Schwabing, during which the Thule Society had come up for discussion. The visit was confirmed by Ritzler who, besides being a member of the *Republikanische Schutztruppe*, was also a member of the Thule Society. He could even pinpoint the time: the search would take place at 10 a.m. To fend off the attack, Sebottendorff requested Mrs Riemann-Bucherer to hold a singing hour in the morning and to have all the Thule Society sisters come. When the chief commissioner arrived, the introductory song *Beglückt darf nun dich, o Heimat, ich schauen*, sounded to him. Countess Westarp, the second secretary, reported to the chief commissioner, who immediately asked: 'What is this society?'

'Oh, this is an association for the betterment of the Germanic race!'

'What?'

'An association for the betterment of the Germanic race, chief commissioner.'

'What are you actually performing here?'
 'You hear, we are singing.'
 'You are practising anti-Semitic propaganda, I know it! You are fooling me, I will have you and all your supporters arrested! I have come to search your house!'

'Go ahead,' Sebottendorff said, 'I cannot stop you, but first I want a statement from you, Mr Chief Commissioner. My authority extends a little further than you think. You see, I have been leader of the Thule Society for over six months now and intend to remain so for a long time. You, Mr Chief Commissioner, have been in office since two days and may remain so for another two or three days, after which someone else will step in. If you, Mr Chief Commissioner, arrest me here or any of my people or all of them for all I care, then my people, no matter where they find one, will pick up a Jew, drag him through the streets and say he stole a host. Then, Mr Chief Commissioner, you will have a pogrom that will wipe you out too.'

'That's madness.'

'Maybe, but my madness is effective.'

'Surely you do not want to - you are trying to trick me.'

'That is far from me, but after all, it need not come to that. You see, in principle we pursue a common goal, only our paths differ. Why won't we tolerate each other?'

'Yes, we could go together.'

'No, that is impossible. You want to achieve the goal through internationalism, I through the national, through the *völkisch* movement. Let's wait and see, who reaches his goal first.'

'Quite right, Mr Baron, should you be suspected of anything, I will warn you.'

'I will be very grateful to you. If you are suspected of anything, I will send you a message.'

With that, he left and with him his officials, including two members of the *Kampfbund* of Thule.

The second event had almost gone wrong, but here too happy circumstances came to the rescue. While handing out the *Rote Hand,* a Thule man had been caught; he fled and was chased. When he reached Marstallstraße, the whole troop ran after him. The Thule Society's holds were crammed in no time. Fortunately, there were a few people from the *Kampfbund* present, who had just come from the communist sections to report. These, with their red sleeve bands, immediately sprang into action and pushed the crowd back. Since then, two members of the *Kampfbund* always stood guard as communists.

The *Rote Hand* was a satirical joke magazine published once and distributed in huge numbers.

In March 1919, Sebottendorff included the war invalids Hanns Georg Müller on the editorial board of the *Münchener Beobachter*. On 5 May 1919, Sebottendorff commissioned Hans Georg Grassinger to improve the layout of the *Beobachter* and print the newspaper in a larger format. Grassinger came from the opposition in the Landdag against Eisner via Witzgall at Thule. Starting with No. 16 of 17 May 1919, Hanns Georg Müller was solely responsible for the *Beobachter*. The sports section took care of Valentin Büchold, first delegate of the student contact *Hansea* and member of Thule.

On 24 May 1919, the *Beobachter* (No. 17) appeared in the new format with a circulation of 10,000 copies. With No. 22 of 28 June 1919, the newspaper appeared once, from No. 23 of 2 July 1919 twice a week with eight pages. On 9 August 1919 with No. 34, the *Münchener Beobachter* appeared for the first time under the name *Völkischer Beobachter*.

Of the articles in the *Beobachter* from that time, the following are printed here:

Israelis at the top in Germany!

The 'German' revolution brought the following Jews to the top:

Arndt, press chief at Prussian Ministry of War Ed. Bernstein, Reich Ministry of Finance
Dr Oskar Cohn, Reich Ministry of Justice Eisner, Bavarian prime minister
Fulda, interior minister in Hesse Futran, director-general at the Prussian Ministry of Culture
Dr Max Grünwald, press officer at the state ministry of economy Dr Haas, Minister of the Interior in Baden Haase,
Foreign Affairs and Colonies in the Reich Prof Dr Jaffé, Minister of Finance
Dr Herz, chairman of the Justice Commission Heimann, president of the People's Council in Berlin Heymann, minister of culture in Württemberg Hirsch, prime minister in Prussia
Dr Löwe, national service for demobilisation
Dr Laufenberg, chairman of the Workers' Council Hamburg Dr Landsberg, chairman of the Council of People's Commissars
Dr Hugo Preuß, state secretary of the interior Rosenfeld, state council in Berlin
Dr Kurt Rosenfeld, Minister of Justice in Prussia Schlefinger, Plenipotentiary at the Ministry of War Simon, Director of Foreign Affairs
Simon, minister of trade in Prussia
Sinzheimer, chief of police in Frankfurt am Main Stadthagen, representative for Lippe Thalheimer, fi-

nance minister in Württemberg Weyl, minister in Hesse Wurm, food minister

A fine, German company together!

The following brief notes from the *Munich Beobachter* shed light on those times:

Bolshevik education

At the command posts here locally, many young people report wanting to go to the border guard. Now our wise government does not want these volunteers to do anything, they are sent to the local regiments, where they are fed at state expense. They do not have to do anything and are thus guaranteed to be surrendered to Bolshevism. This is how the government raises its troops.

Dr Levien is one of the leaders of the communists. In the Puchheim prison camp, he led the Russians to believe that he would soon be president of Bavaria. Soon the puppets were dancing again in Bavaria, because they would get enough land to stay here. Those Bolsheviks are coming, one would have to help them from here. Dr Levien, suffering from severe syphilis, then had himself photographed with the prisoners.

Socialisation committee

Professor Jaffé, hitherto finance minister, has become the president of this college. If he continues in the way he has been killing our finances, we are in for a treat.

Wouldn't it be better if Mr Jaffé left for Jerusalem with competent haste to find a job there? It would be wonderful if he could take his friend Bonn with him; after all, his activities at the trade academy are not worth a pinch.

How well-known the *Beobachter* and how good the propaganda was shows the following incident, which would have major consequences.

One day, the *Beobachter* received a call. There was a well-known hotel owner from Füssen on the phone, who told that a few days ago Mrs Eisner and Mr Landauer had arrived in Füssen in a former court car. They were planning to take up residence in Schloss Hohenschwangau. Since Mrs Eisner had a cold, they had sent for a doctor, who advised against making Füssen their permanent residence because of the climate. Neurenberg or the flatlands would be more suitable.

The next morning, the chambermaid had found Landauer and Ms Eisner in bed in no uncertain terms.

The Jew Eisner had left his first wife in dire poverty in Nuremberg. His second wife, who had a considerable pension, had been his secretary. She had been diligently involved in politics and had also interfered in political affairs on several occasions. Sebottendorff reported on this in the *Beobachter* under the headline 'Revolution!

The day after the publication of the *Beobachter*, on a Monday, Sebottendorff was walking on Karlsplatz in München and heard a newspaper vendor shouting: 'A

Great German slanders Mrs Eisner! Sebottendorff disgraces the late prime minister!'

He walked up to the salesman, who was selling the newspaper *Der Republikaner,* and asked:

'Come here, what have you got there?' 'Well, you should read that.'
He bought an issue and flipped it open. On the second page, under the headline: 'Kurt Eisner's widow vilified lowly by a Great German,' was a response from Leib, the owner of the magazine *Der Republikaner*. The article read:

'Time has not yet erased the deep impression made by the cowardly murder of our unforgettable friend and promoter of a happy world peace everywhere. Still the great sorrow for the brave founder of the Bavarian Republic is not over, or there is already a Great-German fanatic who dares to tarnish the honour of the sorely tried widow of the distinguished deceased in an extraordinarily vicious manner.

A certain Rudolf Sebottendorff, who a short time ago could proudly call himself Rudolf von Sebottendorff, in a magazine published in Munich, of which he is editor, brings against Mrs Eisner the lowest conceivable accusations with the undeniable intention of dragging the affected woman morally and morally through the mud.

Ms Eisner is associated with a well-known left-wing socialist leader, whose name is mentioned, in the most compromitory form; moreover, it is claimed that she took a pleasure trip to Füssen with him in a former court car.

And what happened in reality?

According to the information I have received, Mrs Eisner did not fall only slightly ill on her way home to Munich. She spent several days in a hotel in Füssen, because the attending doctor thought it was impractical to continue the journey by train. In this helpless state, Mrs Eisner turned to a friend of her late husband, who then committed the crime of helping her in this certainly not enviable situation by taking her to her home in Munich in a hire car.

This is what Ms Eisner's pleasure trip looked like!

That which is simply a serious human duty is twisted briskly and with real Great German love for truth is turned into a dirty trick.

This case is typical of the sniping from the anti-revolutionary side, from a rabble that has still not given up hope that one day things will go their way again. Indeed, Sebottendorff's slanderous scribble (dated 9 spring month 1919) bears the title: 'Revolution', in which he claims that Mrs Eisner was quite involved in foreign policy. This last allegation is as made up as the fairy-tale pleasure trip. It was thus the firm intention of the sad Great-German hero to deliberately hit the revolution with untruths. In doing so, he did not shy away from dragging the impeccable reputation a woman through the mud (one who has already been severely affected by the disgraceful act of a creeping murderer), and to cast suspicion on a political opponent who has so chivalrously taken care of his friend's widow, in such a lowly manner. Mrs Eisner is determined to bring to justice whoever attacked her honour in such a cowardly manner. However, one cannot escape the fearful feeling that the reactionary elements seem to have a good reason to feel safer than ever in the Republic of Bavaria, so safe that they believe they can afford anything. How long will it be before certain newspapers can once again open their floodgates undisturbed and dirty everything that can even remotely be associated with the revolution.'

'Well, what's that supposed to be. That's a dirty trick, my dear, that article, what are they doing with that Sebottendorff now?'

'We'll come and get it tonight.'

'Oh yes, I'd like to experience that. Where does this scoundrel live?'

'At the Siegestor he would live.'

'Geez, that's in my district. Give me another 10 of those *Republikaner*, I'll take them so everyone can read them.'

'That's fine, tonight at six o'clock we'll come and get it. There's more of him in the paper.'

Indeed, the *Republikaner* contained a second article dealing with Sebottendorff. This read:

The Great German, the Russian and the Republican

Russian Bolshevism made its entry into Munich. Even the *Munich Kindl* (the figure representing a monk in the Munich coat of arms) shivered at this news and icicles ran down his back, because right near the wisdom carousel of our good fathers, on Marienplatz, that dangerous monster held its orgies. The blame, of course, goes to the *Republikaner*. The only Great-German organ in München, headed by a certain engineer Rudolf Sebottendorff, discovered the unprecedented and, by means of the following scribble, saved our beloved Munich from a certain doom:

'Russian Bolshevism and the German Republikaner. The *Republikaner*, known as not very glorious, whose strategies we will not judge here, has been sold by a Russian in a fairly large square here on the spot for a few days. Kind seeks kind.'

That the *Republikaner* has only been around for four months not only in Munich but also in Bavaria, and is known on the other side of the white-and-blue border posts, is true. However, that the newspaper is described as lacklustre by a Great German liege newspaper only adds to its honour. As for the Russian: this is a prisoner of war who, driven by hunger, had left a Bavarian prison camp and, as he previously did for weeks with other newspapers, now wants to earn an honest living by selling the *Republikaner*. That I gave him the opportunity to do so is human, but certainly not un- German.

When Sebottendorff finds it really humane to denounce a defenceless prisoner of war to the police as a Bolshevik and thereby take away his bit of bread because he cannot return to his homeland through the fault of criminal militarism, then we must regret that this unique German, called Sebottendorff, did not fall on the field of 'honour', yes, then it is highly regrettable that millions of men had to lose their lives for such a mentality. It is not the one who sees in the foreigner the human being who violates the German mentality, rather the half idiotic *furor teutonicus* who puts national intolerance above humanity does so. This can create pus pits in a Greater German mind, making one see a dangerous Bolshevik in an innocent prisoner of war. However, I would like to grant some extenuating circumstances to the author of the gloriously unknown magazine. After all, he is among the deeply unfortunate starvationers who only a few days ago lost the proud word '*von*'. Sebottendorff no doubt lost his mind with the word '*von*' too.

Leib.

The case looked pretty serious anyway. The two articles were aimed at inciting people. For no reason, one does not turn a small note that really could not mean a report to the police into an article or nail a 'juncker' to the pillory.

'So at six you want to get the villain?'
'Yes, tonight at six.'

Arriving at boarding house *Döring* at the Siegestor, Sebottendorff asked owner Hornstein for the key to the backdoor through which one could enter the courtyard of the Serenis simus.

'Tonight I will be visited, Mr Hornstein, *Spartakus'* people want to pick me up. Do not be alarmed when you see me at the search.'

'Do take care, Mr Baron.'
'Yes, yes, I am watching out.'
Exactly at 6 o'clock, the *Republikanische Schutzwehr* appeared on two trucks, accompanied by a few people from Schwabing district. Sebottendorff silently joined them. They seized a few sheets of runic manuscripts, a few unimportant letters and, since they were in the building anyway, the adjoining rooms were also searched. In one of these rooms lived Baroness Mikusch whose son was stations chief during the war in Haidar Pasha. A picture of Baroness Mikusch in Turkish uniform, was on his mother's desk. It was known to Sebottendorff that Captain Mikusch was in Czechoslovakia. When the soldiers saw the photo, one of them shouted:

'That's Sebottendorff.'

'Quite right, he's a Turk,' mused another soldier. A third, pushing forward, joined them: 'And a monocle he wears too, the villain.'

'You know, that picture should be confiscated and everyone should have it with them so we can finally catch the villain,' Sebottendorff stoked.

'Right you are. The picture will be confiscated,' the captain concluded.

During the following days, copies of the photo were handed out in the city so that everyone would immediately recognise and apprehend Sebottendorff.

Ms Eisner never filed charges of insult. Landauer was arrested at the capture of Munich and shot dead on the way to the police station during an escape attempt.

Beobachter No. 13 of 5 April 1919 would be the last issue to appear until the liberation of council rule in Munich. No. 14 of 12 April 1919 could no longer be published because on that day the *Beobachter* was banned. As a result of this ban, Büchold published the *Beobachter* the following Saturday only as a sports magazine. The sports magazine was intended for the horse races in Daglfing. Through this magazine, Schülein, a civil servant, became aware of the student Valentin Büchold. By influencing Büchold's father, Schülein managed to prevent Büchold from continuing his studies.

The *Deutschvölkische Schutz und Trutzbund* was publicised in Germany through the following advertisement:

Take Jews into preventive detention, then there will be peace in the country!

Jews incite to communist revolution. Jews incite the people.

Jews are pushing to the top everywhere.

Jews prevent Germans from agreeing. Therefore, away with Jewish schemers and troublemakers.

Germany for Germans, that's the slogan. Men and women of German blood unite in the *Deutscher Schutz- und Trutzbund*.

A report on the first public meeting of the *Schutz- und Trutzbund* appeared in the *Völkische Beobachter* Nr. 68 of 6 December 1919:

> From the movement

Lecture Gottfried Feder. On Monday 1 December 1919, the *Deutschvölkischer Schutz- und Trutzbund* held its first public meeting. In the fully occupied concert hall of the *Wagner Hotel* in Munich, engineer Gottfried Feder spoke on the theme: 'Mammonism and how to combat this world disease by breaking the slavish obligation to pay interest.' Using convincing, numerical reports, the speaker painted a picture of the enormous debt of the German people; a debt that was the cause of the moral and social decay of our social life. At length, he analysed the state of the German people's wealth, not only by economic- capitalist standards, but also on its *völkisch* merits. It is not only in arbitrarily assumed numbers, in labour power, in motivation, in labour possibilities that the national capacity is expressed. It is wrong to attribute an intrinsic value to money. Money is not a commodity, but a reward for work done. The speaker dealt with the *Freigeld Bewegung* to which we will return in detail. With the appreciation of money as its own value, fate begins for working and creating humanity. Interest on loans is the source of mammonism, of the golden international; it creates the effortless and endless influx of goods, puts enormous pressure on the self-sustained pursuit of profit and thereby causes enormous damage. The pure desire for profit - not money - is the demonic pursuit of the total exploitation of peoples' labour power. Its political effect led to the world war. The whole world was plunged into a bloodbath to bring to an end the work, which was in Germany's way. Next, the speaker elaborated on the interest rate problem. The credit issue is not affected by the interest rate problem in everyday life. Interest has nothing to do with saving either. What is decisive is the fact that the German people year after year 15,000 million, mostly in the form of taxes, is extorted so that the state can pay the interest on the huge borrowed capital. Value-creating labour must first regain its value, all products must rise in price - indirect taxes take care of that - as much as the coverage of those levies amounts to, and so the whole people must bear that huge interest burden. The people do get a little piece of it, which in the meantime disappears without a trace via indirect taxes. Sharp and clear, the speaker outlined the concepts of borrowed capital and industrial capital, citing the truthful and stunning order of magnitude, and drew the conclusion. It would be tantamount to detracting from the weight of these terrible facts if one did not take into account Gottfried Feder's argument, in this very limited framework, that wipes away every narrow-minded inconsequence. A stormy, minutes-long round of applause rewarded the speaker who, with true conviction and unrelenting clarity, created the redemptive prospect, which our people are so yearning for today. The meeting proceeded without incident and may be considered a success of the *Völkische Bewegung*.

VIII
Thule's *Kampfbund* and the counter-revolution of 1919

As already mentioned, at the beginning of the revolution in 1918, there was cause to establish a *Kampfbund*. Its actual establishment, however, took place only after Eisner's death.

Until then, there was still hope of eroding the government from within, bringing the right-wing parties together in a strong *völkisch* unity and uniting the front soldiers in a *völkisch* party. It had been decided to create such a party and the call had gone out. Even in the social democratic party, especially in the Bavarian one, people began to realise that the foreigners, as they called the Jews, were to blame for the whole 'mess'. The aforementioned call issued by the III Army Corps over Munich shows clearly enough how the matter was thought of among the front soldiers.

Eisner's death and subsequent events had made it clear, however, that it had to come to a brawl. The organisation of the *Bund* was settled in a few hours, each member taking the place assigned to him without protest.

There were first two departments that were independent of each other and did not know each other either.

The first division under first lieutenant Heinz Kurz was engaged in recruitment for the *Freikorps*, especially for the *Freikorps Epp*. To fall in with the *Left Socialists*, the government had issued an order forbidding recruiting. It was feared that Epp would one day march into Bavaria if the subjects joined the corps.

The announcement read:

In order to maintain public safety, recruitment offices for volunteers, recruitment campaigns in newspapers and advertising posters in Bavaria are hereby banned. Violations will be punished, insofar as this is not provided for by law with a hefty penalty, with imprisonment of up to one year, or in extenuating circumstances with imprisonment or a fine of up to 1,500 marks. The above decision shall take effect with the publication in the State Gazette'.

W.g. Simon	W.g. Schneppenhorst
Landes-Soldatenrat	Minister for Military Affairs

Until the time the Hoffmann government moved to Bamberg, it was not difficult to bring the people across the border as travellers. It was only when the sharp border control at Bamberg began that people were sent back. These gathered in Munich and visited the Thule premises. It became dangerous to have such a large crowd together; they attracted attention and they wanted something to do. Sebottendorff decided to take them outside the city, not too far from Munich so that one would have them immediately at hand, and also not so close that the red guards would be alerted to them.

First lieutenant Kurz was in contact with the farmers in Eching and so an agreement was reached with them, that people could gather there, protecting the area from looting by the red guards. In command was Captain Römer.

The *Bund*'s second department, intelligence, was in the hands of Lieutenant Edgar Kraus. Kraus was the son of the first chief prosecutor in Augsburg, who later achieved fame in the Bavarian *Femeprozeß*. As a 17-year-old ensign, Kraus had fought from the beginning of the world war until the bitter end. He had endeared himself to his people and now it turned out that they were behind him. The captain of the first squadron *Schwere Reiter* was also commander of cavalry. Egetemayer maintained contact with government troops with his people. He first informed the *Kampfbund*, where messages were edited and passed on.

However, through this contact, soldiers and military units in Munich could be directly affected as well.

In every communist region there were people from the *Kampfbund*, usually as writers or secretaries, who brought their reports to the Marstallstraße every evening. The reports thus received were collected and sent by the last train to Augsburg and from there to Bamberg. Important matters were passed on by telephone from Augsburg.

The Hoffmann government had approached Sebottendorff through a well-known Augsburger lawyer and asked him if he would be active for the government.

To make the necessary appointment, Sebottendorff had travelled to Augsburg and taken a room at the *Goldene Lamm*, a small boarding house where he did not stand out. There it was agreed that the government's publications would be multiplied by Sebottendorff. He was ordered to organise the counter-revolution by all means so that the Hoffmann government would soon be back in power in Munich. With this order, all the actions of the *Kampfbund* were covered as legal. As with the arms case at the time, Sebottendorff was also warned in Augsburg by a curious pre-fall. Something about the negotiations had to have leaked out. The sailors had decided to pick up Sebottendorff early in the morning at the *Goldene Lamm*. However, he had travelled to Munich on the first train and had just arrived at the Thule Society office when he received a telephone call from Augsburg, informing him of the incident.

On the one hand, this way the *Kampfbund*'s freedom to act was secured; on the other hand, the funds were still lacking. Now Baron Malsen and Werner von Heimburg came into the picture, receiving from citizens in Munich the money needed to carry out various actions. The money matters, which for understandable reasons were handled without receipts, were - until Sebottendorff's departure - settled by Johann Ott.

People in Eching were equipped with weapons bought from the Red Guards. For a rifle one paid an average of 60 to 80 marks, for a *Mauser pistol* with ammunition 10 marks; egg-shaped hand grenades cost 1 mark, steel hand grenades 3 marks. The weapons were brought to Eching by students Witzgall and Stecher.

The two were caught more than once in the process, but they always managed to talk their way out of it.

Through Kraus' intelligence service, the *Kampfbund* found out everything planned by the councils and thus managed to obstruct major actions of the Red Army more than once. On three occasions, the entire vehicle fleet was crippled by the changing of magnets, the tanks of the aircraft in Schleißheim were damaged and rendered unusable. Municipalities where people wanted to appellate could be warned.

Despite all the enthusiasm, the situation was still critical enough. People who were in communist regions were in particular danger of being turned on; sometimes Sebottendorff needed all his powers of persuasion to bring back doubters.

As the Munich government tried to prevent the departure of all men between 16 and 60, train tickets for free travel were reprinted with the permission of the transport ministry, and couriers travelled as railway officials. The stamps found when people rolled up the Thule Society were used for this purpose.

The Thule Society was accused of forging the stamps. This was completely unnecessary; the forgeries, if any, were made in the regions themselves and the stamps were bought. Just as carelessly as with the stamps, the clubs for communists handled membership cards and leave letters. Everything was for sale. Every member of the *Kampfbund* had a real membership of the Spartakus Union, obviously with another name on it. If the leadership of communist groups changed very quickly, copies were bought to protect their own.

In Munich, other and smaller groups were formed. Captain Mayer, for instance, reorganised the civilian guard. NCOs and dismissed policemen formed their own associations in which members of the *Kampfbund* were in charge. The organisation had thus become so strong that none would dare to strike a blow. The chairman of the soldiers' council and commander of the city was Seyffertitz, behind whom the garrison stood with the exception of the garderegiment and a few small sections that were strictly communist. Seyffertitz wanted to declare a military dictatorship and the Hoffmann government had promised him the proxy. Two representatives of the government would hand Seyffertitz the proxies on Saturday before Palm Sunday, which would then be presented to the meeting of the soldiers' councils. Before the start of the battle, the government had planes dropped a leaflet, which Sebottendorff reprinted and distributed. The text read:

Citizens of Munich!

Outrage is flaring up across the country over the tyranny prevailing in Munich. Aliens and fantasists reign among you. You are confused and discouraged. Reflect and take courage!

The whole country stands up. All of northern Bavaria stands firmly behind the Hoffmann-Segitz government. The situation is improving hour by hour. In Würzburg on Wednesday, a communist *coup* was completely put down, the hostages were released, the spartak rioters, including Sauber and Hagemeister from Munich, were arrested with their entire supporters.

With the exception of a few individuals who were led astray, all workers throw themselves enthousiastically into the struggle against Bolshevism. The peasants of entire gangs rise up to protect the socialist government. The soldiers radically purge the anarchist nests.

Things are also starting to loosen up in southern Bavaria. The Swabian and Old Bavarian peasants are rising up against the pigsty in Munich. The claim that the *Freikorps Epp* is approaching to overthrow the government in Bamberg is pure deception. Bavaria does not need outside help.

How long do you, citizens of Munich, want to stand by? Resist! Down with tyranny! Long live the Free State of Bavaria! Long live the Hoffmann-Segitz government!
    Bamberg, 10 April 1919.

The Social Democratic *Landespartei*

Sebottendorff had sent a member of the Thule Society, the railway official Kf, to Bamberg on 8 April 1919 with precise plans for a coup. The government did not consider this man trustworthy enough. One held him under pretexts until Saturday afternoon and did not let him return to Munich until all agreements had been made there. If all went well, a member of the Social Democratic Party, the lawyer Ewinger, would immediately represent the government.

It was agreed that on the night from Saturday to Sunday, the night before Palm Sunday, the Communist leaders would be arrested and taken directly to Eichstätt. Schneppenhorst would immediately move artillery, foot soldiers and cavalry from Ingolstadt so that these units would be in Munich on Sunday morning.

The troops were to consist of 6,000 reliable men, who were to act as a combat unit with a special mission, while the garrison in Munich would provide guard duty until the legitimate government arrived in Munich. The men in Eching were to be armed on the arrival of the government troops and occupy Schleißheim airfield.

Seifertietz had summoned the garrison and was waiting for proxies from the government. Instead of proxies, people appeared at 11 pm reporting that the garderegiment commander had picked up the proxies. The proxies, however, were on their way to the executive council. Despite this, the actions were not suspended. The arrest teams sprang into action immediately, but were only partially successful. The wife of the arrested Mühsam was able to alert most officials telephonically. Fechenbach, Mühsam and about 20 other leaders could be caught and were taken to the Central Station, where Aschenbrenner was in command. From the Central Station, the detainees were taken to Eichstätt and placed in police custody there.

On the morning of Palm Sunday, Munich had been liberated, the communists had disappeared, the councils had gone into hiding.

The joy was great and the streets were full of enthusiastic people. In Ludwigstraße, a car was stopped by early churchgoers, whose occupants wanted to hand out communist appeals. The occupants were beaten and the pamphlets were burnt with the car.

Schneppenhorst, however, did not keep his word. The expected troops did not arrive.

By noon, the situation became really critical. Cars belonging to communists equipped with machine guns, raced through the streets and there were deaths and injuries.

Gatherings were reported from everywhere. Bamberg assured by phone that the troops should arrive in Munich any minute.

Sebottendorff sent people out in small groups, but they were sent back. 'Officers and students could not be used, their own people would go on strike.'

The attempt to move the troops lying in barracks into action failed.

Thus happened, what had to happen: the *coup* had to be considered failed and any further action would be futile. At 6 pm, Seyffertitz evacuated the army museum. He managed to get away without being attacked. At 9 o'clock, Central Station, which Aschenbrenner had managed to hold until then, fell in the hope that government troops would still come. The Communists had taken the station under heavy mortar fire at that time. However, Aschenbrenner and his men were able to escape without too many losses too.

As a result of the attempted coup, the *Republikanische Schutzwehr* was now disbanded and the police completely disarmed. A 'workers' guard' was formed, armed in the barracks and used as a security force. As late as Sunday evening, the main post office was occupied by the 'workers' guard' and all telephone traffic to the outside was cut off. Augsburg and Rosenheim, where the Council government had taken refuge for a few days, were recaptured.

Schneppenhorst later claimed that he had given the orders on time and that the troops should certainly have arrived in Munich on time. The failure had been due to a series of unfortunate coincidences. Cargo cars had got stuck etc. We have to believe him; things were sabotaged from the other side.

The troops did not enter Dachau until Monday evening, where they clashed with the Red Guards led by Toller. The 'battle of Dachau' with which the Jew Toller flaunted was limited to a few shots in which one man was wounded by a graze. Captain Römer of the troops from Eching was able to give the retreat of the government troops, that looked more like a flee attempt, cover.

In the process, he was captured and locked up in the fire station. However, he managed to escape and even find a bicycle, so that he was able to make a concise report to Sebottendorff as early as four in the morning. Then the cavalry of the government troops had entered Dachau unhindered, where they had found an angry mob. Women had scolded soldiers and tried to pull them off the horses. When the red troops then opened fire, the bulk had to give way.

'What is to become of that,' Römer concluded his discourse. 'The people in Eching don't know where they stand; we are too poorly armed to resist any longer. And they know for sure that we are in Eching; tomorrow, or the day after tomorrow, they will attack. By the way, I shared my captivity with a certain Klöppel. The man confessed that he came from you and he had a lot of money with him.'

'I had sent Klöppel to you with money. He also had to take money to Freilassing to the hunters there.'

'He has not told me anything about that and to be honest, I do not trust the man, he is too eloquent and above all, too confused. He will probably stick with the red guards. If that is the case, we are all the more in danger.'

'Let me think for a moment, captain. Can you get to Eichstätt with your men?'

'Yes? - How much time do you need?'

'Three days!'

'Very well, captain, you will be in Eching tomorrow, preferably this afternoon. If you march tomorrow, you can be in Eichstätt by Saturday at the latest. On my orders, could you occupy the barracks in Eichstätt, arm yourself there and wait for me to send you a message?'

'What are you up to, Mr Baron?'

'I want to go to Bamberg and get permission there to set up a *Freikorps*. Then you and the people in Eching will form the core of the new organisation.'

'Please give me the order in writing, I will go back today.'

The order was issued in two copies, because Captain Römer wanted to send his brother to Eching via another route, just to be sure. It was also agreed that the Treuchtlingen railway station from Munich should be occupied immediately to keep the road to Eichstätt clear.

To occupy the Treuchtlingen junction, Sebottendorff assigned Lieutenant Kraus, who left on Wednesday morning. Kraus took a few people selected from the *Kampfbund* with him. He had been ordered to occupy the station and forward the arriving troops to Eichstätt.

He himself was to start recruiting immediately for the *Freikorps* to be set up there.

On the same afternoon, First Lieutenant Kurz travelled to Bamberg with orders to wait there for Sebottendorff's arrival.

The departure of so many 'railway officials' had to be conspicuous; however, with the help of clever manoeuvres, they all managed to get away from Munich. Only Lieutenant Arndt was detained, as he looked too young for a railway official. However, he was bold enough to return and leave again with a new train ticket as an assistant. On Wednesday evening, 16 April 1919, almost all the people of the *Kampfbund* were on their way. Now only Thule had to be secured. Kf and Deby took on the task of getting rid of the Society's card system, which, together with Sebottendorff's papers and the Society's documents, was in two military suitcases bearing the initials R.v.S. Those who wanted to continue voluntarily were made aware that they were in danger as soon as it became known in Munich that Sebottendorff was in the process of setting up a *Freikorps*.

Countess Westarp, Johann Ott, Valentin Büchold and many others, including Kf and Deby, offered to continue working. While final measures were thus being taken, Ritzler, who was formerly with the *Republikanische Schutzwehr*, appeared and informed that a warrant for Sebottendorff's arrest had been issued. The warrant could be stopped until 8 p.m., after which Sebottendorff was to be found neither in the Thule Society nor at home.

Sebottendorff therefore had no time to stay any longer in Munich, as the fate of the people in Eching and Treuchtlingen depended on him. One more time he warned to be careful, advised to work from different locations, again requested to immediately bring the suitcases to safety and left. In boarding house *Döring*, he warned Baroness Mikusch and Miss Bierbaumer that they were in danger and asked them to immediately pack everything they needed for a few days and to be at the Hotel *Deutscher Hof*, where rooms had been reserved, no later than 7 o'clock.

Sebottendorff was well known at the Hotel *Deutscher Hof*. He informed the old clerk Siegfried that he was staying here under the name of railway official Kallenbach.

At night, the hotel was searched twice by the 'workers' guard'. The room of railway official Kallenbach was skipped, but both ladies were searched. Miss Bierbaumer pretended to be a communist who had just arrived from Hungary and was left alone. Baroness Mikusch was not bothered any further.

As the train left at 6 a.m. and there was no thought of sleeping after the late-night visitation, the three decided that Sebottendorff would try to get to the station with his briefcase and the ladies' luggage and the ladies would follow.

As he came down the steps of the hotel, a bag in each hand, he saw that the vestibule was occupied. Even though, the clerk met him quickly and said, 'sir, do you want to go to the station already?'

'Yes, Siegfried, I have to go with the train, my mother-in-law in Nuremberg is dying and if I'm not there, I won't get anything.'

'All right, sir, I'll take you away.'
 'Well no, Siegfried, you are busy here anyway.'

'I have nothing to do here, those are the gentlemen of the 'workers' guard', they are looking for one Sebottendorff.'

'Aha, well then I wish them good luck. I hope they get the guy.'

At the station, everything was cordoned off; the sentries would not let anyone pass without the commander's permission. While Sebottendorff was negotiating with the sentries and showing his free ticket, an official, a station chief, entered the hall. 'Hey colleague,' Sebottendorff called out, 'come here. Look, I have to go to Nuremberg today, here's my ticket, but the guard won't let me through.'

'Surely the order does not apply to railway officials, come on, let sir through, he is a colleague after all.'

So Sebottendorff entered the hall where he met the two ladies who had bought tickets.

The train was very full, many Red Guards were travelling to Augsburg, there was an excited mood in the *compartment*, everyone was happy to leave Munich. Among the passengers was the editor of the *Münchener Neuesten Nachrichten*, Dr Hohenstätter, with whom Sebottendorff had become acquainted and with whom he had another small evening in Augsburg. The train did not continue; everyone had to get off in Augsburg. Only the four passengers wanted to travel further: Sebottendorff, who had free travel as a railway official, the two ladies and Dr Hohenstätter. The conductor advised them to wait in the restaurant on the station square. When it was possible for a train to leave, he would alert them.

After that adventure in the *Goldene Lamm,* Augsburg was a very dangerous place for Sebottendorff. He had to reckon with the fact that he was wanted and that the relevant authorities in Augsburg were already aware of it. Fortunately, it did not take long. An official came to tell him that 'the Prussians wanted their carriages back' and that an express train would leave in a few minutes. If the ladies and the other gentleman wanted to come along, they had to quickly go and get permission from the mayor. That too succeeded, and at the last minute the three four travellers were just able to catch the departing train.

In Bamberg, Sebottendorff met First Lieutenant Kurz. Seyffertitz was also there; he made every effort to have the council of ministers meet immediately, so that Sebottendorff could report the same evening. Here, they still knew nothing of the battle of Dachau and of the flight of the governement troops. On that evening, the council of ministers decided to enlist the help of the *Freikorps Epp*. It was Professor Stempfle in particular who championed the *Freikorps Epp* very vigorously. Sebottendorff received the desired authorisation which was issued by Minister Schneppenhorst and the *Landessoldatenrat* on 19 April

1919. At the same time, he received several other proxies. The III Army Corps in Nuremberg was ordered to give him every support.

Copies were made immediately via a notary in Bamberg. A second power of attorney was sent to Captain Römer. Corresponding messages went to Regensburg, Würzburg and other places. Sebottendorff then returned to Nuremberg on 19 April 1919 and moved into the Hotel *Fürstenhof*, where he set up his headquarters.

It is still necessary to report on the Munich situation and on things that are easily forgotten and show what would have become of Germany if Bolshevism had triumphed. It is quickly forgotten what terror and atrocities Munich was exposed to at the time. Nowhere in Germany could a council rule last so long, nowhere so deeply intervene in life as precisely in Munich.

As already mentioned, the city and its immediate surroundings formed a communist island in the state. The borders were guarded by the Red Guards, who controlled all incoming and outgoing traffic; not only travellers, but goods traffic as well.

Farmers who did not live directly in areas occupied by red guards no longer delivered anything to Munich. The lack of food was frightening. Since little milk was available in the city, large numbers of children died. A committee that complained to Leviné-Niessen received the reply: 'Let those bourgeois angels rot, every child that dies is one less enemy of the proletariat.'

Under the pretext of searching for contraband, the 'workers' guards' penetrated the houses and took away what they found. Care homes, hospitals and convents were systematically looted. To unleash the mob on a property, it was enough to prove that hammered foodstuffs were there.

In addition to the control of foodstuffs, the ongoing arrest of hostages instilled terror in the citizens.

Two reports on such incidents are reproduced here. On 23 April 1919, the *Münchener Neuesten Nachrichten* reported:

On Tuesday after Easter, at 6 am, a truck with 10 armed soldiers and labourers appeared on the Bavaria ring and began rounding up hostages. They forced their way into several houses and declared a total of 13 people, including invalids and the elderly, to be arrested. In part, the arrest proceeded in an exceptionally rough manner. They could not show an arrest warrant, afterwards a soldier showed a piece of paper, signed by the revolutionary leader of Westend district, which read: The bearer is authorised to arrest hostages.

The choice of persons had apparently been made on the basis of an address book, because the list also included a certain chief official von Grundherr, the chief of police, who had died in 1917. The detainees included a 68- year-old teacher, a pensioner who was nervously ill and also had bladder issues, a captain b.d., a Protestant clergyman and a chief official of the Ministry of Transport. The latter had a legitimation certificate from people's commissioner Paulukum, with which he was under the protection of the Council government and could not be arrested. The soldier's reply was succinct: 'We know that excuse.'

The hostages were transported on an open truck to the *Guldein school* in a temperature of 2 degrees-unless the temperature was zero, where they were housed in the unheated gymnasium. At 10am, they were taken to the police station in Astallerstraße and detained there in two police cells.

As if the treatment was not lamentable enough, they had to listen to threats of execution and walling as well. One soldier explained that 1,500 hostages had been rounded up in Munich, who would be sent to meet the government troops as they approached. In the late afternoon, the hostages were told that a member of the *Vollzugsrat* was present. By bribing the guard, the hostages managed to speak to him. The guard called the arrest an arbitrary act and it was thanks to his actions that the hostages were released in the evening. The last one to leave the cell was the minister. The guard had strongly resisted his release, with a soldier declaring: 'You are a clergyman by profession and the Council government sees in every clergyman a dangerous individual because the church is against the Council government'. At 7:30 in the evening, however, the clergyman too was released.

The soldier's information, that 1,400 or 1,500 hostages would be shot, was based on a report from the commander's office. This proposed that the hostages should be herded together on Theresienwiese and shot with machine guns should the government troops advance. This proposal was rejected by 6 votes to 7.

About a memory of the arrest of the hostages, a *Transrhenania* student writes in the 1929 *Korpszeitung* No. 2:

'Among the various forms of government Munich had to tolerate at that time was a so-called *Zentral-rat*. This was divided into departments, in which more or less questionable elements, who were supposed to provide the people with a beautiful and dignified life and were themselves fishing in murky waters in the process. These lords did not feel entirely secure on their thrones and felt the need to protect themselves against eventual attacks. They felt that arresting hostages from influential circles, was appropriate.

It was on a spring morning in 1919. We couple of young activists with the final diploma for the a.H. - which we were not allowed to show - in our pockets, were sitting in the *Neue Börse*, when we received the message from the president of the presidial corps, that we had to go straight to an a.o.S.C. What we heard there was very surprising. The *Zentralrat* had asked the weapon-bearing communist students in Munich to take hostages.

The farmers' council occupied a couple of the best *suites* in the Hotel *Bayerischer Hof* and stayed there at the community's expense, not exactly rural. Here we were arraigned and told that the *Zentralrat* adhered uncompromisingly to its position and that the rumours regarding an imminent action by the students forced the council to take the announced measures.'

The author, Mr Max Schmitt, then talks about the negotiations and describes his passage to Stadelheim, where he was received by the later police chief Pöhner. The latter told him that he could not do much for the hostages because he himself was under strict supervision, but he would do what he could. The reporter then enters a cell where he finds four fellow students. Over a communal dinner, he gets to know the other hostages.

'It must be admitted that in selecting these hostages, the gentlemen of the *Zentralrat* had proved that they had a feel for and understanding of quality. Around the table sat the Commanding General von F., General von L., Colonel K. von Kr., *Reichsrat* von A., the fanatically national-minded bookseller and publisher Lehmann and many other high-ranking personalities, whose names I have forgotten over the years. These men had been in detention continuously for 14 days...'

Who remembers when Sontheimer held a pre-dawn lecture with light pictures in the halls of *Munich Kindl* for thousands of schoolchildren, explaining how to prevent pregnancy. Who remembers that in all the command posts, in the guard rooms, women and girls shamelessly hung around and that, for example, in the *Residenz* (former palace of the Bavarian king - transl.) the children watched through the windows what was happening there, that interrogations took place, with the interrogator having his girlfriend on his lap!

In early April, there had been a very heavy snowfall, which remained long after Easter. Why even clear the snow, there was a strike every two days anyway.

Those who picked up pamphlets thrown off by planes had to clean the toilets in barracks, schools and guardrooms for punishment.

When the money ran out, the banks' vaults were emptied. However, the gold from the *Reichsbank* and the Prussian embassy could be brought to Berlin with the help of the *Kampfbund*. Likewise, the *Kampfbund* managed to keep the crates stored in the *Residenz* out of the hands of the red guards.

The streets were no longer swept at all. Munich had literally and figuratively become a pigsty. It was time it was cleaned out.

IX
Entry of the *Freikorps Oberland* in Munich

On Easter Sunday 1919, Sebottendorff appeared before the commander of the III Army Corps, where he handed over his proxies. In accordance with the measures already taken, Eichstätt was designated as the station of the *Freikorps Oberland*.

The government's order read:

By decision of the council of ministers and the *Landessoldatenrat*, this authorised Rudolf von Sebottendorff to establish the *Freikorps Oberland* in Treuchtlingen.

Bamberg, 19 April 1919.

The *Landessoldatenrat*	The Minister of Military Affairs
Mr Simon	w.g. Schneppenhorst

Sebottendorff was assigned two administrators for his staff. At the suggestion of First Lieutenant Kurz, Major Ritter von Beth was asked to take on the military leadership of the corps. An unpleasant matter was concluded. The aforementioned Klöppel turned up and tried to get money from private individuals for the corps. He was taken into preventive custody in Eichstätt until the capture of Munich on Sebottendorff's initiative. The corps did not receive or take a penny from private individuals. However, the station did accept cigarettes and other donations for the *Freikorps*.

After another office and an inn were rented, a visit was made in the afternoon to Rothenburg ob der Tauber, where a recruitment meeting was planned. However, the then reigning First Lord Mayor Siebert declared that such a meeting was not necessary, as he would take the necessary initiatives himself. Indeed, applications began to flow as early as Tuesday after Easter and were highest in Rothenburg. First Mayor Siebert had already done a lot of preparatory work.

On the same day, recruitment drives and recruitment offices were set up in Ansbach and Gunzenhausen. The same took place in other towns on Easter Monday. Volunteers who had signed up were looked after at the guesthouse; and those who arrived in the afternoon were forwarded to the individual corps on the same day. Those who arrived in the afternoon could sleep in the boarding house, were given money for food and, after being properly looked after, were forwarded the next day.

On Tuesday after Easter, Sebottendorff visited Weißenburg and Treuchtlingen, where Lieutenant Kraus was having a very difficult time. He had gone out without legitimacy, but he had managed to hold out. He had gathered 10 men around him, had recruited and sent a whole crowd of candidates to Eichstätt.

In Eichstätt, Sebottendorff informed Captain Römer that Major von Beth had taken charge and asked him to look after things until the leader's arrival.

Treuchtlingen would be occupied from the corps; Kraus would go to Nuremberg with his men.

There, the service of the headquarters, set up as a focal point, had expanded. It not only had to recruit, but also organise arms transports. His loyal helpers in this were Lieutenant Karl Schwabe, Lieutenant Arndt and Lieutenant von Feilitzsch.

Major von Beth had appointed an adjutant, named Kupfer, and with him he clashed several times. He tried to second the men in Treuchtlingen to Eichstätt; only after a vehement protest was he forced to abandon this. Then he complained that the *Freikorps Oberland* was short of men; the station would send more men to the other corps. As it turned out later, Kupfer did not like Sebottendorff's anti-Semitic leanings; hence he was obstructive.

The corps was assigned a third administrator.

Bad news had come from Munich via a courier, Dr Kummer, a member of the *Teutonic Order*. Things would go on there like on a dovecote, people very publicly worked against the Council government. These reports were confirmed by a courier from machine factory *Augsburg-Nuremberg*. Sebottendorff was at the *Freikorps'* march off Eichstätt on 24 April 1919 and had bad luck on the way back shortly before Treuchtlingen. The stationmaster ordered an empty train to stop. Here Sebottendorff met the courier, who was carrying Reichert, a Red Army officer, as a prisoner.

The courier had been in Marstallstraße in the morning and had encountered Kf, who had ignored his warnings and felt perfectly safe.

The courier said that at least 100 free train tickets had been issued on this day and that the activities could not be kept secret for long. The Thule Society could be rolled up at any moment.

The tickets, after Lieutenant Rudolf Heß had checked them beforehand, were issued by Ott. However, Heß would also have leave today for the *Freikorps Regensburg*.

These reports prompted Sebottendorff to send Prince Thurn und Taxis, who arrived the same evening with messages, back to Munich with the order to urge everyone to be especially careful; in addtition, he had to make sure that the two military suitcases had been taken away.

As fate would have it, the prince could not reach Munich the next day. Train traffic was jammed, he did not arrive in Munich until 26 April 1919 and by then the accident had already happened. The prince himself was arrested at the *Parkhotel*. The office at the *Vier Jahreszeiten* had been rounded up; the secretary, Countess Westarp, taken away.

However, the *Freikorps Oberland* power station heard nothing about it.

In the afternoon of 26 April 1919, Sebottendorff received an urgent request to appear at the commandant's office. There he was informed that the advance of the Reich troops in Nuremberg had become known, that the Spartak Union was planning a *coup* and that gatherings could already be observed in the streets.

Unfortunately, the emphatic order had been given at Bamberg not to use arms under any circumstances. The rabble would know that. It was now a matter of getting this order revoked; for that Sebottendorff was the right man. He had to leave for Bamberg immediately.

Arriving in Bamberg, Major Paulus, despite the resistance of Schneppenhorst's adjutant, succeeded in convincing the minister council that it was very dangerous to have an uprising in the back of the advancing troops, that one would save the lives of thousands of people by putting ten people against the wall.

With orders to fire in case of emergency, Sebottendorff returned in time, just when the cornered troops wanted to retreat.

The orders of the supreme command, General von Möhl, under whom all the *Freikorps*, all Prussian and Würt- tembergian divisions belonged, were so struck that by 2 May 1919 the encirclement of Munich would have been complete. On 1 May, because of the May

Day celebration of the workers, they did not want to attack.

Since the *Zentrale Oberland* had yet to carry out an arms transport to Tölz, they set out on 29 April 1919 to arrive in Rosenheim and Tölz via Ingolstadt where arms, hand grenades and blankets were to be received. Unfortunately, poor means of transport and delayed delivery held up the troops in Ingolstadt; added to this was a battle at Kolbermoor and so they did not arrive in Munich until 3 May, where they learned that seven people from Thule had been gruesomely murdered and two hussars executed. Karl Stecher of Thule's *Kampfbund* had been killed in the street fighting around Munich. The *Zentrale Oberland* moved into Thule's office. In the *Vier Jahreszeiten*, General von Epp had also taken quarters. The *Freikorps Oberland* had distinguished itself under Major von Beth. It had entered the city from the Maximilianeum and there had been no losses. The *Freikorps Oberland* was the nucleus of today's *S.A. Hochland* and of the first German S.A. divisions in general.

The *Freikorps Chiemgau*, which was also served by the *Zentrale Oberland*, had been established by R. Kanzler, a senior official. He had received a power of attorney from the government in Bamberg to establish the corps, and his decisive action enabled it to attack, capture and occupy the railway station near the village of Haar on 27 April. As a result, the military leadership had completed the encirclement of Munich two days earlier, as they did not have to take the diversions via Mühldorf - Wasserburg. In this attack, Lieutenant Wiedemann, who had been a member of the *Kampfbund* of Thule until 14 April, was killed.

A brief report on the Munich capture follows here:

With the attack at Haar, the encirclement of Munich was already complete by 30 April. 1 May was a rest day; if the Red Army did not capitulate, the attack would take place on 2 May. There were signs, however, that the Raden government would surrender.

The assassination of Thule's staff prevented this surrender and ensured that individual troops were already moved without command on 1 May and the units in the city itself went on the attack.

On 2 May, the street fighting intensified, shots were fired from the rooftops everywhere, many women took part in the fighting, the bitterness of the troops increased the more resistance was offered. However, they still managed to occupy most of the government buildings in Munich on this day.

On Saturday, 3 May 1919, there was still heavy fighting around the station. On 4 May, the fighting diminished, but raids still occurred. It was still very restless until 10 May, with attacks on patrols and individual posts almost every night. General von Epp was taken under fire by a sniper, but fortunately not hit.

To avenge the people of Thule, Sebottendorff immediately called in Kraus's intelligence service. As main culprits, the three Jews Axelrod, Levien and Leviné-Niessen came into consideration.

Axelrod, it was soon established, had fled with the help of Chief Constable Mairgünther on 29 April. He was found on 16 May by an agent of the *Freikorps Oberland* intelligence service in Achental with two companions, arrested by the police and sentenced to 15 years' imprisonment by the military court. On 20 September 1919, the day on which the seven workers he misled in Stadelheim died, Axelrod was transported to Berlin by the Hoffmann government in a first-class wagon and extradited to the Raden government of Russia. The Ebert-Scheidemann government had claimed him and Hoffmann had complied with the request.

Levien was able to escape across the border. He was later arrested in Vienna, but not extradited. Levien currently has a job in Soviet Russia.

The third, Leviné-Niessen, was caught by the central's intelligence service. Kraus had found out that Professor Salz from Heidelberg had entrusted Leviné to architect Zimmer. Zimmer had taken him to painter Schmitt, at 20 Schneckenburgerstraße, who was in the process of getting Leviné other identity papers. Kraus persuaded the police to hand Schmitt the identity papers and had Ott pursue Zimmer. While Ott followed Zimmer's trail, Ott was pursued by Witzgall and Schödel in a commandeered car, who then passed on to Kraus where Schmitt had gone.

At the time, Kraus had contacted adjutant Kupfer of the *Freikorps Oberland*. However, the latter had rejected the arrest of people. Lieutenant Kraus then turned to General von Epp, who immediately gave the order to arrest people. At midnight, the block of houses was surrounded. Only after a long phone call was the door opened. Schmitt denied that there were any other people in the house apart from him, and when Kraus asked him straight out about Leviné, he replied mockingly: 'You must know that better than me.' In the studio, the cut beard and head hair of the wanted were found. Leviné himself was taken off the roof.

In the premises, Ott found a large stock of new shoes, clothes and other items from theft and confiscation.

The military court sentenced Leviné to death. The sentence was carried out.

Soon after moving in, Major von Beth handed over the *FreiKorps Oberland* to Major Petri. The latter in turn handed it over to the *Reichswehr*. In a conversation Sebottendorff had with General Ritter von Epp, the general promised that the name of the *Freikorps* would live on in the first battalion of the *Bayerische Schützenbrigade*. The corps later distinguished itself in the occupation of the Ruhr (in 1923 - transl.) and then in Silesia, under Major Horadam, in the assault on Annaberg. Shortly before its dissolution, the city of Munich gave a gala performance of *Die Fledermaus* at the *Gartentheater* in honour of the corps. The *Zentrale Oberland* had been disbanded earlier. However, before the station disappeared, the intelligence service still managed to catch someone. Lieutenant Kraus, with the permission of the Italian authorities, was able to arrest the notorious member of the Red Soldiers' Council Buditsch in Innsbruck and hand him over to the *Lüttwitz* corps in Berlin.

To follow up on the mournful satire, it should be mentioned here that adjutant Kupfer of the *Freikorps Oberland*, in the courtyard of the barracks, solemnly burned the *Münchener Beobachter* and ensured that Sebottendorff was reprimanded by the supreme command, because of his anti-Semitic activities. The letter stated that by spreading the anti-Semitic *Beobachter*, Sebottendorff had violated the supreme principle of keeping soldiers far from politics. On the great merits Sebottendorff acquired in setting up the organisations, one might expect him to stop making anti-Semitic propaganda.

The following is known about the employees of the *Zentrale Oberland* about their subsequent lives:

First lieutenant Kurz studied philology, obtained a doctorate and a leadership position in the SS.

Lieutenant Kraus went to the Baltic countries after the disbandment of the station, distinguished himself there, joined the police in Berlin and, on the initiative of Chief Commissioner Pöhner, was brought to Munich to set up troops for special assignments. Today, he is a captain in the *Grüne Landespolizei*.

Lieutenant Karl Schwabe is the famous Afrika pilot.

Lieutenant Parcus had many adventures in his life, which he testifies to in his book *Schiggi-Schiggi*.

Karl Witzgall was killed in a car accident a few years later.

Johann Ott became head of publishing house *Municher Beobachter, Verlag Franz Eher Nachf.* in 1919 and is accountant today.

Schödel has a motorbike factory in Erlangen.

X
The victims of Thule - murder of Thule members

As already mentioned, Sebottendorff's representatives in the Marstallstraße worked diligently during his absence. However, they relied too much on the luck they had had so far. Nor had they learned to step into the breach when the chips were down. During the period from 18 April 1919 until Thule was disbanded by the revolutionary police, more than 500 free train tickets were issued. Passengers were put on a list, which was in the main hall.

On the afternoon of 26 April 1919, the police intervened and sent a commando *Arbeiterwehr* and some sailors to clear the Thule Society, i.e. the recruitment office located there. They found only secretary Countess Westarp there, who was interrogated, taken to the police station and let go again. During the interrogation several people appeared who were also interrogated and let go again.

That was firstly Griehl, who had agreed with Kf and Dietrich Eckart to meet at the Thule office. As his name was not found on the list of train passengers, he was released.

Eckart and Kf had come by car and felt that something was going on and were therefore able to escape. How much Kf underestimated the danger was shown by the fact that on the same day he tried to get into another office; he thought he could continue his work. If he had not forgotten to remove the military suitcases in the office, nothing would have happened. The manager of the fellowship, Weber and his wife, were alerted by porter Sell when they came up the corridor, and they in turn were able to alert other members, such as Dannehl's niece, who appeared with a backpack full of pamphlets. She said she had made a mistake on the stairs and wanted to go to the laundry. Through Dannehl, other members were alerted. An officer who worked with Ott on issuing free train tickets was also released when he declared that he had only come to give the editor of the *Beobachter* a beating because he was still sending him that scurrilous magazine. The sailor was sorry that the officer had not got hold of the fellow and let him go.

Everything shows, especially the release of the countess at the police station, that the intention was to abolish the recruitment office and they were satisfied with that. But now two more circumstances came into play, which set other things in motion.

One had taken the two military suitcases, the anti-Semitic posters and pamphlets to the police headquarters, where Axelrod, the plenipotentiary of the Russian soviets, had seen them. He had now discovered the source of the anti- Semitic propaganda so disturbing to him. And as if the devil played with it: on the same day, the harvest began to ripen. The Bavarian worker had had enough of the Jewish mess. At the councils' congress, the councils called Levien a 'cursed Jew-bender', labelled the 'Jew-boy' as a misleader of the workers and forced him to resign his position.

Leviné-Niessen had to resign as well. Both Jews left the *Vollzugsrat*, but this did not render them powerless. At the War Ministry sat their best friend, Commander Egelhofer, who was directly under Seidel, the commander of the *Luitpold Gymnasium* where there were about 800 Red Guardsmen.

When Levien and Leviné-Niessen heard through Axelrod of Thule's anti-Semitic propaganda, which they blamed for their debacle, their plan was made: the people of Thule had to die. However, since they already knew exactly about the situation on 26 April, in their delusions of power, the death of the Thule members had to give them the greatest possible reputation. The risk was that the Raden government and the Red Army would capitulate. If that happened, of course, they had gained nothing. It had to come to a battle, blood had to flow. As long as the enemy brothers could not come together, chances still existed for them. If the red army did not go to battle, they had to be forced to defend themselves. One had to get the enemies to attack. This could happen, when shortly before the catastrophe, blood of civilians flowed. The roles were divided in the sense that Levien and Leviné-Niessen secured the Thule members to be picked up, while the workers in the *Luitpold gymnasium*, who were to commit the murder, were incited to murder. Axelrod would see to it that the execution of the deed was made known to the troops outside. The plan succeeded. Mehrer was ordered to issue the arrest warrants based on the lists found, and the city commander followed the order given by Egelhofer.

Seidel was let loose with his gang and it was only thanks to the fact, that most of the Thule members had been warned and were able to get to safety, that only seven were caught. This was fortunate because all the members, more than two hundred, were searched. The police were in every house. Lawyer Dahn only escaped arrest because his landlord was so thoughtful. Riemann, Gaubatz, Griehl, in short, all those who were on the list were searched.

Riemann had warned the countess a few days before the arrest. 'Sister, great politics is being practised here, which is nothing for a woman. We are sticking our necks out, but please stay away.' To which she had replied: 'I am a German woman and will do my duty.' On the day before the arrest, on 25 April, Büchold said to her: 'Sister Heila, here, since Sebottendorff has left, things are not looking rosy. It is better if you do not come tomorrow, I do not trust the matter. I am going to one of the upcoming free corps.' Countess Westarp told Griehl this and, when she was afraid, he also advised her to stay away. He himself had to go to Marstallstraße the next day and would excuse her. But out of a sense of duty, the countess had gone to work anyway. After being released for the second time, she had come home to pick up some laundry. As she was preparing dinner, she was arrested for the third time and taken to the city command. There, they had just gathered the Thule members who were the least guilty and had therefore not been warned. Among them were Walter Nauhaus and Walter Deike whom they had arrested at Nauhaus' home, baron Seidlitz whom they had taken from his workshop, and Captain Utsch. A little later they arrived with Daumenlang.

While Utsch, who was not a member but still a guest of Thule, was released after the interrogation, the others were taken to the police headquarters. Most importantly, however, the interrogation held by Egelhofer included Levien, the Levien who had to leave the *Vollzugsrat* the next day.

On the night of 26-27 April, the diabolical plan to murder the Thule members began to take firm shape. It was a diabolical plan because it was aimed at regaining power through this murder and maintaining itself *coûte que coûte*. And if it could not stay in power, blood was spilled. After all, the perpetrators were Germans killing their brothers. And Levien knew how to treat Germans: after all, in the murder trial, Schicklhofer said how enthusiastic he had been 'about Levien's speeches'. Still Levien's words went from mouth to mouth and were believed: 'Eye for an eye, tooth for a tooth, chest to chest, shot for shot, stab for stab.

Egelhofer wrote the phamflet qualifying the captured Thule members as looters. This important link in the chain read:

Reactionary thieves and looters arrested!

On Saturday afternoon, 26 April 1919, by order of the Council Government, a gang of criminals dangerous to public safety were rounded up and imprisoned at the posh Hotel *Vier Jahreszeiten*. They were mostly ladies and gentlemen from the so-called better circles. Among them were a first lieutenant and a countess.

These people counterfeited and forged military stamps and used them for thefts and looting at the highest level by carrying out seizures.

They confiscated huge amounts of goods of all kinds and predatorily requisitioned cattle from farmers in the countryside.

These criminals are arch-reactionaries, agents and colporteers of the white guard, 'inciters against the Raden republic who ruthlessly attack the black-market trade' and are therefore hated to the core by black traders and war profiteers.

Of course, they identified the Raden Republic as the instigator and perpetrator of these lootings and found credence, because, after all, the victims could not have known that they were being robbed by criminals using forged stamps.

The name Egelhofer was misused by forging a facsimile. The well-conceived plan was to create false identities to commit crimes in the name of Egelhofer and the government, thereby simultaneously enriching themselves and making the Raden Republic bad and hated. The facsimile, the stamp bearing Egelhofer's name, is unvalid. Only his personal autograph written in ink is valid. With this, the criminal and highly traitorous plan was thwarted and nullified.

Munich, 27 April 1919   R. Egelhofer

Now the captured Thule members still had to be taken to where the killers could get to them; to the *Luitpold Gymnasium*. That was the only place where the planned act could be carried out. Seidel, who was in command there, collected the prisoners from the main office and took them to the gymnasium. The transport was carried out on foot. Daumenlang tried to flee, but was caught up with and beaten to blood.

The Thule members were locked in a cellar at night with other prisoners. During the day, they had to peel potatoes. Countess Westarp was forced to clean rooms and had to sleep in a secluded shack in the guardhouse.

On 28 April 1919, the circle around Munich was tightening. By 29 April, after a short battle, Starnberg had been taken; Fürstenfeldbruck was in the hands of the government troops; it was time to carry out the deed.

Axelrod fled on that day with the help of Chief Commissioner Mairgünther. The night before, however, another meeting of the three Jews had taken place in the *Luitpold gymnasium*, followed by a nighttime viewing of the victims. People had descended to the basement and viewed the Thule members there by candlelight.

Prince Thurn und Taxis who was arrested by Seidel at the *Park Hotel* had joined them.

On 29 April, Baron Teuchert of the *Regensburg Freikorps* had been captured on a reconnaissance mission, and because his name appeared on the Thule Society's list, the city command took him to the *Luitpold Gymnasium*.

There, seven Thule members were now being held.

Now the beast in man had to be awakened, and for this they used the two white guards, the two Hussars captured at the front. They were incited through the most fantastical fairy tales. Under threats, Seidel forced the two hussars to make statements, which he immediately had printed and published.

That is how the crime was prepared and that is how it was committed. On 30 April 1919, at 10 o'clock in the morning, the two Hussars were put against the wall.

The following are both police disclosures, the unofficial report of agency Hoffmann, a report from *Ein Jahr bayerischer Revolution im Bilde* (A year of revolution in Bavaria in pictures) - Photoreport Hoffmann - and Chief Public Prosecutor Hoffmann's attached complaint, filed during the murder trial.

Announcement 1

The heinous act committed by bestial people (the shooting of hostages in the *Luitpold Gymnasium*) must be punished as soon as possible. The police chief holds it as his most sacred duty to ensure that all those involved receive their deserved punishment. To establish the facts irrefutably, all persons under threat of punishment are requested to provide relevant information. In particular the names of all soldiers who served under their commander in the *Luitpold Gymnasium* should become known, so that an unambiguous picture of these inhumans is obtained. Written or oral testimonies are received daily at the Ettstraße police station.

Munich, 3 May 1919   Chief Commissioner Vollnhals

Announcement 2

The names of the hostages put to death in the *Luitpold Gymnasium* have been ascertained down to two members of the shooters' division. The names read:

Walter Nauhaus of Munich
Baron Karl von Teuchert of Regensburg Wilhelm Seidlitz
   of Munich
Walter Deike of Munich
Countess Heila von Westarp of Munich
Prince Gustav Maria v. Thurn und Taxis of Munich Anton Daumenlang of Munich
Professor Berger of Munich

An accurate report on the killings is made public immediately through the official Hoffmann news agency. It was irrefutably established that the unfortunate hostages were shot to death without any prior interrogation. The two soldiers were executed in the morning at 10 am, the remaining hostages in the afternoon between 4 and 5 am in the courtyard of the *Luitpold Gymnasium*. All the convicts, including Countess Westarp, behaved with bravely and dignity until their last moments. All but Baron von Teuchert, who faced death head-on, were mowed down in the back. The gruesome injuries to three victims were caused by gunshots at close range. Mutilation of the executed did not take place. However, some of the corpses must have been robbed at night. The execution order was given by commander Fritz Seidel of Chemnitz and his deputy Willi Haußmann of Munich. It was not established whether they acted on orders from the supreme command. Willi Haußmann killed himself yesterday, at the moment he was to be arrested in his home. All the other people involved are being prosecuted extremely vigorously and all means are being used to arrest and bring those guilty to justice.

Munich, 4 May 1919   Chief Commissioner Vollnhals

The names of the men who were murdered along with the Thule members are: corporal at the Hussars Fritz Linnenbrügger of Bielefeld, married. Hussar Walter Hindorf of Weißenfels a.d. Saale. Professor Berger of Munich, Jew.

    Official report by press agency Hoffmann

On the evening of 30 April, a rumour spread like wildfire in Munich that hostages had been shot in the *Luitpold Gymnasium* and that the bodies had been mutilated. The police directorate, which, after the departure of the communist chief Mairgünther, had been taken over by some cold-blooded officials of the military police and was under the leadership of chief commissionary Vollnhals, was the first to take on the task of clarifying the facts regarding the shooting of the ten hostages. On 1 May morning, the bodies were taken to the forensic institute, where a meticulous investigation was set in motion. Schillerstraße was completely under fire from the Spartakists who had installed two heavy machine guns and a cannon there, and it was not possible for the officials to reach the forensic institute. The attempt was repeated several times during the night and they tried to get into Schillerstraße with the weak forces available at the time. As no reinforcements came from outside, it was not yet possible to break through. Schillerstrasse was cleared in the morning hours. Identification began immediately. Meanwhile, the facts were recorded by many witnesses. According to the unanimous testimonies, the execution of the hostages took place as follows:

The hostages were locked in the cellar overnight, and on 28 April, two more soldiers from the divisional guard were rounded up, whose names have not yet been determined. They were beaten and told they would be shot. As a result, the mood among the hostages was very depressed; all the more so because the political management, which was under communist leadership, had the persons arrested in the *Vier Jahreszeiten* brought in a day before. Their names are: Walter Nauhaus, Walter Deike, Max Aumiller, Heila von Westarp and Anton Daumenlang. These hostages were already informed of the fate that awaited them at the police station. They were therefore terribly nervous. First secretary Daumenlang cried bitterly and it made a deep impression on everyone when he told them he was completely innocent and did not know why he was here. He was married and had a child and wanted to be released. Daumenlang was covered in blood when he was brought. He had wanted to escape and had therefore been roughly mistreated. Apparently, the plan was to put the hostages to death even then.

On 30 April, at 10am, the two soldiers delivered by the Red Guards were executed. One told that he was the father of a family and lived in Berlin, while the other was a 19- or 20-year-old unmarried man. The young soldier was horribly beaten and mistreated. The two soldiers were taken to the courtyard, had to stand against the wall, came under fire and collapsed. The remaining hostages had to watch. With that, it was certain that they too would suffer the same fate. The hostages wrote farewell letters and heard in the afternoon that Levien would come. Why he came, no one knows. yet. Commander Fritz Seidel now ordered his deputy Willi Haußmann to select the hostages to be executed. Haußmann entered the hostages' room with a scribe and dictated the scribe the names of the individual persons in no particular order. After selecting eight hostages, he took a red pencil, underlined the names and wrote: shoot them. Next, the hostages were taken to the courtyard and at the alarm signal, about 200 soldiers gathered in the courtyard of the *Luitpold Gymnasium*. Another 150 to 200 soldiers watched from the windows. In addition, in the courtyard stood 8 to 10 men including soldiers, sailors and a civilian wearing a lether car coat.

The civilian was smiling and looking forward to the things to come. The victims stood close together in a corner between two trees. In the courtyard stood the writer and Haußmann. It is also claimed that Seidel was downstairs at first, but later went upstairs, before the execution, to count the money for the soldier's pay in his office. In front, in the guard, soldiers played mouth harmonica.

After this, the names were called out and the killers lined up about eight meters in front of the wall. First, the victims had to hand over all their valuables and letters to the soldier in command. The first victim was first secretary Daumenlang. He was shot from behind. He was praying. The shots fell irregularly and there is no evidence that an order was given. First secretary Daumenlang was branded a looter by the troops.

Who was shot second could not be properly determined. The victim was shot again by the civilian afterwards; from close range at the head, shattering the skull.

The third to be executed was first lieutenant von Teuchert, who would not turn around but stood up straight and said to the soldier: 'I look death in the eyes.'

Meanwhile, Prince von Thurn und Taxis, because he said that he was not the wanted Thurn und Taxis, but another, was once again set apart, since the soldiers expressly demanded that under no circumstances innocent people were be killed.

Seidel, who was sitting at his desk with a woman, simply said: 'Out with it, with us there is no negotiating, it is yes or no.' Next was probably professor Berger shot dead, presumably using *dum- dum* bullets, as the upper half of his face was completely shattered. Fifth was probably Walter Nauhaus, who was shot from behind too. Sixth, Friedrich Wilhelm von Seidlitz was killed.

The seventh victim was Countess Westarp. She asked if she could write. This was granted to her and she wrote on the back of a soldier for about 10 to 15 minutes. She told the soldier: 'I am innocent, please do not make a corpse of me.' She gave the letter to the writer, held her hands in front of her face and fell down on the other corpses, struck by a few bullets.

Last to go was Prince Thurn und Taxis. He was very composed and calm and still gave orders, in case any of the other hostages were released, that they should report their execution at the *Park Hotel*. Prince Thurn und Taxis must also have been hit by *dum-dum* bullets, because the upper part of his face was totally obliterated.

An eyewitness recounts that around 4 o'clock, a poster was put up in the *Luitpold Gymnasium*, on the back of which the following was written in pencil: 'Shoot 22 people, but select the best victims, w.g. Egelhofer.'

That the supreme command gave the order is further evident from the farewell letter of Willi Haußmann who committed suicide.

Egelhofer's secretary claims that when Egelhofer heard of the execution, he said, with tears in his eyes, 'I did not want that.' So far it has not been proven how things are connected. One thing is certain: Seidel, Haußmann and consorts seem to have been possessed of utter bestial cruelty and barbarity. The corpses were neither mutilated nor robbed by the soldiers. The victims were probably looted by corpse robbers at night.

News of the terrible event spread across the city with lightning speed. This fact caused citizens to arm themselves in unison and small troops also marched into the city and occupied certain neighbourhoods earlier than envisaged in the military plans.

Nothing can be said about the judicial proceedings yet. The case is in the hands of the public prosecutor. All perpetrators will be prosecuted and tried as soon as possible.

The preliminary investigation and trial that began on 1 September 1919 revealed so much barbarity that cannot be described here. Even the photographs of the victims cannot be printed here for that reason - they are hideous. However, the investigation yielded a picture of the situation that differs slightly from the description above. It can be found in the book: 'One Year of the Bavarian Revolution in Pictures', a photo report by Hoffmann.

The flag out! There it goes!

Afternoon, four o'clock. In the hostage room, the detainees sit. Some are reading, others are playing cards.

Daumenlang sits wailing because of wife and child. There, Haußmann arrives with two writers to whom he dictates the names. 'First the ones from *Vier Jahreszeiten*.' Hesselmann composes the groups. 'First, those, then those, then those.'

One suspects this means death. Only Professor Berger does not, he is not among the people of Thule; on the contrary, he is a Jew.

The other peers want to keep him back - but he pushes forward, thinking this is for the interrogation. The sentries send him back. 'You do not belong'. But he won't leave - he is pushing to die soon. The sentries come and pick off the first group. In front is Daumenlang with folded hands. Meanwhile, the entire gymnasium is in turmoil. As the doomed victims come down the corridor, someone shouts, 'The flag out! There it goes!', and they run - what devilish direction - with the blood-red flag after the poor victims. The courtyard is teeming with soldiers; six to eight hundred men are downstairs. There is a search for gunmen.

Haußmann is humane. The doomed may write a few more lines to their loved ones. Letters that will never reach them. There, already the second group is taken to the courtyard. Among them is Countess Westarp.

'Against the wall with that whore!', the soldiers shout. 'Let me live one more hour,' begs the countess, 'do not make me a corpse.' She too is granted mercy and allowed to write another letter on the back of a scribe. Meanwhile, Daumenlang falls first. He dies praying.

Lieutenant von Teuchert and Nauhaus follow, bravely looking the killers in the eye.

Trembling all over, the countess writes her resignation letter. The spectators grow impatient. 'Let them write in shorthand. Against the wall with her! Finished now!' Then a nurse - the *Red Cross* sign on his arm - grabs her roughly and pulls her forward. Unconsciously, she collapses. She is given a few moments to recover. The alarm signal sounds, the sirens scream: 'Now comes the climax of the execution.' Smiling 'ladies' appear in front of the windows. There is harmonica playing and dancing. In the canteen, the waitress, that fine piece from Blood Gymnasium, calls to the guests to come to the window. Everyone is in the greatest excitement.

Then they bring the last group, including Prince Thurn und Taxis and the unsuspecting Professor Berger, who still thinks he is going to the interrogation. He remains standing, when he sees the corpses lying around. He wants to pull away. Numerous hands reach for him and pull out the man's beard. Meanwhile, the countess has regained consciousness. For another moment she leans against a tree, she cries, then she walks determinedly and upright to the wall. Shots pop. A bullet hits the poor woman straight in the heart.

At that moment, as a last-minute help, the War Ministry adjutant, the art peeler Seyler, appears. He sees how there is an argument around Professor Berger whom he knows. But before he fully understands what is going on, Berger too is up against the wall. Shots pop!

Then Seyler plunges into the crowd, where the very Prince Thurn und Taxis swears to be innocent. 'I want to be interrogated again, I am the wrong one'. Seyler pulls him out of the crowd and drags him into the gymnasium. There he encounters Seidel, who himself is trembling all over.

'How did you guys get it into your heads? ... Who gave the order? ... I am the adjutant of the war ministry! '

Seidel shouts at him: 'Get out of here, with us today the bullets are cheap.'

Seyler flees: 'Not a moment longer in this hell.'

One more time, Thurn und Taxis is brought to Seidel, who has to pay the salary.

'I don't have time now. How many have already been shot?' 'Seven.'

'Eight we must have.'

A few minutes later, the monarch falls.

The tension has subsided, people look at the dead. Someone spits the countess in the face and lifts her legs.

In a special room, the shooters gather. There is extra wine and cigarettes. The harmonica is still being played. It is nearing ten. From the ground floor in the commander's room, cheerful dance steps can be heard.

Seidel has finished paying off the soldiers. He has been busy today.

Sixty thousand marks were left of the pay. Seidel shares the amount with the others. 'Money from refugees,' he says.

The indictment according to the text designed by the first chief public prosecutor Heinz Hoffmann. Less important parts have been omitted.

'When once our present age with its fermenting, bubbling and buldering will be history, the grandchildren of the present generation will be full of glory and amazement at the heroism and titanic strength with which the German struggled for four years against the oppressive power of a hostile world.

The battle is over, the war is lost.

However, the most terrible of all wars, the fratricidal war, undermined our poor homeland that was far from the terror of war and the horror and fear of battle.

We are vanquished. Then our homeland becomes the scene of the sad consequences of war, coming from a dastardly quarter from everywhere and nowhere. To describe these, we Germans in our homeland cannot find a comparison even in the animal kingdom. For that, we must borrow a foreign word: hyenas of the battlefield.

An act of that kind of body robbing by such scum should be tried. The murder of hostages of 30 April 1919 at the *Luitpold Gymnasium* in Munich.'

The prosecutor now reasons the jurisdiction of the *People's Court* and its legality which was challenged by several defenders, and then continues:

'The act on trial was murder. There was no struggle at the scene. Completely defenceless people were slaughtered, no semblance of justice was attached to the act. Rioters and a murderous mob carried it out. Moreover, it was not even attempted to give the murder any semblance of justice. No real interrogation, no investigation, no trace of actual guilt, no attempt at trial. 'We do not give a shit about the tribunal,' Commander Seidel has said. One could not express his contempt for justice more clearly. Hostages were killed, civilian hostages, men of the *Reichswehr*! Well aware that a German word is incapable of expressing the this *culmination* of blood hatred, they invented, nay, borrowed, because their own creativity was lacking, the French word '*bourgeoisie*'. This is probably the same for the real agitators, which for the French means the beautiful word *boches* (= moffs).

The board of the *Kommunistische Partei Deutschlands*, Westend section has uttered this tall tale here: the man who, as he himself says, is a man who says what's on his mind, who, over drinks, wrings the necks of the hostages like cats, who thinks it an honourable task to take the corpses from the gymnasium to the Isar transport, is accompanied by a red gardist, who goes along for that reason alone to steal clothes from the corpses for his friend and domestic servant. Hyenas of the battlefield! One will, my lords, perhaps tell you how terribly dangerous the people of Thule are. Advocate Liebknecht proclaimed not without a certain emphasis himself on Friday that it did not at all occur to him to want to claim that the dead were guilty, even ever to claim guilt.

But what does a trial that should be dedicated to a just punishment for the death of the victims have to do with the alleged acts of the still living members of the association? While not even all the hostages were members of Thule!

After these sessions, where is the man who has the courage to speak of the guilt of death of the grey professor Ber- ger, or of policeman Nies, who had already been dragged to the place of execution? Baron Teuchert, Prince Thurn und Taxis, Countess Westarp, Baron von Seidlitz were probably victims of their nobility more than of their membership of Thule.

'A diamond in our hand is the prince,' a red gardist has said. As a prince, and not a member of Thule, the prince was arrested several times! Baron Teuchert was even caught outside, not as a member of Thule! The countess did not appear to be guilty, even Egelhofer and Levien stated this. Their affiliation did not seem suspicious either.

'Pick the best' was written on Egelhofer's murder paper to Seidel. The Thule members from the *Vier Jahreszeiten* are widely known among the agitators in the gymnasium. What does this prove? That it comes down to murder. It comes down to murder.

There was no fighting in the gymnasium; there was absolutely nothing to justify killing people. At the field kitchen, killing was done, not at the front. The act involved killing hostages.

Generally, it was said: hostages are being shot! Guilty or innocent, that was as unimportant as whether they were old or young, whether they were men or women. For the immediate execution - and only that should be tried here – it is unimportant whether the Thule members were anti- Semites or that Berger himself was a Jew.

On 30 April in the courtyard of the gymnasium, the abject murder. In the place meant to educate the youth in humanity. In the morning the two Hussars, in the afternoon the remaining eight hostages! On a dung heap in the corner they are shot! What barbarity!

Yet not the entire grammar school had become a hideous hell at the time, where of the dozens of human brains, hardly one among them that was not filled with a thought that should not see the light of day. The little sinners were the day thieves who stole food, drink and clothing or wages and did their utmost to get out from under the service. Others were out to fulfil their service as the terror of the citizens by stealing and plundering as they understood it. Indeed, many were too lazy to seek out the *bourgeois*, they stole in the gymnasium itself.

Oh, irony! One generally defends the crude action of the commander and the lower gods in the gymnasium there- with, that their barking tone was necessary to maintain some semblance of order among the gentlemen. What did these agitators not discredit the zealous German non- commissioned officer because of his tone as a slave-driver! Free men they promised to make and among themselves they must bark if necessary.

And who was barking? It is very interesting, in a psychological and criminal sense, to review the gentlemen. The commander-in-chief Egelhofer came from the navy, a penal prisoner escaped in Cologne. Seidel was never a soldier. It is interesting to note that, just when he was in command, Seidel was overworked and had taken leave - I mean: had asked for it - using an excuse, and that he admits to having falsified pay slips. The World War brought this strange force from the port of Trieste here. In the captivity, he immediately fell ill again and wanted to go to the lazaret. Haußmann, the second commander, was also absent from work because of his nerves. Pfister suffered a severe nervous breakdown on the morning of the execution. Schicklhofer, the first group commander, was a stoker. On his many sailings, he saw the world, brought syphilis and was addicted to alcohol; both threatened to consume body and mind for a long time. Hesselmann, the first writer and place-substitute commander, walking around in a worn officer's uniform, who imagined himself to be a great film actor and was exposed here as a marriage swindler, has been convicted of repeated theft before. Fehmer has been punished for pimping before and was therefore well suited for the trust post as head of care. Vagrancy is the crime of umbrella repairer Huber.

Völkl has been repeatedly punished as a recidivist for theft. Pürzer is a psychopath and even the commander's porter, Schmittele, is straight out of the penal colony.

Truly a beautiful bunch to command!

And my lords, a little statistics on the criminology of this case. Seven of the 16 defendants are of illegitimate descent; two, Hesselmann and Schicklhofer, have disrupted marriages; three are inferior psychopaths - a witness described Egelhofer as megalomaniac - and when war broke out, of all 16 'heroes', only four were adults and 12 were minors.

No wonder that with these top officials the selection in the grammar school became a mess. Everyone did what they wanted, or rather, everyone didn't do what they didn't want, despite the barking tone inherited from the old fatherland.

The touching complaint of Sergeant Schicklhofer - who, in his touching modesty, only allowed himself to be called a non-commissioned officer - that he and the others were so often invited to go to the fair and that he could not possibly comply, because he could not be missed in the gymnasium, must also be mentioned here. Moreover, it should be mentioned here that the signatures on the leave letters, by the hundreds, were forged by people in the gymnasium itself.

Those who might suspect plundering and falsifying while looking through the fog of the betrayal by the bourgeoisie, will note that this society was man enough to commit all these dark deeds themselves, and in whatever manner was necessary.

What do the rector and beadle of the grammar school say? Nothing was safe! What does Hesselmann say? The room is being plundered! Why does the high lord's love give up her 'honorary job' at the *Red Cross* office? For the sake of a comrade sex crime! Barbarism and crime squared!

Someone from the red guard wanted to see hostages: one takes him to three noble pigs. 'This is what hostages look like.' This barbarity at least made it clear where the fresh entrails, found in the blood gymnasium and mistaken for human organs in the initial excitement, came from.

Rude was the tone! Beatings were dealt. The prisoners were threatened with death from the start. Their families, wives and children were told, 'They are going to die.' Arriving at the gymnasium, anyone who felt entitled to open his mouth said, 'Your life is over, you will die!'

The two Hussars, the poor countess, the old professor are treated roughly and rudely, they are shamelessly scolded and mocked until the sacred moment when they must die a guiltless death for their bourgeoise status. 'Bastard, old whore, bastard' are expressions that are thrown in their faces on their last walk!

Furthermore, one could meet the 'ladies' there who had so scolded, what in the face of a real lady so brazenly and sound cynical. There were 'ladies' in the gymnasium too. If a witness saw correctly, these fine 'ladies' even stood at the window to watch the horrific scene. One lovely wife exclaimed joyfully: 'Mine too is joining in.' And what a noble representative of her sex our defendant Hannes describes in the 'lady' who has traded her artistic profession for that of a communist waitress in the *Lutepold gymnasium*. She encourages her Hanns to shoot a fellow sister, whom she does not know at all, who has never harmed her! And when he fails to take aim, she clarifies in realistic terms! What an abyss of cruelty!

Can one believe that there is something even more horrific, even more gruesome? But from that 'lady's' own mouth we hear things that are even more inhuman. She goes to the kitchen to get her *lunch* and in passing, perhaps because it will taste better to her, she looks at the corpses of the poor, murdered soldiers. She stands on a chair in the canteen so that nothing escapes her either! Yes, she then, this 'lady', went to view the corpses. Corpses that the experienced expert, who has been active on the battlefield, has said of that he has never seen anything so horrific!

Poor Countess! Not in life and not in death was she left alone by her torturers. She was scolded, one locked her in the cellar under death threats, she was forced under death threats to clean Schicklhofer's room! She is rudely interrupted: 'Now it is enough', when she wants to write her last letter, which never arrived at the addressee. One punches her and pushes her forward under the addition of obscenities. The dead person - one shudders at such lowliness - is lifted by the legs by a brute. One gives her a kick and one spits in her noble face. Truly a martyr!

Never will the veil be lifted from where came the suspicious caretaking that the gentlemen platoon commanders allowed the lady to do. They forced the countess, or as they said - they allowed her - to sleep in their room! The very Schicklhofer, the adept of Levien, alluded to something terrible. He had noticed that in the room next door, which he too was not allowed to enter, the poor countess was being interrogated behind closed doors! O poorest of the poor!

Another unfortunate person is still convulsing while dying; he gets a mercy shot. 'Screw him, he doesn't need a mercy shot!' people say. Another targets the boots of the executed. What have I said before? From everywhere and nowhere hyenas approach the battlefield, corpse robbery!

And now to the offence itself. With regard to the arrest and detention, I may refer to the indictment, which was fully upheld in open court. I may already note here, that in properly assessing the offences, I will follow the suggestion of the President, who conceives both executions as a complex of consecutive murders.

Once again, I must stress that during the trial it was not proven that none of the dead was really guilty. Advocate Liebknecht's solemn statement also established this.

Why fratricide? There was a bloodthirsty mood among the Red Guards, the agitators had stirred things up considerably during the meetings. One place, however, was dangerous in Munich, the *Luitpold Gymnasium*. Seidel with his radical following was to be feared, said the councils, whom Seidel claimed were his bosses.

In case of important prisoners of the *Luitpold Gymnasium,* whichever highest ranking officer was present was in charge. Higher authorities ensured custody and, in the case of selected victims, certain death. A start was made with the pupils of the police school: Nies escaped death shortly before the scaffold. The communist Jung, the dangerous man whose only crime was that he had resisted madness in driving two thousand Munich workers into certain death, was the second type of dangerous prisoners, *Reichswehr* and members of the Thule Society was the last and most important group.

Why this now? This question was fully clarified in open court. With a cynical pretence, a secret group of thugs sought to assert themselves during the last days of the councils. Lie was piled on lie, one smear campaign followed another. Behind the scenes of this trial, outlandish agitators and stooges emerged. They were exposed as those who were increasingly inciting instincts to ever greater bloodlust!

Seidel and Egelhofer are adepts of Levien, his loyal followers ready for any outrage.

The same applies to Haußmann!

Levien is present at that interrogation of the Thule members. Leviné and Levien secretly visit the prisoners, especially the Thule members, in the deepest secrecy as criminals do, who do not want to betray themselves!

Secret talks and meetings take place in the *Luitpold Gymnasium*! And between interrogation and that nocturnal visit to the victims lies that hypocritical, systematic inciting that casts a bright torchlight in the gymnasium corridors.

We have all experienced it here. First, the billboards in town: 'Looters will be shot!' Yes, in Miesbach a man was shot dead, who was totally innocent. He was killed because he was suspected of betraying the Red Guards, but his execution was presented as a fair punishment for looting. That was how it was written on the billboard!

Did not the communist Seidel himself also loot? The alleged confiscation of the five silver shaving devices was plunder under the posture of an office he did not hold.

A pamphlet was cast off in the city: 'Reactionary thieves and plunderers, high-ranking forgers and looters have been found!' This pamphlet did not concern Mr von Sebottendorff or anyone else who was not caught, but it was bloodthirsty slander written on the heads of the victims.

Never has greater lowliness been displayed!

One blackens the one who is known to be most innocent, the Countess! Not the member of the Thule Society - the Countess they wanted to kill!

At the time, *confrère* Sauter, one would not have doubted the nobility of baron von Sebottendorff, but insisted: they had caught a baron as well!

One fired up the comrades against the looters first. The infernal machine was loaded, all they needed was a fuse!

That was the murder of the Hussars! The interrogation was not about finding out the truth from anyone. Seidel draws his pistol and forces the most blatant lies, so one can use it to incite. Every click of the pistol forces a 'yes', and everything is very delicately put down on paper, taken by the commander, Mr Seidel, with his own hands to the printing office and distributed as a pamphlet at night - as a seditious magazine among the disaffected workers in Munich!

This is how the fire is set, the murder of the Thule members prepared! No doubt, the murder in the gymnasium is a continuation of this inciting. After the murder of the Hussars, a citizen comes to Seidel and asks: 'Do you have data, that the executed were Noske dogs and killers of Liebknecht?' Only then does Mr Seidel have the corpses examined for papers, which must provide this evidence. However, one does not find the evidence. What a boundless mountain of hypocritical lies! And these people later have the shameless audacity to drag their own people through the mud with lowly lies: 'Our people were so violent and so barbaric, that we knew no more advice, otherwise we would have prevented it."

The prosecutor then addressed the individual charges. He had set three conditions under which a person could be charged:

1. That he was in the gymnasium as a red guardsman or whoever might be armed;
2. That he was there during the commission of the murder;
3. That he was somehow directly or indirectly involved in the murder of the hostages.

The defence could not claim, that he (= officer of jus- tition - transl.) had dragged people to the accused bench, of whom nothing could be proved other than that they had made a careless statement.

Here, only the offence itself had to be tried. The defendants he had here were guilty. He then formulated his demands.

The court sentenced six defendants to death on the 15th day of the trial, while the others received long prison sentences.

As the entire ministry ratified the sentence, the executions were carried out in the courtyard of the Stadelheim prison.

If now, after 14 years, it is possible to talk openly about the killers, it must be taken into account, that the real killers were the three Jews who held and wanted to hold on to power. From their minds sprang the diabolical plan to destroy the enemy. Those who carried out the plan, the killers, were misguided victims.

This way, lawyers Sauter and Liebknecht could have saved the killers' heads.

However, this path was not passable, as it would have revealed the prevailing ideologies.

Therefore, they tried to spin the matter so that the Thule Society became the culprit. To understand this properly, one should consider the smear campaign unleashed against the Thule Society's founder Sebottendorff after the Munich occupation.

Again, only Jews took part in this smear campaign. They provided the material, which Liebknecht and Sauter had used in the murder trial.

The *Beobachter* No 45 of 17 September 1919 contained the following article on the hostage killing.

Behind the scenes

Long articles were written about it in other newspapers. Only we remained silent more than anyone else to this day. Since for us, everything was at stake, for us, the question of whether we were ruthless truth-fighters or unscrupulous agitators was important. Again and again we had pointed out the connection between Jews and Bolshevism, again and again we had contradicted the fateful legend that the leaders of the Raden Republic in Munich and elsewhere were Jews only by chance; Jews who fought for the fraternisation of the people out of pure idealism and only with pain in their hearts crossed corpses. People laughed at us as if we were fools, or blamed selfish motives with regard to our information. Russia was drowning in blood: the German leaders did not believe it. Hungary turned into a mess: the German workers did not want to see it. Wilfulness and murder raged through Munich: people still kept their eyes shut tightly. But more menacing and increasingly urgent the question was asked: Who is to blame for the death and misfortune of so many thousands?

Finally came the dreaded hostage killing trial. It presented a shocking picture of immeasurable cruelty and diabolical lowliness. The world stared speechlessly at the staggering spectacle and slowly, very slowly with an inescapable inner necessity, the roads converged on a point: Haußmann, Seidel, and the very blackened Egelhofer were mere hangmen. Two names, however, stand in the brightest light at the conclusion of the preliminary investigation: Levien and Leviné. And another third had fallen under their spell: Toller, who had narrowly escaped. They were the ones directing the players from behind the scenes. They paired the murder with sophisticated atrocities. On their orders, members of the Thule Society were handed over to death, on their orders, they were compressed into a damp pen like cattle for slaughter.

They have committed the heinous crime that will cry to heaven as long as there are people of German blood. They have raped Heila von Westarp, the most innocent of all, destroying her mentally and physically long before her physical death. With a hellish lowliness, they vented their Asian lust and ruthlessness on her. A true stroke of luck that the tortured woman died. Her life was broken, eternally tormented she would have dragged on.

And why did they do this? Remember, German worker: not as punishment for alleged offences against the sacred ideology of the Raden Republic. They wanted to destroy and dishonour what was alien to their essence. The only thing that really hindered their lordliness was the German. How they had shed all noble blood in Russia and acted with ruthless harshness against everything non-Jewish in Hungary, so everything that rightly still bears the German name had to be ruined.

The hideous murder of the seven Thule members and three other hostages was dealt with in two sessions of the Munich *People's Court*.

During the 15 days during which treatment took place, from September 1 - 18, 1919, a hell of moral frenzy and debauchery opened up. It was an orgy of power psychosis and bloodlust in its most unrestrained form, displayed in those days by a number of crazed individuals. On the other hand, the real culprits, such as Levien, Leviné- Niessen, Axelrod and his comrades, Toller and Mühsam and numerous others not excepted, were emphatically discussed. The Jews were the driving force, they were the agitators behind this vile crime. Condemned were the workers seduced and blinded by them.

To get a better idea of what kind of killers, the 'executors of justice' were, here is a list of those convicted.

The main defendant, 25-year-old businessman Fritz Seidel, was given the death penalty twice for each murder for committing two murders.

Fritz Seidel was found not to have been in the field during the war. Instead, he had forged pay slips, embezzling considerable sums. As command of the *Luitpold Gymnasium*, he was also accused of stealing four silver razors. Of the last salary he had to pay on 30 April, he pocketed 60,000 marks. He had intended to use this amount to prepare his escape. He was the cruellest individual and knew no compassion.

40-year-old Johann Schicklhofer, who was charged with two murders as well, received the same sentence.

He had fought in the war, but had had to leave the service early due to a nervous breakdown. For mistreating animals, he had been punished earlier. Additionally, it was established during the hearing that he was a notorious alcoholic. Moreover, he suffered from various abattoir diseases.

For committing one murder were sentenced to death:

The 21-year-old mechanic Josef Widl. - The 21-year-old baker's servant Georg Pürzer. He was rejected for service after three months due to obvious weakness. - The 29- year-old coachman Johann Fehmer. He already had a lot on his criminal record as a brothel keeper. - The 23-year- old unskilled labourer Josef Seidl who had entered military service as a farmhand in July 1916 and wore the Iron Cross I without being entitled to it. He had already been convicted repeatedly of theft, vagrancy, embezzlement and desertion.

For complicity in murder were sentenced to 15 years in prison:

The 34-year-old carpenter Johannes Rick. He was discharged from military service in 1916 due to weak nerves. - The 24-year-old businessman Karl Gsell. - The 24-year-old artist Bernhard Hesselmann who had been discharged from military service because of gas poisoning. This degenerate individual had been repeatedly convicted of theft. He wore a threadbare officer's uniform and passed himself off as a film star. He also appeared not to be averse to matrimonial scams. It was he who had robbed the bodies of the murdered hostages. - The 43- year-old machine bench worker Georg Lermer. - The 25-year-old bench worker Johann Hannes. - The 23-year-old umbrella operator Georg Huber. He had not been able to fight during the war due to psychological problems and had already been convicted of vagrancy and other offences. - The 19-year-old banker Johann Riethmeyer.

Those sentenced to death were deprived of all civil rights forever; the rest lost their civil rights for a period of 10 years.

Three suspects were acquitted.

A few weeks later, a second hearing took place, in which 27-year-old unskilled labourer Alois Kammerstätter was sentenced to death. He had previously pleaded guilty to desertion.

Sentenced to 15 years in prison:

The 18-year-old waiter Luitpold Debus. - The 23-year-old student and Russian prisoner of war Andreas Strelenko. - The 21-year-old day labourer Rudolf Greiner, who had been previously convicted of desertion as well.

Willi Haußmann, the deputy commander of the *Luitpold Gymnasium*, who had given the direct order to kill the hostages, shot himself at the very moment he was to be arrested. Under his act, the hostages had suffered the most.

Rudolf Egelhofer, the commander of the Red Army, signed the order to kill 22 hostages. He was a marine and 21 years old. For participating in the sailor uprising, he had been sentenced to death earlier, but managed to escape. Among his comrades, he was called the sailor 'with the tango hairdo'. During an escape attempt, he was shot dead on 1 May 1919.

XI
The Thule Society after the murder of the hostages

The murdered members of the Thule Society:

1. Heila Countess von Westarp joined the Thule Society as a second secretary in February 1919. She had been born in 1886 and had left her family to go through life as a working woman. The countess had done a course in arts and crafts, then worked as a hat-gardener, and was content and grateful when she got a modest job at the bread-card distributy. In January, the authorities learned that she was a countess and dismissed her for that reason.
2. Walter Nauhaus was born on 20 September 1892 in Botschabelo, Transvaal, the son of the superintendent of the mission district, had volunteered at the beginning of the war and was badly wounded as early as the first battles in the west. When he had to leave the service in 1916 as cured but rejected, he went to Professor Wackerle's school in Berlin to be trained as a sculptor. In 1917, he came into contact with the *Germanic orders* and left for Munich with Professor Wackerle.
3. Walter Deike, Nauhaus's friend, was born in Magdeburg in 1894. He too volunteered for the army and was badly wounded as early as the first battles in 1914. He was three-quarters disabled. Deike at-

tended the arts and crafts school in Munich. In July 1918, he joined the Nauhaus group.
4. Born in 1891 in Langenbielau (Silesia), Friedrich Wilhelm *Freiherr* von Seidlitz was a grandson of Frederick the Great's famous general. He too had participated in the war from the beginning and was wounded several times. Since September 1918, he had been a member of the Thule Society. Seidlitz was a painter and an artist at heart. At parties, he played the piano and harmonium masterfully.
5. Anton Daumenlang, first secretary at the railways, was born in Königshofen on 16 September 1870 and married in 1898. He left behind wife and daughter. His hobbyhorse was heraldry and genealogy. He had become a member of Thule in January 1919.
6. Gustav Franz Maria *Prinz* von Thurn und Taxis was born in Dresden in 1888 and had joined the Thule Society without being a member. He had also fought during the campaign and had gone to Nuremberg, having been arrested several times because of his stand. He returned to Munich to warn Thule.
7. Franz Karl *Freiherr* von Teuchert was born on 20 July 1900 in Marburg, Styria. At the beginning of the war, he joined the volunteer riflemen and at the end of the war he went to Regensburg to train. He had joined the *Freikorps Regensburg*. In January 1919, he had joined Thule.

It is probably unnecessary to say that these seven Thule members knew what they died for and why they were killed.

However, they did fight for their lives while they still had hope. When the time came that all hope was gone, they all stepped in front of the misguided workers, who had to murder them for a judas wage, proudly and with their heads held high.

The Thule members were the first victims to die for the swastika.

From the moment they saw Levien at the interrogation in the Ministry of War, they knew that only a miracle could save them.

They were sure they would die when they saw the three Jews on that night visit. Even then, they knew that death was decided and inevitable.

What else is it to die fresh and cheerful in battle, than to have to wait four days for the hour to come.

When they swore they were innocent, they meant the plunder they were accused of.

They all knew very well what awaited them, that the hatred with which the Jews persecuted them was boundless. Nauhaus in particular had no illusions about this He was the oldest member, after all, and in many a conversation he had said he would die in harness. Deike, too, was on notice. When painter Seyler, Egelhofer's adjutant, declared in the War Ministry that the two had behaved cowardly, it was a misstatement: both knew they had fallen into the clutches of the Jews.

Sebottendorff had warned the countess at parting. She had said: 'Are you leaving, brother? Will you leave me here, if only I eat my earned bread.' As late as 25 April, the countess expressed her thoughts of death to Brother Griehl and nevertheless went to work the next morning. When they went home one day and said goodbye at the Siegestor, Seidlitz said: 'Believe me, master, our movement will only become something when the Jews are tempted to put some of us against the wall.' 'And if we are?' 'Well, at least you will know what for and why.'

Thurn und Taxis was certainly not a convinced anti-Semite, as the others were. He was a bit soft-hearted and yet he went out to warn his brethren. 'I have a protective charisma, and if it comes to that, well, it is no big deal, after all, one knows what for.'

No, the Thule members faced death with their heads held high and consciously. They died as heroes, as martyrs for their cause.

No one resisted when it came to the final passage. With heads held high, they surrendered to the bullets. Daumen praying, he still thought of wife and child, Nauhaus, Seidlitz and Teuchert turned their faces to the killers. Deike, the prince, the countess died with their heads held high and with dignity.

Ten determined men could have saved them, but they were not there and the one they secretly hoped for knew nothing. No message had been sent to him. He came too late, he could only take revenge.

A common grave could not be constructed for the Thule members. Seidlitz, Thurn und Taxis and Teuchert were interred in the family grave at home. Deike and Nauhaus rest in a common grave. Two days after the countess' burial, the mourning lodge took place at the Thule Society. Over the lectern was a captured communist flag. In the place of the hammer and sickle, a sister had applied the swastika in the white field, the swastika that adorned all the walls of the lodge, for which the Thule members had died.

When Sebottendorff said in his speech that the sacrifice had not been in vain, that the movement will keep drawing new strength from this sacrifice, it did not look like this would come true. A tough internal struggle began that would bring an end to the Society. It had served its purpose, it had to disappear so that something new could come, which was already on the horizon. A few weeks after Sebottendorff left, Adolf Hitler entered the rooms of Thule and took part in that great day of struggle on which, led by Dannehl, the whole of Munich was covered with pamphlets and posters.

It was not only issues of a financial nature that forced Sebottendorff to resign. These could have been overcome.

However, he had given the movement a large part of his and his wife's wealth and it was impossible to sustain the three foundations he had created in the long run. His monthly incomes were constantly shrinking. But it was not that. It was the attack of the Jews, the attack of the Social Democratic Party, that forced him to resign. He was the founder of the movement, he was easy prey; him they could hit and him they had to hit.

There were mainly two reasons for these attacks.

The first was: one had to deprive the coming trial for the murder of the hostages of its sharpness by diverting public attention with a trial for libel. This was the same trick that was later successfully pulled off through the staged *Femeprozesse,* to distract the public from the financial scandals.

The second trigger was, that the Jews, alarmed by anti-Semitic propaganda, no longer wanted to support the Social Democrats financially and sought cooperation with the *Unabhängigen*. The first warning was given to Sebottendorff from Frankfurt am Main; it was then published in the 1919 *Deutsche Zeitung* Nr. 291 in Berlin. Mr Timmermann, legal adviser to the *Staatsverein*, had taken up the matter. Negotiations on subsidies were conducted by him with the *Unabhängigen* in Weimar. The point was to limit the actions of the anti-Semites once they came to power. The Jews were willing to provide all financial and other support. So the Social Democrats ran the risk that this rich financial source would dry up if they did not act.

Munich, the centre of the dangerous movement, had to be tackled and here they could tackle it. They had declared 'material' against Sebottendorff.

The initial material had been assembled by official Schülein, the brother of the *Geheimer Kommerzienrat* Schülein.

Sebottendorff had attacked the sapphire factory in which Schülein and his brother participated in the *Beobachter*. A mediator who offered money for a recall had been thrown out on the street. Schülein had contacted the well- known lawyer Alsberg in Berlin, who was a friend of Liesbeth Seidler. Alsberg was financially interested in Sebottendorff; after all, when he married Mrs Iffland, the Jew who administered the estate had given notice, and Alsberg had tried to get the marriage annulled through *Polizeirat* Heindl in Dresden, the later *Legationsrat* at the Foreign Office.

Sebottendorff had been light-hearted enough. He had never asked what would come next, but had acted in the manner that seemed right to him; not according to the law, but according to his conscience.

By means of an irrevocable power of attorney he had placed his assets and those of his wife in the hands of a baptised Jew, who was an honorary judge at a commercial law firm and an in-law relative of his. Due to this power of attorney, his assets were seized and he was later placed under guardianship of profligacy.

Sebottendorff had received Turkish citizenship in 1911. Coming from a bourgeois family, he was born in Hoyerswerda and was adopted under Turkish law by Baron Heinrich von Sebottendorff. This adoption, because it was not valid in Germany, had been ratified by the last two members of the Sebottendorff family Siegmund Sebottendorff von der Rose had recognised him as a member of the family in Wiesbaden in 1914, and his wife had ratified the adoption with a notary in Baden Baden after her husband's death.

However, these papers had fallen into the hands of the Bolsheviks, as had the papers of the civil registry. When Munich was taken, Auer's foster son, the well-known social democrat Buisson, had obtained these papers and not returned them - they had thus been 'looted'.

So here they could get to grips with the matter. Under the title: 'Strange stories', the *Munich Post* published a pamphlet accusing Sebottendorff of:

- That he bore a false name,
- That he had cowardly abandoned the Thule Society,
- That he had become a Turk to evade military service,
- That he had collected money without clearing it,
- That he was under guardianship.

With this, they wanted to force Sebottendorff to file a libel lawsuit. Another string in their bow.

Under the influence of the aforementioned Schülein, who collaborated with trade-judge Spitzer, Mr Timmermann, lawyer Alsberg and *Polizeitrat* Heindl, they had put together a splendid document, which had to be absolutely scathing. Then came the scandal, which would certainly have cast the trial for the murder of the hostages in a different light.

On the hunt, then, Sebottendorff had to go. He had to sue for libel. Yet he did not begrudge them that pleasure. If those seven Thule members had sacrificed themselves for ideology, Sebottendorff had to sacrifice himself for the movement. He had to leave so as not to smother the sapling. True, he had had the opportunity to prove his innocence, but the dust raised by the ruling parties would have covered everything and ruined Thule, the *Beobachter* and the party.

And what was worst, they knew the names of the people who had collaborated. They could have taken them on too, hundreds of people would have suffered.

As his successor as leader, Sebottendorff appointed lawyer Hanns Dahn, which was confirmed by the *Germanic orders*. Unfortunately, Dahn did not remain president for long. An opposition of youth forced him to resign. His place was taken by Johannes Hering.

XII
From the Thule Society emerged organisations

The following independent organisations emerged from the Thule Society:

the *Deutsche Arbeiterverein*, later *Deutsche Arbeiterpartei* (DAP) and the *Deutsch-Sozialistische Arbeitsgemeinschaft*, later *Deutsch-Sozialistische Partei* (DSP) with its organ: *Münchener Beobachter*, later *Völkischer Beobachter*.

At the Christmas meeting of 1918, the *Germanic Order* decided to issue the following appeal to the German people. The appeal was printed in the *Allgemeine OrdensNachrichten* Nr. 15 of December 1918 and was released to the lodges for further distribution.

'To the German people!

World War, revolution and insurrection are behind us! We have gone through misery, blood and humiliation and yet everything has stayed the same, yes, it threatens to be even worse than before. Only the form of government has changed and there are other leaders, but capitalism and Jewry will reemerge under democracy more than ever. Constantly you, German people, will be sucked out, face usury and be doomed to trouble and worry. Why is this and must it remain so forever? The reason for the unhappiness lies in the fact that the struggle against the aforementioned powers has hitherto been conducted separately. Both are closely linked.

Social democracy is only waging a war of convenience against capitalism because their leaders are Jews and capitalists!

However, those who know the Jews fight in vain against Judaism, because the basis of their state structure is capitalist; therefore, both fronts must collapse.

To change this and finally give the German people real freedom, a *Deutsch-Sozialistische Partei* must be formed. *German-völkisch* and socialistic.

Lasalle, the founder of German social democracy, had to know his friends as a Jew when he said, 'A people's movement must not pander to capitalists and Jews. Where these act as leaders, there they also pursue their own goals.'

The new Socialist Party accepts only men born in Germany. It is of course at the forefront of political reform; will leave democracy untouched for the time being, but does not, however, want a democracy on the Western model with a Jewish-plutocratic top, but a free people's state in which capitalism and Judaism are vanquished.

She is not satisfied with pure parliamentarianism, where executive power lies solely with the deputies. She always demands a referendum for new, fundamental laws, in order to eliminate the risk of mismanagement among the parties.

Its main demands are of a radical nature; the party does not engage in sham reforms. It tackles the roots of *völkisch* and social distress.

Capitalism and Judaism hitherto stood in the way of such reshaping. All our parties were more or less, consciously or unconsciously, servants of one or the other power or even both. That is why, so far, all work has been useless and produced only sham reforms. The new party has no pardon, but is completely uncapitalist and Jew-free. It is guided solely by the prosperity of the whole and strives for the equal distribution of consumer goods and the healthening and promotion of the German, so badly affected popular power. However, not by means of a new revolution and sudden change should the new goal be pursued, for that is always in the opposite direction, but along legal paths through the phased demolition of the present state of affairs and the building of the future.

The main cause of our distress lies in our distorted basic law, in our social law and in our money being.

Accordingly, we demand:

1. Free proprietary land, because the cancer that harms economy, businesses and households, as well as individual peoples, lies in land tax. The debt burden on German land (before the war 100 billion) results in all the social and economic wrongdoings: tenements, dilapidation,

infant mortality, epidemics, poverty, crime, pauperisation and popular dislocation.

This can be remedied by making German land - regardless of private ownership - state property, in other words, that the sale of land between two private parties is henceforth ruled out. Land loses its character as a commodity. Merchandise is characterised by this, that it is fungible. Land is irreplaceable. Anyone who wants or needs to sell can only do so to the municipality. The latter gives the land to interested parties, either temporarily or on a long lease. This way, land may not be used to raise capital in future. The land is declared untaxable. Accordingly, personal credit instead of the current collateralised credit is to be promoted. All current mortgages will become, if they are not already, irrevocable, short-term repayment mortgages, with interest rates also reduced. In this way, German land will gradually become free in favour of a truly great housing policy. Even for the simplest man, it becomes possible again, to live on his own piece of land in his own little house. The genesis of overcapitalisation lies in the current free marketability and taxability of land. With free land, there is no overcapitalisation.

2. Replacing current Roman law with a German general law. Our current fundamental law is based on Roman law, therefore all encroachments on our public life are breaches of law. Roman law was introduced 400 years ago by princes and their higher clergy.

In vain, the people resisted it, knowing that with the foreign law, the ground and other privileges were being knocked out from under their feet. The peasant wars, the first social revolution, was a bloody struggle against foreign law. Again and again, the peasants demanded the reintroduction of the old German law.

Today we are again making the same demand, and it is up to you, people of Germany, that our desire remains unheard once again. This problem is more important than it may seem to most of us; it is the core around which our future existence revolves. Roman law arose at a time when Jew-infested Rome was going under; it is anti-social, protecting private gain at the expense of the community. It is the law of the refined and the clever. On this un- German basis, the Jew always trumps the German. Facts prove it. Therefore, the German people must be given a right according to their nature and disposition, according to the old principle: common interest prevails over individual interest. The deeply ingrained greed, unreasonableness and immorality that are commonplace in trade and commerce, the Jewishisation of our people, are due to Roman law. Likewise, the development of our economy into an outspoken interest economy that finally brought the world under the leadership of the Jewish race, the war and the misery of recent years.

3. Nationalisation of finance. Our money system is in the hands of private individuals, especially Jews and other foreign individuals. This in itself is an impossibility, because money is the blood of the national popular body. The state as the representative of the people can only truly govern if it possesses the power of disposal over money and the monetary system. Today, money is

alienated from its purpose as a convenient medium of exchange between work and wages, goods and purchase price, manufacturer and consumer. Money today serves to make even more money through manipulations of banks and exchanges, without real labour.

For most of our people who live on labour, money is nothing but a medium of exchange until today. There is no reason to let it become an unhealthy means of enrichment for the benefit of a small number of pickpockets and speculators and at the expense of the working people. Only real work should be rewarded and paid for.

Our real savings and credit institutions must become nationalised banks, which do not make huge profits for the benefit of shareholders and do not pay princely salaries or directors' fees. New banks and enterprises must be checked by the National Economic Council we will create to see if they really meet a need and are in the interest of the community. Future credit worthiness will no longer relate to business but to people. It follows that, as in the past, a business will be based on the competence, soundness and virtue of the individual, which will bring the necessary calm and natural growth to our economy.

Stock market speculation is ruled out as unnecessary and harmful, as stock trading is banned.

Our currency must be reorganised. Eternal interest, interpreted as a condition under which capital is immortal - cleverly conceived by its immoral inventors and protectors - would be replaced by an interest service that gradually replaces capital. Here, the interest slavery originating from the East would end forever.

These are the three main points and the three main egos of the new party. This will solve the unresolved problems of overcapitalisation and Jewishness for the benefit of the entire German people.

Whoever has German blood in his veins and agrees to these demands and declarations is our man. However, whoever does not want to see and thereby supports the current usury system, or whoever is too gullible, can quietly stay with his party.

We are sure of the victory of our thoughts, as always truth triumphs over guile and deceit! The interest economy will collapse, people will find each other as people in a natural life in the sense of a loving community that makes everyone happy. Further consequences that follow logically from the three main demands are:

4. Gradual reform of our economy in the sense that it becomes a true people's economy.

5. Restriction of our large land holdings according to the yield of individual pieces of land for housing. State land must be parceled out, wasteland built on.

6. A fair distribution of taxes that prevents the creation of excessive wealth.

7. Organisation of our trade according to natural principles, so that goods reach consumers by the cheapest and shortest route from the manufacturer. Without eliminating honest brokering, all the unnoble middlemen, who only somehow create avoidable profit mark-ups and make goods more expensive, must disappear. Our necessities of life, especially our foodstuffs, do not need thousands of idle hands.

8. In the case of major, fundamental laws and constitutional amendments, parliament has only an advisory role. The people will decide by voting yes or no.

9. Establishing a National Economic Council that will determine measure and purpose according to further perspectives of our entire economy. The council will be guided solely by the country's prosperity. The members of the council - not capitalists and Jews - must have been in practical life and distinguished themselves in the service of the community.

10. Creating a truly independent German press. Considering, that our press is 90 per cent in Jewish- capitalist hands, largely run by Jews and dependent on Jewish big-advertisers, a fundamental reform is necessary. At present, the mood of the people is not reflected by the press, but artificially created to realise the self-seeking plans of capitalists and Jews without people seeing through these plans.

We demand: a German newspaper may only call itself a company if it is German and its editors are Germans.

Newspapers that do not fulfil this condition must be described at the top by the name of the newspaper as being Jewish.

11.Fundamental change in Germans' attitudes towards Jews. Examining the laws and religion of Jews. Today's citizenship equivalence is based on the mistaken belief, that the issue is about difference in religion. Today, scientific research and proven facts leave no doubt that the Jewish problem is a racial problem, which has nothing to do with religious belief. It has to do with the question: do we German people want to continue to allow ourselves to be controlled politically, economically and spiritually in the future by a vanishing minority of a racially alien people who consciously feel themselves as such and deliberately keep themselves pure of blood and aloof by means of laws and religion - which flow together in the case of the Jews? This is a matter of our honour, all the more so because it is obvious to the simplest man today that the innate lordliness and greed of the Jew has a destructive influence on our people.

We demand: The new Germany for the German, not for the Jew! The Jews are absolutely a foreign people, they may enjoy the protection and benefits of the state, but no longer have the right to be representatives, leaders, teachers of the people. The Jewish people may, according to the number of individuals, send representatives to the German parliament. The Jewish people include baptised Jews and halve Jews.

12. Protection of the German worker from foreign labour that depresses wages and livelihoods of the German worker.

In general, our national economy should be run in such a way that we can sustain ourselves as much as possible.

At the centre of all our politics, administration and economy should no longer be the merchandise as it has been until now, but the German people. Our German people are our wealth.

We do not want to become ever richer in money and earthly luxuries that benefit only a small part of the population, but we want to be rich in contented, powerful people who have a secure income and live on their own piece of land. By means of these principles and demands, which our party promotes and which are free of any obligation and patronisation, it is possible to definitively bring down the interest economy and the Jews who still devour and ruin the peoples. After we have pushed through our demands, even after the first gradual demolition of the present interest economy, a sigh of relief will pass through the German people. In the place of the few who amass more and more treasures, and the many who have to wear themselves out throughout their lives, there will be an even distribution of all consumer goods. Just as enormous wealth, ostentation and luxury will disappear, so too will poverty and unemployment be banished. Honesty and righteousness will push appearances, deceit and cunning into the background.

Our inflated floor prices, rising rents, the ever-rising cost of livelihood, all of which is the natural consequence of the interest economy, will naturally decline. National wealth will be distributed correctly and fairly and not accumulate in the hands of unscrupulous people, as it has done so far. Our whole life will become simpler, cheaper and more beautiful. Instead of haste, stress and eternal worries, there will once again be peace, contentment and stability in the hearts of the sorely tried German people.

The *Deutsch-Sozialistische Partei* is a party for the less well- off strata of the population, such as workers, civil servants, artisans, craftsmen, small independents and farmers, teachers, settlers and technicians. Those who see things clearly will join us without delay. False Jewish socialism and the interest economy must dissipate like chaff in the wind.'

The Grand Lodge's guidelines were discussed with Harrer soon after Sebottendorff's return. Harrer was against describing the movement as a party. He was of the opinion that this would draw too much attention to opponents; a workers' association would attract less attention. Harrer continued to lead the workers' association and moved the headquarters to Herrnstraße.

The events surrounding Eisner's death limited political work at the time. After public order was restored, the *Beobachter* reappeared on 10 May 1919 with No 15. About the same time, the *Deutsch-Sozialistische Arbeitsgemeinschaft* was founded, the later *Deutsch-Sozialistische Partei*, of which the *Beobachter* became the organ. Its political programme was published in the *Beobachter* No 18 of 31 May 1919. At this time, the D.S.P. also appeared in contact with the *Nationalsozialistische Partei* in Austria. On 9 August of the same year, the newspaper appeared alongside the *Münchener Beobachter,* for the first time as a Reich edition also un der the name *Völkischer Beobachter* with a combined circulation of 10,000 copies. On 4 October 1919 with No. 50, a circulation of 17,800 copies had already been achieved. The newspaper had eight pages and appeared twice a week.

Chairman of the *Deutsch-Sozialistische Partei* was Hans Georg Grassinger. The office of the D.S.P. was in Thierschstraße 15 (Publisher *Franz Eher Nachf.*). The *Deutsch-Sozialistische Partei* made a lot of propaganda for the movement with its newspapers *Münchener Beobachter* and *Völkischer Beobachter*. The *Münchener Beobachter* was distributed in Munich, the *Völkischer Beobachter* throughout the empire. The *Völkischer Beobachter* taught many thousands of fighters the basic tenets of National Socialism. The newspaper managed to appear even during the general strike - resulting from the Kapp-Putsch (March 1920) - despite the high risk. At the time, the newspaper was set and printed at another address by Grassinger together with editors Sesselmann, Müller, Wieser and Laforce.

Important people who later held and still hold leading positions in the NSDAP were members and collaborators of Thule, the newspaper and the party. Harrer of the DAP was also a collaborator at the *Beobachter*. Karl Harrer died on 6 September 1926 in Munich from the effects of the serious injuries he had received on the western front during the war.

When, in the autumn of 1919, the *Beobachter* could no longer be printed on *I.G. Weiß'schen Buchdruckerei*'s high- speed presses, Grassinger negotiated with regard to printing the newspaper on a rotary machine with a few large printing firms. With the exception of *M. Müller & Sohn,* the other firms rejected printing the *Beobachter*. Since 14 October 1919, from No. 53 onwards, the *Beobachter* has been printed by *M. Müller & Sohn*.

Not uninterestingly, Drexler gave his first political brochure: *Mein politisches Erwachen, aus dem Tagebuch eines deutschen sozialistischen Arbeiters* (*My* Political Awakening, from the Diary of a German Socialist Worker) to Karl Harrer as a 'founder of the *Deutsche Arbeiterpartei* and tireless fighter for justice and truth'. Presumably this is the same pamphlet mentioned by Adolf Hitler in his book *Mein Kampf,* published by *Franz Eher Nachf.* Publishers in Munich, when describing his first meeting with the Deutsche *Arbeiterpartei*. The brochure was published in 1919 by *Deutscher Volksverlag*, Munich.

The *Deutsche Arbeiterpartei* did not gain much influence for the time being and was mainly confined to Munich. Only when, due to that decisive confluence of circumstances in the autumn of 1919, Adolf Hitler came to strengthen the party's then thin ranks, came the turning point that was of great historical significance for the entire German people.

There was the following report about the first lecture evening of the *Deutsche Arbeiterpartei* in the *Völkischer Beobachter* Nr. 55 of 22 Octo- ber 1919:

From the movement

The DAP (*Deutsche Arbeiterpartei*), Munich branch, held a lecture evening on Thursday, 16 October, in the hall of the *Hofbräukeller*, which was very well attended and went quietly and inspiringly. As the speaker was prevented from speaking, Dr Erich Kühn, editor of the monthly magazine *Deutschlands Erneuerung*, spoke on the theme: 'The Jewish question - a German question'. In his introductory remarks, the chairman warned against allowing the anti-Semite problem to become a fashion problem. He stressed the urgent need for everyone to try to penetrate as deeply as possible into the Jewish question. This would enable them to deepen their own understanding of anti-Semitism so that they could resort to the right means. Using a large number of confessions by leading Jewish statesmen, politicians, scholars, poets and philosophers about their own race, the speaker proved that German anti-Semitism is justified. Judaism is known as a community closed in on itself for thousands of years and hostile to all other peoples, as an element hostile to culture and morality, as the bearer of a materialistic ideology. It is high time to start working on the solution of this 'German question' and to draw the right conclusions. The following statement should be emphasised in the process:

'Any person who proves to be equal to the Jew's 'dialectical gift and art of persuasion'; any person who successfully resists the seductive arts of Jewish-materialist luxury living; any person who does not allow Jewish slogans, pseudo-science and *trends* to alienate him from his orientation; any person who, from the bottom of his heart, castigates his fellow citizens for immoral behaviour, wants to preserve by word and deed the harm and ruin resulting from Jewish deception - who is called an anti- Semite by the Jew.'

The speaker received prolonged applause.

The discussion was particularly lively. Mr Hitler of the *Deutsche Arbeiterpartei,* in a blazing speech, dealt with the need to work together against the common enemy of the people and pointed in particular to the support of a German press, so that the people could find out, what Jewish newspapers were concealing. Mr Kreller of the *Deutscher Schutz- und Trutzbund,* called for participation in the propaganda work for the referendum against the immigration of Jews from the East, and in connection with this, pointed out the outcome of the trial on the murder of the hostages. The chairman confirmed that, according to Seidel's statement, Professor Berger's (Jew) resignation letter had already been signed and it was therefore clear that the Jews' appeal concerning Berger was unfounded. Mr Sesselmann of the *Deutsch-Sozialistische Partei* briefly described the aim of anti-Semitism, demanded mutual financial support and urged unity.

In the closing remarks, the chairman warned against propagating anti-Semitism by means of troublemaking.

'Through perseverance and diligent, *völkish* work and constant education, we must achieve our goal.'

No. 63 of the *Völkischer Beobachter* of 19 November 1919, brought an account of the second lecture evening of the DAP.

From the movement

The *Deutsche Arbeiter Partei*, Munich branch, organised a lecture evening on 11 November 1919 in the upper room of the *Eberlbräukeller*. Speakers were: Mr Hitler on 'Brest- Litovsk and Versailles' and Mr I. Mayer on 'Experiences from the war and the revolution of a German living abroad'. After a brief word of welcome, the chairman gave the floor to the first speaker, Mr Hitler. The speaker extraordinarily skilfully contrasted the *Schand- und Gewaltfrieden*, as much of the German (!) press called the Brest-Litovsk peace treaty, with the so-called *Verständigungsfrieden* of Versailles so mendaciously and nonsensically demanded in the same press. The images that Mr Hitler painted of the two peace treaties for the attentive audience were in sharp contrast with each other and made many hearts boil. Through shouting, the audience showed its agreement with the speech of the extraordinarily spirited speaker. The speaker met with enthusiastic approval when he called the German republic a free state of the *entente*, whose freedoms within its borders consisted of the fact that people's exploiters, usurers, black marketeers and smugglers were allowed to squeeze out the people in the most despicable way with impunity. With thunderous, oft-repeated applause, Mr Hitler was thanked for his thorough speech. After heartfelt words of thanks, the chairman went into detail on the party's most urgent goals, emphasising in particular the removal of Jews from all public functions, abolition of interest rule as per Feder's proposals and fighting usury and black-marketeering with all vigour. The exposition received lively applause. Subsequently, Mr Franz Dannehl of the Thule Society, on a few passages from the magazine *Der Revolutionär* (the publisher is the Jew Lederer from Mannheim). One can hardly think it possible that such vile lies and allegations were allowed to be published in Germany. However, genuine *völkisch* magazines such as the *Völkische Beobachter*, which truthfully depict the conditions and want to show a blinded government how to help the German people move forward again and free them from their domestic torturers, are banned as seditious magazines. A storm of indignation swept through the hall when these low-level antics of Lederer became known.

Now came the second lecture. Mr Mayer described his escape from Barcelona after the outbreak of the World War in an extraordinarily humorous way, while not forgetting the serious aspects of his adventures. The speaker received great applause and a lively discussion ensued. Finally, the meeting adopted two resolutions: one against the banning of the *Völkische Beobachter* by Noske, the other against the activities of the parliamentary enquiry committee.

From the *Völkischer Beobachter* No 17 of 28 February 1920, we bring you the report of the 'First large public people's meeting' of the *Deutsche Arbeiterpartei*.

From the movement

On Tuesday, 24 February 1920, the *Deutsche Arbeiterpartei* went public for the first time. At the very busy meeting in the hall of the *Hofbräuhaus,* Dr Johannes Dingfelder spoke as a guest of the *Deutsche Arbeiterpartei*, on the theme: 'What we need'. In a popular way, overlooking the social confusion from the lofty vantage point of a doctor and friend of man, the speaker led the audience back to the cause of the people's need. We have lost touch with the forces of nature, neglected the law of order, disregarded the world and creation law of cause and effect. On this, however, man's creative work is founded. Work = arbot - is the divine solar commandment - means to create solar goods, commodities of life for the ennoblement of mankind. We have despised this law, the law of movement, and surrendered to pleasure-seeking and unemployment benefit, following the example of a foreign people. There is a law of love, most despised by the Bolsheviks. To expect help against it from abroad is cowardly and undignified. 'Help yourselves' is the motto and that means abandoning international madness, thinking *völkisch* and believing in our people and their real leaders. - That was the essence of an excellent lecture which, although it also contained unpopular truths, was rewarded with a resounding applause. -

Hitler (*Deutsche Arbeiterpartei*) now sketched striking political images that drew stormy applause, but also provoked protests from the 'prejudiced' opposors present in large numbers. The speaker summarised the party programme, which was broadly in line with that of the *Deutsch-Sozialistische Partei*. Following this, the following resolution was adopted unanimously: More than two thousand Germans, from all working classes, gathered in the hall of the *Hofbräuhaus* on Tuesday, 24 February 1920, protested sharply against the allocation of 20,000 kilos of wheat flour to the Jewish community, when there was no bread to be had for 10,000 seriously ill people. - The discussion was very lively. The meeting gave the impression, that a movement is underway, which will continue under all circumstances.

With the revival of the *Deutsche Arbeiterpartei* by Hitler, the *Deutsch-Sozialistische Partei* increasingly faded into the background. Julias Streicher had initiated a movement in Nuremberg. Members of the *Germanic orders* there, the Thule Society and the *Deutsch-Sozilistische Partei* had united and aligned themselves with Adolf Hitler.

Marxist socialists and communists had sent people to the meeting on 4 November 1921, which took place in the ballroom of the *Hofbräuhaus* in Munich, to blow things up. The hall was crammed full and therefore cordoned off by the police. Hitler spoke for an hour and a half; the hall listened breathlessly. A man who had become angry started shouting and suddenly jumped up. 'Freedom,' he roared and, almost at the conclusion of Hitler's speech, threw a beer glass that flew right past the *Führer*'s head. That was the sign for battle. Beer glasses flew around, shots rang out, blood flowed. The still small S.A. pounced on the opponents, one after the other flew out, the rest fled. What remained were pale, exhausted and wounded men. And who had organised this Marxist terror? Mr Buisson, the foster son of Erhard Auer, the man from the police headquarters, who had withheld Sebottendorff's papers.

Hitler himself had been standing behind the lectern and suddenly the chairman, Hermann Esser, stood up and shouted: 'The meeting continues. The speaker has the floor.' The preparation work was done, the first battle had been won. The *Nationalsozialistische Deutsche Arbeiterpartei* led by Adolf Hitler was coming. The movement was seeking its way.

The *Heil und Sieg*, the greeting of the Thule members, turned Hitler into the *Sieg Heil* of the Germans!

The *Völkischer Beobachter* made the *Führer* the battle magazine of the National Socialist movement of Greater Germany.

The swastika made Hitler the symbol of the victorious NSDAP.

XIII
Origin and growth of the *Völkischer Beobachter*

Members of the movement often ask how it is that the *Völkischer Beobachter* has so many volumes, after all, the NSDAP is only 14 years old. Here, we will elaborate on the origins and growth of the newspaper using data from the trade register. We find the first entry in volume III, No. 125, page 63, of the Munich district court: minutes of 6 December 1901. Editor Frans Eher states that he is the owner and publisher of the *Münchener Beobachter*. He has owned the publishing house since the mid-1900s. The registration and disposition of the subscription take place on the same day.

Before this entry, the *Münchener Beobachter* was published as the trade journal of the butchers' guild. The next entry dates from 1918.

Through the mediation of the lawyer Dr Georg Gaubatz, the publisher and the newspaper were taken over from Franz Eher's widow. This was necessary because the new newspaper could not be published at the time because of paper rationing.

As the owner of the publishing house, Käthe Bierbaumer, a member of the *Teutonic Order*, was registered. The relevant inscriptions read with a short table of contents:

31 July 1918: Franz Eher died on 22 June, the sole heir being his widow who sold the firm to Käthe Bierbaumer.

14 September 1918: Mrs Eher appears, hands over the certificate of inheritance and declares, that she has sold the publishing house to Käthe Bierbaumer, Bad Aibling, Parkstraße 335.

17 September 1918: Käthe Bierbaumer, identifying herself with her passport, will sign with: *Verlag Franz Eher Nachf.* Registration and publication follow.

The *Beobachter* had hardly any subscribers when it took over; the first issue appeared on 1 July 1918. As the responsible editor, Rudolf von Sebottendorff signed on.

In March 1919, Sebottendorff included the writer Hanns Georg Müller on the editorial board; for Number 17 of 24 May 1919, Müller alone was responsible.

In the reorganisation after the wheel era in May 1919, Sebottendorff split the publishing house of the *Beobachter* completely from Thule. In Tierschstraße, where the publishing house is still located, Grassinger rented the parterre space (formerly café-restaurant *Zum Hansahaus*) on a hire-purchase basis. Ott took over the commercial management of the publishing house. Laforce was given the advertising department.

In March 1919, Sebottendorff had become acquainted with baker Max Sesselmann, and since he was looking for an articulate worker for the movement, he hired Sesselmann.

When it was decided in July that Sebottendorff would take his leave, matters were thus settled through the following tender:

Käthe Bierbaumer states, that the appearing gentlemen Hanns Georg Müller, Wilhelm Laforce, Max Sesselmann, Johann Ott are authorised to sign all three jointly. Order of registration and publication dated 15 July 1919.

On 9 August 1919, on the day issue 34 of the *Münchener Beobachter* was published, the newspaper was first named *Völkischer Beobachter* for part of its circulation.

It later turned out that Sebottendorff had been mistaken about editors Sesselmann and Müller. The work and behaviour towards the other contributors did not correspond to what Sebottendorff, nor publisher Käthe Bierbaumer expected of them. Hostilities occurred.

After Sebottendorff left, the newspaper's owner, Käthe Bierbaumer, also had to leave. To achieve this, the rumour was circulated that she was a Jewess. People talked about Sebottendorff and his 'Jewish friend'. Never before had anyone been spoken of so outrageously evil, and the bad thing was that the rumour was spread by popular opinion. A smear campaign was also started against Sebottendorff himself. People circulated the article 'Strange stories' in copies endorsed by legal adviser Dr Först. All over Germany the article was imprinted and because copies were also sent from *völkisch* circles, without indicating where they came from, it was believed. Bierbaumer gave in to the hostile treatment and also left Munich.

Several times, Sesselmann, who had managed to place himself at the top of the publishing house, had to travel to Constance to get money from Sebottendorff again and again. At last, the owners of the publishing house became aware of the matter: a lot of money was being squandered on lawsuits involving editors because they had insufficient evidence.

To clear the way here and eliminate incompetent forces, Sebottendorff asked his sister Dora Kunze and Käthe Bierbaumer to come to Konstanz. On 30 September 1919, through a notary, the publishing house *Franz Eher Nachf.* was converted into a limited liability company. The relevant extracts from the commercial register read:

Register deed of the Munich district court, No 1649/19. Capital 120,000 marks, thereof:

Miss Käthe Bierbaumer
110,000 Mark

Mrs Dora Kunze, née Glauer, at Lauban
10,000 Mark

Deposited Miss Bierbaumer by contribution of the firm *Franz Eher Nachf.* in Munich, with all rights, assets and inventory of the firm

110.000 Mark

Paid in cash to Ms Dora Kunze
10.000 Mark

Supplement: notarial Munich XVI:
Chairman Miss Käthe Bierbaumer, Munich, Thierschstraße 15,

Lawyer Dahn for Mrs Dora Kunze, Lauban. Correction: Value of property contribution
91,600 Mark

Cash value 18,400 Mark

Managing director of the publishing house: Franz Xaver Eder, merchant in Munich. Following this, Miss Bierbaumer donated 50,000 Marks in shares to the publishing house for the attention of Mr Eder and gave a further 13,500 Marks in shares, leaving Miss Bierbaum with 46,500 and Mrs Dora Kunze with 10,000 Marks in shares in the company. The intrinsic value of the shares was considerably higher.

The list of associates dated 20 March 1920 includes the following names:

Ir. Gottfried Feder, Munich, with
10,000 Mark

Franz Xaver Eder, merchant, Munich, with
10,000 Mark

Franz Freiherr von Feilitzsch, Munich, with
20,000 Mark

Dr Wilhelm Gutberlet, physician, Munich,
10,000 Mark

Theodor Heuß, manufacturer, Munich, with
10.000 Mark

Juffr. Käthe Bierbaumer, Freiburg/Breisgau
46.500 Mark

Ms Dora Kunze, Lauban
10.000 Mark

Karl Alfred Braun, Munich
3.500 Mark

After a subscription on 17 December 1920, all the shares, except those of Miss Käthe Bierbaumer and Mrs Dora Kunze, were owned by Anton Drexler.

From 11 August 1921 with No 63, Dietrich Eckart signed on as editor-in-chief of the *Völkischer Beobachter*.

On 16 November 1921, Adolf Hitler, Munich, Thierschstraße 15, authenticated with his passport, appears for the first time at the register of the Munich cantonal court as chairman of the *Nationalsozialistische Deutsche Arbeiterpartei* and declares that he owns all the shares. Hitler appointed Joseph Pickl as managing director. Max Amann took charge of the publishing house, now general director of the party publishing house.

XIV
Thule without a founder and the resurgence

A 1926 letter from Johannes Hering, which reached Sebottendorff in Istanbul, contains further information on the developments within the Thule Society.

'As you may recall, I was chairman of Thule for quite a long time after Dahn's resignation, then handed over the chairmanship to Professor Bauer, who performed his duties in an exemplary manner, delivered thoughtful, literary and political lectures himself, but also managed to attract good speakers and outstanding members.

A good politician, he joined the board of the rising German-national party and became a delegate. There was much to do in the social field under his leadership; concert and poetry evenings, and twice a theatre performance took place.

In Bauer's place came Max Sesselmann, whom you recruited, who became a delegate to the state as well. However, he had little time for Thule.

Moreover, we were driven away from our location and after a few meetings in *Fränkischer Hof*, the Thule party bled out. Only two things remain to be done: the ceremony on 30 April in the *Luitpold Gymnasium* and the wreath laying on the graves on All Saints' Day. For that, Bursar Bucherer will send the wreaths with black-white-red ribbons and I will bring the wreaths to the *Wald- und Westfriedhof*. Deby was second chairman for a while...'

One more time there was a big fuss in the Thule Society: when the NSDAP was defeated after 9 November 1923. At that time, under the current first mayor Fiehler, Munich, most party members became members of the Thule Society. This allowed propaganda to continue until Adolf Hitler, who had returned from Landsberg, reorganised things.

In 1925, Thule still had 25 members. Sesselmann changed the statutes, renouncing the leadership principle. In 1926, there were still only five members. When the registration court fined Sesselmann for not sending in a report for a few years, Sesselmann and the second president Wagner, declared that Thule no longer had any members. Based on an order of the registry court of June 1930, the Thule Society was deregistered.

Nor were ceremonies held at the *Lutepold Gymnasium* in recent years. Only in 1933 did one take place again. Sebottendorff was to give a commemorative speech, but this was thwarted by Sesselmann. However, after the ceremony, 75 old Thule members gathered at the Domhof to greet the old master. They agreed to revive Thule and undo the society's dissolution.

Under the chairmanship of court-appointed fiduciary Mr Georg Gaubatz, a general meeting of members took place, at which Sebottendorff was again appointed leader, and Mr Riemann as vice-chairman.

It was further decided to restore the leadership principle through an amendment to the articles of association.

The Walterspiel brothers, owners of hotel *Vier Jahreszeiten*, accommodated Sebottendorff by providing him with the old, historic space for the benefit of Thule. Thus, the 15-year anniversary could be celebrated on 9 September 1933. Actor and brother of Thule Max Bayrhammer gave an introduction, Sebottendorff gave the dedication speech. Professor Stempfle of the *Rehse Institut* gave a humorous speech on Thule's past, and read out, among other things, a 1920 letter from Sebottendorff to teacher Rohmeder, in which Sebottendorff informed that he will not be in Munich again until then when flags with the swastika will proclaim the movement's victory in Germany. At this party, Professor Stempfle also proposed for the first time that a dignified memorial to the first martyrs of the awakening Germany be erected in the city of Munich. First Mayor Fiehler, an honorary member of the Thule Society, who was present, took note of the proposal.

On 31 October 1933, on the eve of All Saints' Day, the Thule Society organised a commemoration of the dead. The sacred sounds of Kistler's *Treueschwur*, performed by the orchestra of the NSDAP's Civil Service Department conducted by Georg Festner, ushered in the ceremony. Actor Max Bayrhammer recited a fatherland poem, *In einer Winternacht*, by D. von Liliencron. Finally, Thule brother Dr Heinz Kurz spoke in a recitation on 'Praise of Death'. On this day, an organ of the Thule Society appeared again for the first time: the *Thule-Bote*. The *Thule-Bote* is published by *Deukula*, Munich, and can be bought at any post office every month for RM1.40.

On All Saints' Day, the Thule brothers laid wreaths on the graves in honourful remembrance of their deceased.

The task of renewing the Thule Society has succeeded. On every Saturday evening, Thule members met again at the historic place where they had unfolded their activities, at the Hotel *Vier Jahreszeiten*. With that, Sebottendorff held that the time had come to put the leadership of the Thule Society in the hands of Brother Franz Dannehl. The leader appointed Dr Heinz Kurz as vice-president and Hanns Georg Grassinger as propaganda leader.

What does the Wala sing, of what is needed? Honour the divine! Avoid the lowly! Love the brethren! Protect the homeland! Be worthy of your ancestors!

Register of persons and cases

Ahlwardt, Hermann (1846 - 1914), teacher and rector in Berlin. Founded an anti-Semitic movement in 1889. In Jewish circles, he was mockingly called the 'rector of Germans'. He was denounced by Jews and, as a result, his movement came to an end.

Alemanni, West Germanic tribe. They were crushed by the Romans in the Battle of Strasbourg in 357, led by Julian Apostata. This prevented the Alemanni from penetrating further into Alsace.

Alldeutscher Verband, (Great German Association). Founded in 1891 by Alfred Hugenberg (see there) and Heinrich Claß (see there) as *Allgemeiner deutscher Verein*. In 1894 the name was changed to *Alldeutscher Verband*. Was one of the most influential *völkisch* organisations with a strong militaristic, nationalistic and anti-Semitic character. The alliance was an inspiration for Hitler's expansionism (*Lebensraum*). In 1919, the *Deutschvölkischer Schutz - und Trutzbund* (see there) was founded as a subsidiary organisation. After Hitler's seizure of power, the *Alldeutscher Verband* lost importance until it was disbanded by Reinhard Heydrich in 1939.

Allgemeine Ordens-Nachrichten, Organ of the *Germanic orders* (see there).

Alsberg, Max (1877 - 1933), lawyer, criminal law reformer and writer. Alsberg was a well-known criminal lawyer. Was boycotted and persecuted in 1933 because of his Jewishness, and had to flee to Switzerland, where he committed suicide. Alsberg also wrote some plays.

Amann, Max (1891 - 1957), politician and publisher. One of the first members of the NSDAP. Participated in the *Hitler-Putsch* of November 1923, for which he spent several months in prison in Landsberg. There, Hitler dictated to him his book *Mein Kampf*, the text of which Amann wrote on the typewriter. Member of the Munich City Council from 1925 - 1933 and of the Reichstag from 1933 - 1945. Since 1925 head of the NSDAP publishing house, where the *Völkischer Beobachter* was published. In 1933, Amann became Reich leader for the press and in 1941 appointed *SS-Obergruppenführer*. Arrested in 1948 and sentenced to 10 years' labour camp under expropriation of pension and assets. Released early in 1953.

Arbeiterwehr, formed the Red Army during the Raden Republic (see there) in Bavaria.

Arco auf Valley, Anton *Graf* von (1897 - 1945), was of Austrian nobility. Assassin of Kurt Eisner (21 February 1919). Was originally sentenced to death, but was granted amnesty. Later considered a hero by the Nazis.

Arndt, Julius (born 1898), lieutenant, son of the cultural historian Arndt in Munich. Fought at the front in the First World War. Member of the *Kampfbund* of Thule and of the *Freikorps Oberland*.

Aschenbrenner, occupied Munich Central Station in the *coup* on Palm Sunday (10 April 1919).

Auer, Erhard (born 1874), left-wing politician. Worked for the *Sozialdemokratische Partei Deutschlands* (SPD) in Bavaria from 1900 - 1921. Member of the Landdag since 1907 and vice-president in 1919. Was severely wounded on 21 February 1919, after Eisner's death was announced, by shots fired by communist Lindner.

Aumiller, Max, owner of hotel *Marienbad*. Was arrested and threatened with execution along with the Thule members.

Axelrod, Tobias. Born in Moscow in 1897, studied linguistics and literature, acted as plenipotentiary for Soviet Russia to the Council Government in Munich. Came to Munich in December 1918 and kept a low profile there until Eisner's death. Leviné, Levien and him formed the triumvirate leading the Council Government. Was arrested after the overthrow of the Council Government and sentenced to 15 years in prison, but finally exchanged for prisoners in Russia.

Ballin, Albert, (1857 - 9.11.1918, suicide), director-general of the Hamburg-America Line.

Peasant Council. Representation of peasants in the council-government during the Raden Republic in Munich (see there).

Bauhütte, In the Middle Ages, the construction guild, especially among masons and stonemasons. Its purpose was to train construction workers and provide work. With regard to the construction of major works, there was a duty of secrecy. There was a close friendship among the members. Later, well-trained non-construction workers were also given access to the guild. These finally formed the majority of members. From this, Freemasonry then emerged in 1717.

Bayrhammer, Max, an actor at the *Münchner Kammerspiele*, Munich's city theatre, was sacked for his anti-Semitic affiliation.

Beth, Ritter von, major. Fought at the front in World War I. Led the *Freikorps Oberland* in 1919.

Belfried, German newspaper published in Belgium during World War I for which Erzberger was responsible.

Berger, Ernst, professor. Was murdered together with the seven Thule members in the courtyard of the *Luitpold Gymnasium*. Thinking he would be released, he had joined them.

Bernstein, Eduard (1850 - 1932), left-wing politician and writer. Led the newspaper *Der Sozialdemokrat* from 1880 to 1890.

Bethmann-Hollweg, Theobald von (1856 - 1921), liberal politician and Reich Chancellor from 1909 - 1917. Nickname: *der Lederne Kanzler.*

Bierbaumer, Käthe, born 1889 in Neustift (Burgenland), Austria. Owner/principal shareholder of publisher *Franz Eher Nachf.*, Munich.

Bismarck, *Fürst* Otto von (1815 - 1898), conservative politician and founder of the First Reich, Reich Chancellor from 1860 - 1890. Dismissed by Kaiser Wilhelm II. Nickname: *der Eiserne Kanzler.*

Bissing, Moritz Ferdinand, *Freiherr* von (1844 - 1917 in Brussels), general. Became governor-general of Belgium in 1914 and sought to divide Belgium into a Flemish and a Walloon part.

Bleichröder, Jewish bank in Berlin, founded by Samuel Bleichröder in 1803.

B'nai B'rith, Hebrew: 'sons of faith', organisation founded in America in 1843 as the *United Order of Bne Briss.* Allied itself with the *Alliance Israelite* and came to Europe in the 1960s. Membership was reserved exclusively for Jews. By 1900, the organisation owned an office in Berlin's Wilhelm Street.

Bodmann, Hans Hermann, *Freiherr* von und zu, member of the Thule Society, of the *Kampfbund* and contributor to the *Beobachter.*

Bonn, rector of the commercial academy in Munich.

Braun, Karl Alfred (b. 1920), shareholder of publishing house
Franz Eher Nachf. GmbH, Munich.

Bruxellois, Name of a newspaper published in Brussels during the First World War.

Büchner, Ludwig (1824 - 1899), physician, champion of materialism, wrote the book *Kraft und Stoff.*

Büchold, Valentin (b. 1898), sports editor of the *Beobachter* and first representative of student body *Hansea*. Came into conflict with the rector of the Bonn Commercial Academy as a result.

Buditsch, called Dietrich, member red Soldiers' Council.

Buisson, Wilhelm, pharmacist and Marxist, foster son of Auer. Was at Munich police headquarters when Liberation troops entered in 1919, where he led a militant group.

Bunge, Hans, member of the Thule Society and of the *Kampfbund*, later leader of the SS bodyguard.

Bürgerwehr, during the revolution militant groups of citizens who protected municipal institutions. During the Raden Republic (see there), such groups existed in several towns in northern Bavaria.

Chandals, (Sanskrit candala). Among Hindus, the lowest caste, the *dalits* or *untouchables*. Also used as a swear word.

Claß, Heinrich (born 1868), lawyer. Together with Alfred Hugenberg (see there) founded the *Alldeutscher Verband* (see there) in 1891.

Commune, Aims to abolish private property in favour of collective property. The Paris *Commune* (18 March - 28 May 1971) was a revolutionary government that overthrew the legitimate French government. The re- volution was bloodily put down by the French government army, killing about 30,000 civilians and 900 soldiers. The 147 members of the *Commune* were executed without any trial. The *Commune* was seen by Karl Marx as the beginning of a social, classless society.

Cyrus, called Cyrus in the Bible - book of Ezra, (565 - 529 BCE) founder of the Persian Empire. In 539 BC, he conquered Babylon, among other places.

Dahn, Hanns, lawyer and member of the Thule Society of which he became leader as Sebottendorff's successor in 1919.

Dannehl, Franz, member of the Thule Society, of which he became leader in 1933, and of the *Kampfbund*. Well-known researcher and collector of butterflies; also composer.

Daumenlang, Anton (1870 - 1919) First secretary with the railways. Engaged in heraldry and genealogy. Was murdered as a hostage in the *Luitpold gymnasium* by red guards on 30 April 1919. Left behind a wife and a 13-year-old daughter.

Debus, Luitpold. Was sentenced to 15 years in prison for involvement in the murder of the hostages in the *Luitpold Gymnasium* on 30 April 1919.

Deby, Theo, member of the Thule Society and the *Kampfbund.*

Deike, Walter, (1892 - 1919), arts and crafts designer. Was murdered as a hostage in the *Luitpold gymnasium* by red guards on 30 April 1919.

Deutscher Arbeiterverein, emerged from the Thule Society (see there), later the ultra-right-wing *Deutsche Arbeiterpartei* of which Karl Harrer and Anton Drexler were chairmen.

Deutsch-Sozialistische Partei, emerged from the Thule Society (see there). The programme of the ultra-right-wing *Deutsch-Sozialistische Partei, An das Deutsche Volk,* was published in December 1918 in No 15 of the *Allgemeine Ordens-Nachrichten* of the *Germanic orders (*see there). First chairman was Hans Georg Grassinger (see there).

Deutschvölkischer Schutz- und Trutzbund. Formed in 1919 from the *Alldeutscher Verband (*see there), and most active, influential anti-Semitic alliance in Germany after World War I. The largest and most important carrier of *völkisch* thought. Its aim was to fight against Judaism and left-wing organisations. At its peak in 1922, the union had 180,000 members. After the assassination of Walther Rathenau (see there) on 24 June 1922, the union was expelled from most of Germany's federal states due to complications associated with the assassination. Members of the union included Dietrich Eckart, Gottfried Feder, Reinhard Heydrich, Julius Streicher and many others.

Dingfelder, Johannes, physician and guest of the Thule Society (see there).

Disraeli, Benjamin, *Earl of Beaconsfield* (1804 - 1881), British Conservative statesman, was twice prime minister in England. Known as a writer for his novels *Conningsby*, *Tancred* etc. He was in charge at the Congress in Berlin in 1879, where the peace of San Stefano was concluded and the Turkish-Russian war ended.

Stab-in-the-back myth. Towards the end of World War I, the German military leadership is said to have claimed that Germany's political leaders (Scheidemann and Erzberger - see there) had not given them enough support to win the war. The lack of this support would have been the stab-in-the-back myth in the back of the military and the reason they had lost the war as well. Far-right circles in Germany, such as e.g. the *Alldeutscher Verband (*see there), which had hoped for conquests of large territories, took advantage of this by claiming in their turn that the war could have been won if the left-wing government had supported the army sufficiently instead of betraying it. This 'stab-in-the-back' had major consequences in Germany in the following years.

Dönme, Jews in the Ottoman Empire, who openly converted to Islam but secretly continued to observe Jewish traditions. The sect was founded by Sabatai Zevi (1626 - 1676), who declared himself to be the Messiah in Damascus. He converted to Islam to escape persecution by the sultan. Later, most of the sect merged into the Turkish population. The Dönme played an important role during the 1918 revolution of the Young Turks who supported Mustafa Kemal (Atatürk). Still today, the Dönme form a very closed sect about which little is known.

Drexler, Anton, metal turner and guest of the Thule company. Joined the *Deutsche Arbeiterverein*, was second president under Karl Harrer, later delegate of the *völkische* bloc in the Bavarian Landdag.

Dschavid, finance minister in Turkey from 1909 - 1919. Was hanged in 1925 for participating in a conspiracy against Mustafa Kemal (Atatürk).

Ebert, Fritz (1871 - 1925), saddler, politician and statesman. Editor of the *Bremer Bürgerzeitung,* and group chairman for the *Sozialdemokratische Partei Deutschlands* (SPD) in Bremen. After Bebel's death in 1913, chairman of the SPD. Reich chancellor for a short time in 1918 and chairman of the Council of People's Commissars in late 1918. After abolition of the monarchy in 1919, first president of the *Weimarer Republik* .

Eck, Klaus, editor of the anti-Semitic newspaper *Miesbacher Anzeiger*.

Eckart, hereafter called Echart Dietrich (1868 - 1923), writer and guest of the Thule Society. One of the earliest key figures in the founding of the NSDAP. Publisher of the anti-Semitic magazine *Auf gut Deutsch*, editor at the *Völkischer Beobachter* from 1921 - 1923. Participated in the *Kapp-Putsch* in 1920 and the *Hitler-Putsch* in 1923.

Eder, Franz Xaver, was appointed managing director of publisher *Franz Eher Nachf.* on 1 October 1919 by the proprietors Bierbaumer and Kunze, after the firm was converted into a partnership. In 1920 he became a partner of *Franz Eher Nachf. GmbH*, Munich.

Egelhofer, Rudolf (1896 - 1919), took part in World War I as a marine. Involved in the sailors' rebellion in 1918 (see there). In February 1919, came with a group of armed sailors from Wilhelmshaven to Munich, where Kurt Eisner (see there) had meanwhile proclaimed the *Freis- tate Bayern*. After Eisner's assassination (21.2.1919), Egelhofer became a member of the *Kommunistische Partei Deutschlands* (KPD) and the revolutionary *Sodatenrat* in Munich. On 13 April 1919, Egelhofer, under Leviné and Levien (see there), becomes city commander and commander of the Red Army, which consists of 20,000 poorly-armed soldiers and workers. In early May 1919, Munich is conquered by the 'white troops' (*Reichswehr* and *Freikorpsen*), during which hundreds of revolutionaries die or are killed. Egelhofer was caught and shot without trial on 3 May.

Eher, Franz (1851 - 1918), editor. From 1900 to 1918 owner of publisher *Franz Eher*, Munich.

Ehrhardt, member Soldiers' Council and responsible editor for the *Zentralrat*'s newspaper.

Eisenhut, left-wing politician and member of the College of Eleven, which formed the *Zentralrat* in the Bavarian Raden Republic (see there) from February to March 1919.

Eisner, Kurt (1867 - 21.2.1919), writer and left-wing politi- cian. Son of a Jewish manufacturer. (That Eisner was actually called Kosmanowski and came from Galicia - now partly Poland, partly Ukraine - is based on anti- Semitic propaganda and has since been refuted. See Bernhard Grau: *Kurt Eisner 1867 - 1919. Eine Biographie. Verlag C.H. Beck*, Munich, 2001). His parents came from Bohemia and Kurt Eisner was born in Berlin. He studied philosophy and worked as a journalist at the *Frankfurter Zeitung* and later at the social-democratic newspaper *Vorwärts* (see there). Due to an article in which he attacked the monarchy, he ended up in prison for nine months. In 1917, he left the *Sozialdemokratische Partei Deutschlands* (SPD) to join the *Unabhängige Sozialdemokratische Partei Deutschlands* (USPD), a leftwing breakaway from the SPD. In 1910, Eisner came to Munich and led the workers' staking at the munitions factory there in 1918. He was convicted of treason and spent six months in *Stadelheim* prison (see there). On 8 November 1918, Eisner organised a meeting on the Theresienwiese in Munich, which led to the revolution. The Bavarian King Ludwig III had to flee and Eisner was declared prime minister of the *Freistaat Bayern*, forming a *Nationalrat*. Using documents, Eisner wanted to prove that Germany was to blame for the outbreak of the First World War. His rapprochement with the *Entente* (see there) also did not go down well with him. This led to a big loss for his party in the elections held in January 1919. When Eisner was on his way to the Landdag in Munich on 21 February 1919 to tender his resignation, he was shot dead by Anton Count Arco auf Valley, upon which the Raden republic (see there) was declared in Munich.

Eller, lawyer in Bad Aibling. During the Raden Republic (see there) in Bavaria, mayor there.

Endres, Fritz (born 1877 - 1963), coppersmith and left- wing politician, member of the SPD. In 1918, he became secretary of the union of metalworkers and president of the *Arbeiter- und Soldatenrat*. During the Raden Republic (see there) in Bavaria minister of justice and later minister of internal affairs.

Engels, Friedrich (1820 - 1895), scientist, philosopher and political theorist. Was, together with Karl Marx (see there), the founder of Marxism and co-wrote '*The Communist Manifesto*' (1848).

Entente, Alliances between countries that faced Germany, Austria-Hungary and the Ottoman Empire in World War I and felt threatened by powerful Germany, mainly England, France, Russia and later the US.

Epp, Franz, *Ritter* von (1868 -1947), general. Began his career as a professional soldier in 1887. Fought in China in 1900 and took part in the Herero genocide in South- West Africa (Namibia) in 1904. During the First World War, he fought on several fronts: including in Western Europe, South Tyrol, Serbia and at Verdun, then again in Romania and northern Italy. He received the *Eiserne Kreuz* II and I in 1914, the *Militär-Max-Joseph-Orden* in 1916 and *Pour le Mérite* in 1918, and was promoted several times. In early 1919, he was ordered by Reich Minister of War Noske to form a *Freikorps*. Since the Bavarian government under prime minister Eisner forbade recruiting soldiers, the *Freikorps Epp* was formed in Ohrdruf, Thuringia, and numbered 700 men. Together with other 'white' units, it put a bloody end to the Raden Republic (see there) in Bavaria in April/May 1919. Subsequently, the *Freikorps* merged into the new *Reichswehr*. In 1927, Epp joined the *Bayerische Volkspartei* and later of the NSDAP, with the leading figures he had contact with. In 1928, he entered the Reichstag as an NSDAP deputy for Bavaria. In 1933, he was appointed Reichsstatthalter in Bavaria.

Erzberger, Matthias (1875 - 1921), politician. Entered the Reichstag in 1903 as a deputy for the left wing of the *Zentrumspartei*. Worked on the peace resolution in 1917 and was a member of the Armistice Commission in 1918/19. Was vice-chancellor from June 1919 to March and also Reich Minister of Finance. In the latter position, he worked on finance reform. Since he had worked for compliance with the Treaty of Versailles, he came into conflict with the extreme right and had to resign. On 26 August 1921, he was assassinated by members of the *Freikorps Oberland*.

Esser, Hermann (born 1900), Member of the National Socialist movement since January 1920. Alderman in Munich. Since 1933 Bavarian minister without portfolio and chief of cabinet.

Falkenhausen, Ludwig, *Freiherr* von. In 1917/18 governor-general of Belgium.

Fechenbach, Felix (1894 - 1933), journalist, politician. From 1912 - 1914 party secretary of the *Sozialdemokrati- sche Partei Deutschlands* (SPD) in Munich. Fought in the World War and was private secretary to Kurt Eisner (see there). Murdered by the Nazis in 1933.

Feder, Gottfried (1883 - 1941), economist and politician. Initially studied architecture and later economics. Advocate of the abolition of so-called 'interest slavery'. Published his work *Das Manifest zur Brechung der Zinsknechtschaft* in 1919. Became a member of the *Deutsche Arbeiterpartei* in 1919, where he also lectured; later a member of the NSDAP and the economic brain of the party. As a deputy in the Reichstag, he advocated interest ban and expropriation of Jewish property. In 1933 secretary of state for economic affairs. When he later fell into disfavour with Hitler, he quit the party.

Fehmer, Johann. Was sentenced to death for involvement in the murder of the hostages in the *Luitpold Gymnasium* on 30 April 1919.

Feilitzsch, Franz, *Freiherr* von. Partner of the publishing house *Franz Eher Nachf. GmbH*, Munich.

Femeprozeß, Judicial process in which crimes with political motives are judged, often behind closed doors. *Femeprozesse* mainly took place in the first years of the *Weimarer Republik* (1918 - 1933), because of the many murders of political opponents of the extreme right. In 1924, more than 400 such murders were committed. Major notoriety was given, for example, to the murder of Matthias Erzberger (see there) and Walther Rathenau (see there).

Fiehler, Karl (1895 - 1969), early politician and National Socialist. Fought in World War II, was wounded and received the *Eiserne Kreuz II.* Joined the NSDAP in 1920 and became a convinced National Socialist. Member of Hitler's *Stoßtrupp* (later SA). After the *Hitler-Putsch* of 8/9 November 1923, was sentenced, along with Hitler, to high treason and went to prison in Landsberg. From 1933 - 1945 first mayor of Munich.

Fimbulwinter - the great winter that precedes the *Ragnarök* (= the great Get). (*Fimbulvetr* from Nordic mythology, as described in the *Edda*).

Först, legal adviser and lawyer.

Frank, Michel Hans (1900 - 1946), lawyer. Fought at the front in World War I in 1917/18 as a soldier and later served in General von Epp's *Freikorps* (see there). Member of the NSDAP in 1919 and legal advisor of the same party. In 1930 deputy in the Reichstag and in 1933 minister of justice in Bavaria. After the invasion of Poland in 1939, governor-general there. During the Nuremberg Trials in 1945/46 sentenced to death for war crimes and hanged on 16 October 1946.

Frauendorfer, Heinrich *Ritter* von, (1855 - 1921), lawyer and politician. In 1918/19 under Kurt Eisner, minister of transport.

Freikorps, Paramilitary units composed partly of demobilised soldiers returning from World War I, partly of volunteers and partly of deserted mercenaries. In total, the combined *Freikorps* had 400,000 men; they were also called the 'white troops'. Since the Treaty of Versailles forbade the action of an official army, they were used by the Friedrich Ebert (SPD) government in 1919 to prevent domestic disturbances, such as the November Revolution, the Spartak Uprising and the leftist Raden republics. After partial lifting of restrictions on the size of the official army, the *Freikorps* were gradually disbanded and merged into the *Reichswehr,* the SA and the SS.

Freikorps Oberland, Was founded in early 1919 by Sebottendorff with support from the cabinet Hoffmann, who fled to Bamberg, with the aim of overthrowing the Raden Republic (see there) in Munich.

Friedrich der Große, (1712 - 1786), king of Prussia.

Friedrich III, (1830 - 1888), German emperor.

Fritsch, Theodor (1852 - 1933), instrument maker and mill builder, publicist and publisher of anti-Semitic writings. Author of the *Antisemitic Catechism* and the *Handbuch der Judenfrage*. Founded *Hammer Verlag* in Leipzig in 1902 and published the *Hammer-Blätter für deutschen Sinn*. It also published a translation of the *Protocols of the Wisemen of Zion*. In 1912, he founded the *Hammerbund* and the *Teutonic Orders*. Members of the Teutonic *orders* again founded the Thule Society (see there). The *Hammerbund* merged into the *Deutschvölkische Schutz- und Trutzbund*. Fritsch himself became a member of the *Deutschvölkische Freiheitspartei* (DVFP). In 1924, he entered the Reichstag for the *Nationalsozialistische Freiheitspartei*.

Furor Teutonicus, The rage and fury with which the Teutonen (a Germanic tribe) at the time attacked the Romans. The expression is first used by Marcus Annaeus Lucanus (39 - 65 AD) in his work Bellum civile.

Gandorfer, left-wing politician, farmers' council and member of the College of Eleven, which formed the *Zentralrat* in the Bavarian Raden Republic from February to March 1919.

Gaubatz, Georg, lawyer and advocate.

Germanic orders, Founded together with the *Reichshammerbund* in 1912 as a secret anti-Semitic society and structured along the lines of the Masonic loos. Members were readers of the magazine *Der Hammer*. The order itself published the *Allgemeine Ordens-Nachrichten (*see there). Before World War I, there were still more than 1,000 members. New members were initiated using rites that contained elements of Freemasonry and Ariosophy (Guido von List), and music by Richard Wagner was performed. After the 1916 split, one branch was called *Walvater* and continued by Hermann Pohl (see there) and Freese. The other branch was continued under the leadership of Philipp Stauff (see there) together with General von Brockhusen. During the war, membership declined rapidly. With the foundation of the Thule Society (see there) in 1918, the *Germanic orders* rapidly lost importance.

Glauer, Adam Rudolf, (1875 - 1945), son of a machinist, adventurer and spy. Glauer amassed a fortune during the Balcan Wars (1912/13). In Istanbul in 1909, he met Baron Heinrich Freiherr von Sebottendorff, who adopted him. Therefore, Glauer was also allowed to bear his name with corresponding title of nobility. In 1920, the adoption was contested, but later recognised as such by his family. See further under Sebottendorff.

Glauer, Dora (1886 - 1921), sister of Adam Rudolf Glauer.

Göbel, Friedrich Wilhelm, (died 1929), designed a tank, the *Landpanzerkreuzer*, in 1913. Sebottendorff (see there) is said to have financed its development. In 1914, the model was shown at the Berlin Stadium. The colossus weighed 550 tonnes and moved on gigantic balls.

The military authorities refused to put the monster into production.

Goldschmidt, left-wing politician and member of the College of Eleven, which formed the *Zentralrat* in the Bavarian Raden Republic from February to March 1919.

Goltz, Colmar, Freiherr von der (1843 - 1916), Prussian general and author of military-historical works. From 23 August to 28 November 1914, governor general of Belgium. Died in the service of the Sultan of Turkey in 1916 of typhoid fever in Baghdad.

Grassinger, Hans Georg, (born 1887), business leader and ultra right-wing politician. Fought at the front as a soldier in World War I. Member of the *Kampfbund* of Thule. Voiced opposition to Eisner (see there) in the Landdag during the council government. Fellow of the *Munich Beobachter* and *Völkische Beobachter* respectively. First chairman of the *Deutsch-Sozialistische Partei* founded in 1918.

Grätz, Heinrich (1871 - 1891), historian at the University of Breslau. Author of *Geschichte der Juden*.

Gesell, Silvio (1862 - 1930), economist and known for his theory of the free economy (*Freiwirtschaft*). For only seven days people's commissioner of finance of the Bavarian Raden Republic.

Greiner, Rudolf. Was sentenced to 15 years in prison for involvement in the murder of the hostages in the *Luitpold Gymnasium* on 30 April 1919.

Great German Confederation - see Alldeutscher Verband.

Gsell, Karl. Was sentenced to 15 years in prison for involvement in the murder of the hostages in the *Luitpold Gymnasium* on 30 April 1919.

Gutberlet, Wilhelm (1870 - 1933), physician. Member of the *Kampfbund* of Thule. Partner of Publisher Franz Eher Nachf. GmbH, Munich.

Haeckel, Ernst (1834 - 1919), biologist, physician, philosopher. Professor at the University of Jena. Promoted the work of Charles Darwin in Germany. His main work is *Die Welträtsel.*

Hagemeister, left-wing politician and member of the College of Eleven, which formed the *Zentralrat* in the Bavarian Raden Republic from February to March 1919.

Halbritter, Ernst, illustrator and member of the editorial board of the *Beobachter*.

Hammerbund, The union formed by the readers of *Der Hammer*, the magazine edited by Theodor Fritzsch (see there).

Hannes, Johann. Was sentenced to 15 years in prison for involvement in the murder of the hostages in the *Luitpold Gymnasium* on 30 April 1919.

Harden, Maximilian (1861 - 1927), his real name was Felix Ernst Witkowski. Publicist, critic, actor and journalist. Moved mainly in the fields of literature and drama. Edited the weekly *Die Zukunft* from 1892 to 1922, in which he published articles on art and politics. Initially a monarchist and an adept of Bismarck. Later he showed his distaste for Germany's war policy. As one of the few, he welcomed the Treaty of Versailles and was convinced of Germany's guilt in the world war. This led to an assassination attempt by members of a *Freikorps*, which he narrowly survived. In 1923, he defected to Switzerland.

Harrer, Karl (1890 - 1926), ultra-right politician and sports journalist with the right-wing *Münchener- Augsburger Abendzeitung*. First chairman of the *Nationalsozialistische Deutsche Arbeiter-Verein*.

Haußmann, Willi. Was involved in the murder of the hostages as deputy commander of the *Luitpold Gymnasium* on 30 April 1919. At the time of his arrest, he committed suicide.

Heindl, *Polizeirat* in Dresden, later *Legationsrat* until 1933 at the Ministry of Foreign Affairs.

Heine, Heinrich (1797 - 1856), poet and journalist of Jewish origin. Converted to Protestantism. His work belongs to the Romantic movement. Worked for some time with Karl Marx together. A prophetic statement by Heine is: *wo man Bücher verbrennt, verbrennt man auch am Ende Men- schen*. Famous poetry collection: *Buch der*

Lieder, which includes *Die Lorelei*. Died in Paris, where he had lived since 1931.

Heise, Karl (1872 - 1939) writer of esoteric works. Gained fame mainly for his *Die Entente-Freimaurerei und der Weltkrieg* (1919). Follower of the ariosophers Guido von List and member of the *Anthroposophischen Gesell- schaft*. Joined the National Socialists.

Hesselmann, Bernhard. Was sentenced to 15 years in prison for involvement in the murder of the hostages in the *Luitpold Gymnasium* on 30 April 1919.

Heß, Rudolf (1872 Alexandria - 1987 Berlin), politician, early Nazi, close associate of Hitler, who appointed him his deputy as chairman of the NSDAP in 1933. Volunteered during World War I. Member of the Thule Society and the *Kampfbund*. Participated in the Hitler-Putsch (*Bierkellerputsch*) in 1923 and was imprisoned with Hitler at Landsberg. As Hitler's private secretary, he edited his *Mein Kampf*. Became chairman of the *Zen tralkommission* of the NSDAP in 1932. Participated in the occupation of Austria, Sudetenland and Poland. After flying to Scotland on his own in May 1941, supposedly with peace proposals, he fell into disgrace and Martin Bor- man became the first man next to Hitler. Sentenced to life imprisonment during the Nuremberg Processes (1945/46). In 1987, committed suicide in Berlin's Spandau prison.

Heuß, Theodor, manufacturer. Partner of Franz Eher Nachf. GmbH, Munich.

Hindorf, Walter. Soldier in the *Husaren-Regiment No. 8*. Was executed at the *Luitpold Gymnasium* on 30 April 1919.

Hitler, Adolf (born 20.4.1889 in Braunau, Austria - 1945 suicide in Berlin). Guest in the Thule society. After high school, he went to Vienna to study architecture. Before finishing art school, he worked as an unskilled labourer. Went to Munich in 1912 where he tries to sell his paintings as a painter. During World War I, he fights as a volunteer in the 16th Bavarian Regiment Infantery *List*, later as a corporal. After 1918, he becomes a training officer in the Reichswehr. In April 1919, Hitler became politically active and joined the *Deutsche Arbeiterpartei* (DAP), of which he became chairman. In February 1920, he founded the *Nationalsozialistische Deutsche Arbeiter Partei (*NSDAP). In a putsch in November 1923, Hitler is arrested and sentenced to five years' imprisonment in Landsberg. During this time, he writes *Mein Kampf*. Is released again in 1924, but is initially banned from speaking. Is appointed Reich Chancellor by president Hindenburg on 30 January 1933.

Hoffmann, Heinz. First public prosecutor in Munich. Was involved in the hostage murder trial.

Hoffmann, Johannes (1867 - 1930), politician. Joined the *Sozialdemokratische Partei Deutschlands* (SPD) in the Landdag in 1908. Was a deputy in the Reichstag from 1912 - 1919. From November 1918 to March 1919 under Kurt Eisner (see there) minister of culture in Bavaria and thereafter prime minister, during which time he and his government defected to Bamberg. Back in Munich, he was forced to resign by the *Freikorps* in March 1920.

Hohenstätter, editor of the *Münchener Neuesten Nachrichten.*

Huber, Georg. Was sentenced to 15 years in prison for involvement in the murder of the hostages in the *Luitpold Gymnasium* on 30 April 1919.

Hugenberg, Alfred (1865 - 1951), politician. Founded the *Alldeutscher Verband (*see there) with Heinrich Claß (see there) in 1891. Until 1919 director-general at Friedrich Krupp AG. Owns Scherlverlag publishing house in 1933. In 1918 co-founder of the conservative, nationalist and anti-Semitic *Deutschnationale Volkspartei* (DNVP), of which he becomes chairman in 1928. In 1933 minister of economic affairs in Hitler's first cabinet.

Iffland, Anna Bertha. Sebottendorff's second wife. Married Sebottendorff in 1915 and divorced in 1928.

International, The First International Workers' Association was founded on 28 September 1864 as an international confederation of socialists and dissolved in 1889 due to conflicts between Marxists and anarchists. A Second International was founded in Paris in 1889. The adherents called themselves Marxists, the anarchists were excluded at the London Congress in 1896. At the outbreak of the First World War, the International fell apart because of disputes about the policy to be pursued with regard to the war. In 1919, under the leadership of the Communist Party of the Soviet Union, the Third In- ternational was founded in Moscow as an alliance between the various communist parties - the *Comintern*. Its aim was: to realise the international revolution and the dictatorship of the proletariat by all means at its disposal. In 1943, the *Comintern* was abandoned because of the Second World War, which had now broken out.

Jaffé, Edgar (1866 - 1921), economist and politician. Member of the *Unabhängige Sozialdemokratische Partei Deutschlands* (USPD). In 1918/18 minister of finance under Kurt Eisner.

Jahreiß, major, was killed by shots from the stands at the opening of the Munich Land Day on 21 February 1919, the same day Eisner was assassinated.

Jakobi, *Arbeiterrat*, responsible editor for the *Zentralrat*'s newspaper.

Calendar, Among the Nazis, people liked to use the old Germanic names for the months. People in NSB circles in the Netherlands also tried to introduce the old names. The old German, resp. old Dutch, resp. current Dutch names read as follows:

Hartung - louw month - January; Hornung - sprokkelmaand - February; Lenzing - spring month -March; Ostermond - grass month - April; Maimond - flowering month - May;

Brachet -summer month - June; Heuert - hay month - July; Ernting - harvest month - August; Separation -

autumn month - Sep- tember; Gilbhard - seed month - October; Neblung - slaughter month - November; Julmond - winter month - December.

Kammerstätter, Alois. Was sentenced to death for involvement in the murder of the hostages in the *Luitpold Gymnasium* on 30 April 1919.

Kampfbund, Fighting squad of an association or group with a political or ideological background to protect their members or intimidate police opponents. Members of right-wing thugs merged into the SA (Sturmabteilung), the thugs of the NSDAP under the command of Ernst Röhm, in the years 1921 - 1923.

Kanzler, Rudolf (1873 – 1956), surveyor, civil servant and politician. Sat as a delegate of the *Deutsche Zentrumspartei* in the Bavarian Landdag from 1905 - 1918. Founder of the *Einwohnerwehr Organisation Kanzler* (Orka), for self- protection of citizens. Had the lead in the establishment of the *Freikorps Chiemgau* in 1919.

Kapp, Wolfgang (1858 New York - 1922 Leipzig) lawyer and politician. His father, Friedrich Kapp, a political activist, had emigrated to America in 1849 after the failed revolution of 1848 and returned to Germany in 1871. An opponent of the Bethmann-Hollweg government (1909 - 1917), he founded the *Deutsche Vaterlandspartei*. In an attempt to overthrow the government of the Weimar Republic, he and General von Lüttwitz staged a coup in Berlin on 13 March 1920. The government fled to Stuttgart and a general strike broke out, causing the coup to fail after five days. Kapp was not prosecuted and finally died of cancer.

Charlemagne, (742 - 814), king of the Franks, Longobards and, from 800, emperor of the Romans. On his numerous campaigns, in 772 he forced the Saxons to become Christians - the Saxon Wars (772 - 804), during which 4,500 Saxons were beheaded near the German town of Verden in 782. His son and successor Louis the Pious had all German sagas and epic poems burned.

Katzenstein, alias Katzi, confidant of Kaiser Wilhelm II.

Koppel, Arthur, major industrialist. Together with Benno Orenstein, he founded Orenstein & Koppel in 1876. The company's activities included the manufacture of earth-moving machinery, escalators, railway equipment, cranes, etc.

Kraus, Edgar, lieutenant. Fought at the front in World War I. Member of the Thule Society and the *Kampfbund* of Thule. Fought the council government in Munich. Leader of the intelligence service of the *Zentrale Oberland*. His investigations led to the arrest of Leviné-Niessen and Buditsch.

Kreß von Kressenstein, Otto, Freiherr (1850 - 1929), ge- neral. From 1912 - 1916 minister of war in Bavaria.

Kreuzzeitung, Officially *Neue Preußische Zeitung*, conser- vative, reactionary and anti-Semitic newspaper published in Berlin from 1848 to 1939. The newspaper 'of the feudal squire and the strict Protestant minister'. An important contributor was Hermann Goedsche, who wrote trivial novels under the name Retcliffe (see there).

Kröpelin, Left-wing politician and member of the College of Eleven, which formed the *Zentralrat* in the Bavarian Raden Republic from February to March 1919.

Kühlmann, Richard von (1873 - 1948), diplomat. From 1917 - 1918 secretary of state for foreign affairs. Made the peace of Brest-Litovsk (3.3.1918) and Bucharest (7.5.1918), settling peace with Soviet Russia.

Kun, Bela (1886 - 1938), politician and Bolshevik. Led the revolution in Hungary and established a council government there from 21 March to 1 August 1919. After the fall of the government, he fled to Russia via Austria. Executed in purges under Stalin in 1938.

Kunze, Dora - see at Glauer, Dora.

Kupfer, Adjutant to Major Beth of *Freikorps Oberland.*

Kurz, Heinz, first lieutenant. Adjutant of *Zentrale Oberland.*

Laforce, Wilhelm (born 1886). Worked in the advertising department of the *Beobachter.* Member of Hitler's *Stoßtrupp* (later SA). Was sentenced to prison in Landsberg together with Hitler for high treason after the Hitler-Putsch of 8/9 November 1923.

Landauer, Gustav (1870 - 1919), writer, anarchist and pacifist. Came to Munich at the invitation of Eisner (see there) to take part in the revolution and was far- according to his cabinet. Withdrew after the coup from politics by the communists led by Leviné (see there). After the defeat of the Raden Republic (see there), he was arrested by soldiers of the *Freikorps* (see there) on 1 May 1919 and murdered a day later in the Stadelheim prison (see there).

Landauer, Hugo. Lawyer and friend of Kurt Eisner (see there).

Lasalle, Ferdinand (1825 - 1864), socialist and politician. Founded the *Allgemeiner Deutscher Arbeiterverein* in 1863, one of the forerunners of the SPD.

Lehmann, Julius Friedrich (1864 - 1935), bookseller and publisher, fierce anti-Semite. Initially published medical literature, but early on supplied Munich with fascist, racist and anti-Semitic literature. Member of the *Deutschnationale Volkspartei* and later of the NSDAP, which he supported financially, as well as its leaders, including Hitler (see there) and Rosenberg (see there). Published, among others, the monthly journal *Deutschlands Erneuerung* in 1917; the journal *Archiv für Rassen- und Gesellschaftsbiologie* in 1922 and the *Zeitschrift für Rassenhygiene* in 1928. For his achievements, the Nazi regime awarded him the highest prize for science, an honorary doctorate at the University of Munich and an honorary membership of the NSDAP.

Leib, publisher of the Munich newspaper *Republikaner*.

Lermer, Georg. Was sentenced to 15 years in prison for involvement in the murder of the hostages in the *Luitpold Gymnasium* on 30 April 1919.

Lessing, Gotthold Ephraim (1729 - 1781), writer and poet of the German Enlightenment and Freemason. Advocate of tolerance and against any form of intolerance. Well-known plays of his are: *Emilia Galotti*, *Minna von Barnhelm* and *Nathan der Weise*.

Levien, Max (1885 Moscow - 1937 Soviet Union), politician and communist. Came to Germany early because of his studies in natural sciences. Took part in the Russian Revolution of 1905/06; later came into contact with Lenin in Switzerland and became a Bolshevik. After his promotion, he obtained German citizenship and served as a volunteer soldier in the First World War. After the war, Levien became chairman of the *Soldatenrat* in Munich. Took part in the founding of the *Kommunistische Partei Deutschlands* (KPD) and published *Die Rote Fahne* in Munich. When the Raden Republic (see there) collapsed in 1919, Levien was arrested but was able to flee to Vienna. Returned to Russia and joined the Russian Communist Party. Was sentenced to death in the Great Suicide in 1936.

Leviné, Eugen (1883 St Petersburg - 1919 Munich), economist and left-wing politician. Came to Germany as early as 1886. Took part in the Russian Revolution in 1905/06. Returned to Germany and studied economics. During World War I, member of the *Unabhängige Sozialdemokratische Partei Deutschlands* (USDP). Co-founder of the Spartakus Union in 1919 and was among the leaders of the newly founded *Kommunistische Partei Deutschlands (*KPD). Came to Munich in 1919 and became leader of the Raden Republic (see there). Arrested after quashing the revolt, convicted of high treason and imprisoned in Stadelheim prison (see there), and executed. (According to Sebottendorff, Leviné was also called Niessen; that would have been his wife's name).

Liebenfels, Jörg Lanz von (1874 - 1954), gnostic and racist. His real name was Adolf Joseph Lanz. From 1893 - 1899 monk in a Cistercian monastery near Vienna. Founded the Order of the New Templars in 1900. Lanz called the racist theories he developed, which he proclaimed as science, ariosophy. From 1905 - 1917, he edited the racist journal *Ostara*. Liebenfels had great influence on Nazi ideology.

Liebermann von Sonnenberg, (1848 - 1911), politician. Together with Stöcker (see there), founded the *Christ- lich-Soziale Arbeiterpartei* in 1878, which later merged into the *Deutschkonservative Partei* (DKP).

Liebknecht, Karl (1871 - 1919) Left-wing politician and pacifist. Studied law and economics and came into contact with Marxism. In 1900, he joined the *Sozialdemokrati- sche Partei Deutschlands* (SPD), which he would later sharply criticise. Elected to the Reichstag in 1912. Together with Rosa Luxemburg, founded the Spartakusbond in 1915, which would merge into the

Kommunistische Partei Deutschlands (KPD) in 1918. Together with Rosa Luxemburg, unleashed the Spartakus revolt in Berlin in January 1919, forcing Friedrich Ebert's government to defect to Weimar. The revolt was bloodily put down and both Liebknecht and Luxemburg were imprisoned, tortured and horribly murdered.

Liebknecht, Theodor (1870 - 1948), lawyer and brother of Karl Liebknecht. Defender in the trial for the murder of the hostages.

Lindner, butcher and communist. Shot Auer in the Beierse Landdag in 1919. Lindner fled to Austria, was arrested and extradited there and sentenced to several years in prison.

Lipp, Franz (1855 - 1937), left-wing politician. Foreign minister during the Bavarian Raden Republic in 1919. Declared war on Switzerland. Best known for his telegram to Lenin (according to Sebottendorff, to Chichitcherin, the foreign minister in Soviet Russia), the contents of which read: 'Proletariat of Upper Bavaria shares in the revelry. Socialists, independent socialists and communists united as a warhammer, together with the peasant union. Liberal bourgeoisie as servant of Prussia completely disarmed. Hoffmann fled to Bamberg, taking with him the key to my ministry's toilet. Prussian politics, of which Hoffmann is the lackey, is trying to cut us off from the north, Berlin, Leipzig, Nuremberg, also from Frankfurt and from the coal region around Essen, and at the same time make us suspect to the Entente as bloodhonours and looters. And all this while Gustav

Noske's hairy gorilla hands are dripping with blood. We get coal and food in abundance from Switzerland and Italy. We want peace forever. Immanuel Kant on eternal peace 1795, Thesis 2-5. Pruisen wants the truce only to take revenge.'

Guido von List, (1848 - 1919), journalist and writer of esoteric, racist works. Following in the footsteps of Liebenfels (see there), List was a popular representative of the *völkisch* movement. List was particularly concerned with Germanic mythology and with theosophy. In 1908, he founded the *Guido-von-List Gesellschaft*. In the same year, his *Das Geheimnis der Runen* was published. Had great influence on the later National Socialists, including Heinrich Himmler.

Luitpold Gymnasium, Named after Prince Regent Lui- tpold von Bayern (1821 - 1912). The gymnasium opened in 1891 and was located at Müllerstraße 5-7 in Munich. The school was used in 1918 to accommodate soldiers returning from the war. In March 1919, it was occupied by red guards. The murder of hostages took place here on 30 April 1919. In 1944, the building was bombed. Now Albert Einstein grammar school.

Linnenbrügger, Fritz (1878 - 1919) Private first class in the Regiment Hussars 1, No. 8. Was one of the victims of the murder of the hostages in the *Luitpold Gymnasium* on 30 April 1919.

Luther, Martin dr (1483 - 1546), theologian and church her- former. Translated the Bible into German and caused a church schism in 1517 by announcing his 95 thesis against the sale of indulgences, whereupon he was banished by the Pope in 1521. This marked the break with the Catholic Church. Luther made anti-Semitic statements in his works.

Luxemburg, Rosa (1871 Zamość, Poland - 1919), Marxist politician. Was forced to flee at the age of 16 because of revolutionary activities and arrived in Switzerland, where she came into contact with Russian revolutionaries. Studies law and obtains a doctorate *magna cum laude*. In 1898 she returned to Poland, where she founded the Social Democratic Party of Poland, but soon had to flee again, this time to Germany. During the First World War, she was repeatedly imprisoned for political activities. There she met Karl Liebknecht (see there) and became the leader of the left wing of the *Sozialdemokratische Partei Deutschlands* (SPD). In 1918, together with Karl Liebknecht, she transforms the Sparatkusbond (see there) into the *Kommunistische Partei Deutschlands* (KPD) and unleashes the Spartakus revolt, forcing Friedrich Ebert's government to defect to Weimar. The revolt is bloodily put down and both Liebknecht and Luxemburg are captured, tortured and murdered by Herman Wilhelm Souchon, a member of a *Freikorps* (see there). Rosa's corpse is thrown into the Landwehr Canal.

Mairgünther, In 1919 chief of police during the Raden Republic (see there) in Bavaria and friend of Axelrod. Provided passports for the benefit of revolutionary leaders so that they could flee.

Malsen-Ponickau, Freiherr von (1895 - 1956). Police officer. Supported the *Kampfbund* of Thule in 1919 and joined the *Freikorps Epp*. Joined the NSDAP in 1930. Worked as chief constable in various towns, including at Dachau concentration camp. Later appointed by Himmler to *SS-Brigadeführer*.

Maenner, (born 1893), bank employee. In 1919 minister of finance during the Raden Republic in Bavaria.

Marx, Karl (1818 Trier - 1883 London), economist and sociologist. Founder of the labour movement. Published the *Communist Manifesto* with Friedrich Engels in 1847. Collaborated in the creation of the First International in 1864. His main work, *Das Kapital*, appeared in 1867.

Sailors' revolt, Started in Kiel in November 1918. Navy sailors refused the order for a decisive battle against England to sail. The merchant navy joined the mutinous sailors, which finally led to the November Revolution and the fall of the monarchy.

Mehrer, In 1919 city commander of Munich during the Raden Republic.

Miesbacher Anzeiger, One of the best-known newspapers in Germany after World War I. Was founded in 1874, initially a liberal, after 1900 conservative newspaper. After World War I, the newspaper led by Klaus Eck (see there) became a forum of the far right and a source of anti- Semitic and National Socialist propaganda. Dietrich Eckart (see there) and Bernhard Stempfle (see there) wrote a.o. for the newspaper. Banned by the Allies in 1945.

Millibauer, (=milkman). Nickname for King Ludwig III of Bavaria, given by leftist politicians, to protest against the sale (alleged or otherwise) of milk and butter to Prussia.

Möhl, Arnold, Ritter von (1867 - 1944) general in the *Reichswehr*. Received supreme command of parts of the Bavarian and Württembergian *Reichswehr* and the joint *Freikorps (*April 1919) at the Munich defeat of the Raden Republic (see there).

Molz, Anni, secretary of the Thule Society.

Mommsen, Theodor (1817 - 1903) historian and archaeologist. Received the Nobel Prize for literature in 1902.

Much, historian and physician.

Mühsam, Erich (1878 - 1934) writer and anarchist. Would initially become a pharmacist. Moved to Munich in 1909, where he published the journal *Kain. Zeitschrift für Menschlichkeit* and became friends with Heinrich Mann, Frank Wedekind and Lion Feutschtwanger, among others. From 1916 - 1918 co-organiser of protests and strikes against the war. Together with Gustav Landauer (see there) and Ernst Toller (see there), proclaimed the Raden Republic on 7 April 1919. After quashing the republic and serving a prison sentence, he goes to Berlin. On the day of the Reich fire on 27 February 1933, he was arrested there and murdered by the Nazis in concen- tration camp Oranienburg in 1934.

Müller, Hanns Georg. Fought at the front in World War I. After 1919 editor of the *Beobachter*.

Nationalversammlung, National Assembly. The government, which was elected on 19 January 1919 and lasted from 6 February 1919 to 6 June 1920. It met mainly in Weimar.

Nauhaus, Walter (1892 - 1919), sculptor. Joined the *Germanic orders* early on. Took part in the First World War and returned as a war invalid. Was killed as a hostage in the *Luitpold Gymnasium* on 30 April 1919.

Neurath, Otto (1882 - 1945), Austrian, economist. Was appointed state commissioner and chairman of the *Zentralwirtschaftsrat* (Economic Affairs) in the Bavarian Council Republic, with the task of socialising business. From this position, Neurath strove for a cashless society. Was arrested after the defeat of the Raden Republic and extradited to Austria.

Niekisch, Ernst (1889 - 1967), educator, politician and writer. Joined the *Sozialdemokratische Partei Deutschlands* (SPD) in 1917. In 1918/19 chairman of the *Zentrale Arbeiter- und Soldatenrat*, Munich. Arrested after the defeat of the Raden Republic (see there) and sentenced to 2 years' imprisonment, which he served together with Ernst Toller (see there) and Erich Mühsam (see there).

From 1919 - 1922 for the *Unabhängige Sozialdemokratsche Partei Deutschlands* (USPD) in the Bavarian Diet. Warned of Hitler's rise to power in 1932 with his publication *Hitler - ein deutsches Verhängnis* (Hitler - a German disaster). Stubbornly opposed National Socialism. Sentenced to life imprisonment in 1937. After World War II in East Berlin. Initially joined the *Kommunistische Partei Deutschlands* (KPD), later the *So- zialistische Einheitspartei Deutschlands* (SED). In 1948 pro- fessor at the Humboldt-Universität (GDR), where the German historian Werner Maser was one of his assistants. After the 17 June 1953 uprising, he withdrew from politics and moved to West Berlin in 1963.

Nies, a pupil at the police school, escaped execution at the Lutepold Gymnasium on 30 April 1919.

Noske, Gustav (1868 - 1946), basket maker, politician. Became a member of the *Sozialdemokratsche Partei Deutschland* (SPD) in 1884. In 1919 in the *Weimarer Nationalversam- mlung*, where, as Reich Minister of War, he was responsible for quelling the Spartakus uprising, in which Karl Liebknecht (see there) and Rosa Luxemburg (see there) were murdered. Subsequently also supported the crushing of several Raden republics, including that in Munich. When he wanted to abolish the *Freikorps* in 1920, it came to the Kapp-Lüttwitz-Putsch on 13 March 1920 in Munich and he was forced to resign as minister.

Osel, deputy of the Bayerische Volkspartei. Was killed by shots from the gallery at the Landdag meeting on 21 February 1919.

Ostara, 1. From Ostern (= Easter). Germanic goddess of spring, feast of the equinox (20 March), when day and night are of equal length and the sun rises in the northern hemisphere; later became the Christian festival of Easter.

2. Name of racist journal edited by Jörg Lanz von Liebenfels (see there).

Ott, Johann, became a member of the Thule Society and of the *Kampfbund* of Thule in 1918, also a commercial employee of the *Münchener Beobachter* and, in 1919, head of publishing house *Münchener Beobachter* (later *Völkischer Beobachter*), *Verlag Franz Eher Nachf.*

Parcus, Leo. Lieutenant. Member of the *Kampfbund* of Thule and of *Freikorps Oberland*.

Pallabene, Chief of Police during the Munich Raden Republic.

Penka, According to Sebottendorff scientist, who proved that all culture came from the north and came exclusively from Aryans.

Pickl, Joseph. Became manager of *Franz Eher Nachf. GmbH*, after the publishing house, where the *Völkischer Beobachter* appeared, was taken over from Hitler by the NSDAP. Employee of Dietyrich Eckart in 1921 (see there).

Pohl, Hermann. Calibrationist in Magdeburg. Founder of an anti-Semitic lodge there and co-founder of the Germanic orders (see there). Died in Berlin in 1925.

Pöhner, Ernst (1870 - 1925) jurist member of the *Alldeutscher Verband (*see there). In 1918 director of the notorious Stadelheim prison and in 1919 chief of police in Munich. Member of the NSDAP and later of the *Deutschnationale Volkspartei* (DNVP). Helped overthrow the government Hoffmann in 1920. Participated in the Hitler-Putsch in 1923 and was sentenced to five years in prison for high treason, but released after three months. Killed in a car accident in 1925.

Polenz, Wilhelm (1861 - 1903), writer. Wrote naturalistic regional novels with anti-Semitic overtones. His famous novel, at the time, *Der Büttnerbauer* (1895), was highly praised by Hitler.

Pückler-Muskau, Hermann Ludwig Heinrich, Fürst von (1785 - 1871), large landowner in Prussia, officer, world traveller, writer.

Pürzer, Georg. Was sentenced to death for involvement in the murder of the hostages in the *Luitpold Gymnasium* on 30 April 1919.

Radek, Karl (1885, Lemberg - formerly Polish, is now Lviv in western Ukraine - 1939), left-wing politician and journalist) His real name was Karol Sobelsohn. Came to Germany in 1907 and joined the *Sozialdemokratische Partei Deutschlands* (SPD). Was expelled from the country in 1913. After the outbreak of the First World War (1914), he goes to Switzerland, where he gets to know Lenin and Zinoviev. Joins the Central Committee of the Communist Party of the Soviet Union in St Petersburg in 1917. Is involved in the Spartakus uprising in Berlin in 1919. Secretary of the *Comintern* in 1920, but expelled from the party in 1927 for supporting Trotsky and the Left Opposition. Arrested in 1936 during the Great Purge on Stalin and sentenced to 10 years' hard labour. Assassinated in 1939 on the order of Beria (head of the NKVD (People's Commissariat for Internal Affairs - predecessor of the KGB - the secret service).

Council republic in Munich, The era of the council revolutions began in early November 1918 with the sailors' revolt (see there) in Kiel. The revolution spread to Munich on 7 November and was led by Kurt Eisner (see there), leader of the *Unabhängige Sozialdemokra- tische Partei Deutschlands* (USDP), which declared the *Freistaat Bayern*, with King Ludwig III having to flee and Eisner himself becoming prime minister. In the January 1919 elections, the USDP suffered a heavy defeat. On 21 February 1919, Eisner resigned and was assassinated in the street. Supporters of Eisner wanted to overthrow the new government led by Johannes Hoffmann (see there) of the *Sozialdemokratsche Partei Deutschlands* (SPD) and, together with the anarchists, proclaimed the Munich Radenrepublik on 7 April 1919 and expelled Hoffmann and his government to Bamberg. The new government, led by the chairman of the *Zentrale Arbeiter- und Soldaten- rat* Ernst Toller (USPD) (see there), who was assisted by the Council of People's Commissars (ministers). At the behest of Hoffmann and the German government, *Freikorpsen (see there)* and *Reichswehr* stormed Munich on

13 April 1919. A red army hastily formed by the communists under the command of Leviné (see there) managed to repel the attack. Meanwhile, the communists joined the Raden government. On 1 May 1919, the *Freikorps Epp* entered Munich, defeated the Red Army and liberated Munich.

Rathenau, Walther (1867 - 1922), industrialist, politician, publicist. Son of Emil Rathenau, founder of the AEG concern. Became chairman of the Supervisory Board in 1915, after his father's death. After World War I, founder of the *Deutsche Demokratische Partei* (DDP). Minister of Reconstruction in 1921 and foreign minister in 1922. Assassinated by far-right officers on 24 June 1922.

Rauscher, Ulrich (1884 - 1933), journalist and diplomat. During the First World War, press chief in the governorate of Belgium. After the war, private secretary to Reichminister President Philipp Scheidemann and in 1919 press chief of the Reich Government. In 1920 ambassador to Georgia and later to Poland.

Republikanische Schutzwehr, A militant group loyal to the Hof- fmann government (see there) led by Heinrich Aschenbrenner (see there), which attempted to overthrow the Radenre- public (see there) on 13 April 1919.

Retcliffe, John, Sir (1815 - 1878), pseudonym of Hermann Goedsche, also called himself *Hofrat* Schneider, among others, writer of anti-Semitic novels. Wrote, among others, the novel Biarritz, which became the source of the later *Protocols of the Wisemen of Zion*.

Rick, Johannes. Was sentenced to 15 years in prison for involvement in the murder of the hostages in the *Luitpold Gymnasium* on 30 April 1919.

Riemann, Hans, teacher. Joined the Thule party in 1919. Member of the NSDAP. Had to give up teaching because of his extreme right-wing affiliation.

Riemann-Bucherer, Gertrud, wife of Hans Riemann and member of the Thule Society. Singing teacher in Munich.

Riethmeyer, Johann. Was sentenced to 15 years in prison for involvement in the murder of the hostages in the *Luitpold Gymnasium* on 30 April 1919.

Ritzler, Konrad (b. 1883), member of the *Republikanische Schutztruppe*, which, under the command of Alfred Seyffertitz (see there), tried unsuccessfully to overthrow the Raden government on Palm Sunday 13. April 1919.

Rohmeder, Wilhelm, teacher and president of the *Deutschen Schulverein* and various *völkische* (see there) groups. Member of the *Germanic orders* (see there).

Rosenberg, Alfred (1893, Tallin, Estonia - 1946 Nuremberg). Experienced the Russian revolution and became an anti-communist. Came to Munich in 1919, joined the Deutsche Arbeiter Partei (DAP), later NS-

DAP. Guest of the Thule Society (see there). Became editor in 1921 and editor-in-chief of the *Völkischer Beobachter* in 1923. After the failed coup of 23 November 1923, he replaced Adolf Hitler (see there) as party leader of the NSDAP. Published his most important work in 1930: *Der Mythos des 20. Jahrhunderts*, in which he attacked both Judaism and Christianity. After taking power in 1933, held various positions within the NSDAP. During the Nuremberg Trials in 1945/46, Rosenberg was convicted of war crimes and crimes against humanity and hanged on 1 October 1946.

Roßhaupter, Albert (born 1878), lacquer worker and left- wing politician. Was minister of war from 9 November 1918 to 17 March 1919 under Kurt Eisner.

Rosicrucians, Occult, secret society allegedly founded in 1484 by the legendary Christian Rosenkreuz. Initially receiving little attention, the movement revived in the 18th century, however, and in the freemasons occupied an important place. Several Rosicrucian movements emerged in the 19th and 20th centuries. Rosicrucian theories also played a role in the founding of Helena Blavatsky's theosophical movement and Rudolf Steiner's anthroposophical movement (see there).

Rothschild, Jewish family, who started a bank in Frankfurt am Main around 1800. Mayer Amschel Rothschild (1744 - 1812) had five sons, who successfully expanded the banking business across Europe. Today, the bank operates in 40 countries and employs 2,800 people.

Ruf, mayor in Bad Aibling.

Runes, 1. Runic writing is the oldest known script used by Germanic peoples in northern Europe. Old Germanic runic series are also called *futhark*.
2. Name of a monthly magazine for the benefit of friends of the *Teutonic orders*.

S.A., Sturm-Abteilung. Formed in 1921, the NSDAP's brawling squad under the command of Ernst Röhm, created from the *Freikorps* (see there). Were also called 'brown-shirts'. After the Hitlerputsch of 8/9 November 1923, both the SA and the NSDAP were temporarily banned. When it took power in 1933, the SA already had 400,000 men. Due to a controversy between Hitler (see there) and Röhm, during the *Night of the Long Knives* (Röhm-Putsch) on 30 June 1934, the entire top of the SA, including Röhm, was eliminated and murdered by Hein- rich Himmler's SS. Thereafter, the SA merged into Himmler's SS.

Salz, Professor at Heidelberg. Helped Leviné (see there) flee in 1919.

Sauber, left-wing politician and member of the College of Eleven, which formed the *Zentralrat* in the Beierse Raden Republic from February to March 1919. Was arrested at the suppression of a communist coup in Würzburg.

Sauter, Munich lawyer. Acted as defence counsel for the nine defendants in the trial surrounding the murder of the hostages of 30 April 1919.

Schaible, Chief official from Baden-Württemberg.

Scheidemann, Philipp (1865 - 1939), book printer, politician. Became a member of the *Sozialdemokratische Partei Deutschlands* (SPD) in 1883. From 1903 to 1933, he was a deputy and vice-chairman respectively in the Reichstag. In 1918, Scheidemann proclaimed the German Republic to get ahead of Karl Liebknecht (see there), who was pursuing a Raden Republic (see there). On 11 November 1918, he became a member of the Council of People's Commissars and, on 13 February 1919, Reich Prime Minister. In June of the same year, he resigned because of disagreements regarding the Treaty of Versailles. Mayor of Kassel from 1920 to 1926. Criticised the extreme right, leading to a failed assassination attempt in 1922. After Hitler's rise to power in 1933, he emigrates to Denmark.

Schicklhofer, Johann. Was sentenced to death for involvement in the murder of the hostages in the *Luitpold Gymnasium* on 30 April 1919.

Schneider, Louis, *Hofrat* (1805 - 1878), actor and writer. Would have written historical novels together with Hermann Goedsche (Retcliffe - see there).

Schneppenhorst, Ernst Wilhelm (1881 - 1945), carpenter. Was a trade union leader from 1906 - 1918. Member of the *Sozialdemokratische Partei Deutschlands* (SPD) and delegate in the Bavarian Landdag. During the Raden Republic in Munich (see there) under Prime Minister Hoffmann (see there) from 18 March to 22 August 1919, Minister of Military Affairs. Resisted the na- tional socialists and had to go into hiding. Was repeatedly arrested and sentenced to prison after 1937. Together with Wilhelm Leuschner, he organised resistance groups. Finally murdered in 1945 shortly before the capitulation by a *Sonderkommando* of the *Reichssicherheitshauptamt*.

Schödel, member of Zentrale Oberland.

Schülein, 1. Lawyer in Munich. 2. *Kommerzienrat,* director of the Löwen brewery in Munich.

Schwabe, Karl. Lieutenant. Fought in the First World War. Member of the *Kampfbund* of the Thule Society in 1918. Also worked for the *Zentrale Oberland.*

Sedlmeier, Hermann (born 1896) lieutenant. Fought as a volunteer in World War I in the Regiment List. Member of the Thule Society and the *Kampfbund.* Founded the *Freikorps Schäfer* in 1919. Later owner of *Ring-Restaurant- Café* in Munich.

Segitz, Martin (1853 - 1927), metal worker, trade union leader and politician. Member of the *Sozialdemokratische Partei Deutschlands* (SPD). Served in the Reichstag as Minister of Demobilisation, among others, and as Minister of the Interior, later of Social Affairs in the Bavarian Diet.

Seidel, Fritz. Was sentenced to death for involvement in the murder of the hostages in the *Luitpold Gymnasium* on 30 April 1919.

Seidl, Josef. Was sentenced to death for involvement in the murder of the hostages in the *Luitpold Gymnasium* on 30 April 1919.

Seidler, Liesbeth. Ex-wife of a restaurant owner in Berlin. She was trained as a clairvoyant by the dentist Dr Hummel around 1909. Was then with the police and kept a salon for gay men, such as Alsberg, Heindl. etc, friend of the Moltke family and of Rudolf Steiner. She became known for the *Sklarek scandal* (the corruption scandal surrounding the Sklarek brothers in Berlin, which occupied minds from 1926 - 1932).

Seidlitz, Friedrich Wilhelm, Freiherr von (1891 - 1919), painter. Member of the Thule Society and the *Kampfbund.* Was murdered as a hostage in the *Luitpold Gymnasium* by red guards on 30 April 1919.

Seyffertitz, Alfred (born 1884), painter. Was chairman of the soldiers' council from 1918/19, city commander in Munich and commander of the *Bayrische Republikanische Landesschutztruppe.*

Sell, Doorman of hotel *Vier Jahreszeiten* (see there) in Munich, where the Thule Society (see there) met.

Semi-Alliancen, List of noblemen who had married Jews, compiled by Baron Wittgenberg (see there) and published in 1914 by Philipp Stauff (see there).

Semi-Gotha, List of all descendants of Jews who were raised to the peerage, compiled along the lines of the

Gotha Almanac (yearbook published in Gotha since 1763), compiled by Baron Wittgenberg (see there) and published in 1914 by Philipp Stauff (see there).

Semi-Kürschner, List of Jews from industry, science and art, compiled by Baron Wittgenberg (see there) and published in 1914 by Philipp Stauff (see there).

Sesselmann, Max. Became a member of the Thule Society in March 1919 and editor of the *Völkischer Beobachter* in July the same year. Was a member of the *völkisch* anti-semi- tische *Deutschsozialistische Partei*. Took part in the Hitler-Putsch in November 1923. Became delegate for the *völkisch* bloc in the Bavarian Landdag. After Sebottendorff was forced to resign the chairmanship of the Thule Society, Sesselmann became one of its leaders. It was also he who, due to lack of interest, dissolved the society in 1930.

Siebert, Ludwig 1874 - 1942), lawyer and politician, member of the *Bayerische Volkspartei*. From 1908 - 1919 first civic master of Rothenburg ob der Tauber, later of Lindau.

Joined the NSDAP in 1931. Enters the Bavarian Landdag as finance minister under Reich Commissioner Franz Ritter von Epp (see there). Becomes prime minister of Bavaria in 1933 and also *SA-Gruppenführer*. From 1933 - 1942 in the Reichstag as deputy for Oberbayern and Sch- waben.

Simon, left-wing politician and member of the College of Eleven, which formed the *Zentralrat* in the Beierse Raden Republic from February to March 1919.

Spartakusbund, Association of Marxist socialists, formed in World War I, which wanted to end capitalism, imperialism and militarism through revolution. Led by Rosa Luxemburg (see there) and Karl Liebknecht (see there), they unleashed an uprising in Kiel in 1918 in response to the sailors' revolt (see there), leading to the November Revolution. In 1919, the Spartakusbund merged into the *Kommunistische Partei Deutschlands* (KPD). The name of the group was taken from Spartacus, the leader of the slave revolt in ancient Rome (73 - 71 BC).

Spitzer, Julius, merchant and lawyer. Commercial judge in Barmen.

S.S., (= Schutzstaffel). Paramilitary organisation of the NSDAP. Established in 1925 as Adolf Hitler's bodyguard. Originated from the S.A. (see there), which was founded on 4. November 1921 and was led by Ernst Röhm.

Stadelheim, Notorious prison in Munich, where many prominent Germans were imprisoned. Built in 1894.

Since 1901, death sentences were also carried out here, most of them in the period from 1933-1945.

Stauff, Philipp (1876 - 1923), educator, publisher and writer. Early on wrote for *völkische* blades. Chairman of the *Guido-von-List-Gesellschaft* and active in the anti-semi- tic *Hammerbund* and, since 1912, in the Germanic orders. In 1913, he published his *Runenhäuser*. In July 1923 comitted suicide in Berlin.

Stecher, Karl. Student. Fought in World War I. Member of the Kampfbund of Thule. Killed on 2 May 1919 while fighting for Munich.

Steiner, Rudolf (1861 - 1926), philosopher, writer, archi- tect and educator. Founder of anthroposophy. Wrote several philosophical works. Also dealt with many other areas of social life.

Stempfle, Bernhard (1882 - 1934), theologian and publicist. Was originally a monk, later professor of theology at the University of Munich. During the First World War a member of the far-right *Organisation Kanzler* (Orka). Wrote under the ps. Redivivus articles for the *Völkischer Beobachter*. From 1922 - 1925 publisher and editor of the fanatically anti-Semitic *Miesbacher Anzeiger (*see there). Was well known in National Socialist circles and involved in political assassinations. Would have co-edited Hitler's *Mein Kampf*. In 1926 went into temporary hiding in Austria. In 1929 manager of the NSDAP archive. Arrested and murdered by the Gestapo or SS during a purge in 1934.

Stiegeler, Hans. Book printer in Munich.

Stöcker, Adolf (1835 - 1909), theologian and politician and an- tisemite. Founded the *Christlich-Soziale Arbeiterpartei* in 1878, which later merged into the *Deutschkonservative Partei* (DKP). Due to a corruption scandal, Stöcker had to leave the party.

Streicher, Julius (1885 - 1946), Nazi leader, journalist and notorious anti-Semite. Fought as a lieutenant in the First

World War. After the war, he founded the anti- Semitic *Deutsch-Sozialistische Partei*, which merged into the NSDAP in 1922. Participated in the Hitler-Putsch of November 1923 and subsequently became party secretary in Nuremberg. Founded the weekly *Der Stürmer* in 1925, which became notorious for its hatred of Jews and sedition. Became Gouwleider of Franconia in 1933. Arrested by the Americans in 1945 and sentenced to the noose at the Nuremberg trials.

Strelenko, Andreas. Was sentenced to 15 years in prison for involvement in the murder of the hostages in the *Luitpold Gymnasium* on 30 April 1919.

Sulla, Lucius Cornelius (138 - 78 BC) Roman general and statesman. Consul and dictator.

Talaat, Mehmet Pasha (1872 Edirne - 1921 Berlin), apo- theker's assistant and politician. Was among the leaders of the Young Turk Revolution in 1908, who staged a coup d'état after the Balkan War (1912/13) and came to power in Turkey. Talaat played a leading role in the genocide of Armenians in 1915. From 1917- 1918 grand vizier (prime minister) of the Ottoman Empire. In October 1918, Talaat was deposed and had to flee. Assassinated by an Armenian in Berlin in 1921.

Teuchert, Franz Karl, Freiherr von (1900 - 1919), first lieutenant. Fought from 1916 -1918 in the First World War . Member of the Thule Society and of *Freikorps Regensburg*. Was murdered as a hostage in the *Luitpold Gymnasium* by red guards on 30 April 1919.

Thule, Also called Ultima Thule. Mythical island in the far north. First mentioned around 400 BC by the Greek mariner and geographer Pytheas of Massalia. Possibly meant Iceland, the Shetland Islands or the Orkney Islands. In the Middle Ages, Thule stood for Iceland. In National Socialist ideology, Thule was the last refuge for the Germanic people, who did not want to convert to Christianity.

Thule-Bote, Organ of the Thule Society (see there). Published by publisher Deukla, Grassinger & Co., Munich, and distributed through the post office.

Thule Society, Anti-Semitic and right-wing extremist organisation, founded in 1918 by Rudolf von Sebottendorff (see there). One of the inspirations of National Socialism. Published the *Münchener Beobachter*, later the *Völkischer Beobachter*. The society supplied a number of leaders of the Nazi regime. In 1919, on the initiative of Karl Harrer (see there) and Anton Drexler (see there), the *Deutsche Arbeiterpartei* (DAP) emerged from the society, of which Hitler (see there) became a member. Shortly afterwards, Hitler transformed the party into the NSDAP. Thereafter, the Thule Society, which had about 200 members, rapidly lost significance.

In 1925, it was disbanded due to lack of interest. In 1933, Sebottendorff tried in vain to revive the society.

Members of the Thule Society were: (*Kampfund* after the name means: also a member of the *Kampfbund* of Thule):

Andersch, Alfred
Annacker, Johan
Arndt, Julius, (alleen *Kampfbund*),
Aßmann, Ludwig,
Baldauf, Georg
Baller, Alfred
Bartels, Fritz
Bauer, Hermann
Bauer, Josephine
Bauer, Ludwig
Baumer, Anna
Bayrhammer, Max
Becker, Berta
Besnard
Bierbaumer, Käthe
Birner, Hedwig
Birner, Max
Block, Nora
Bodmann, Hans Hermann (*Kampfbund*)
Born, Kurt
Brehm, Georg
Bruno, Alfred
Büchold, Valentin
Bunge, Hans (*Kampfbund*)
Closmann, Hans
Closmann, Hugo
Coblitz, Franz
Dahn, Hanns
Dannehl, Franz (*Kampfbund*)
Danner, Mathilde
Daudistel, August
Daumenlang, Anton
Deby, Theo *(Kampfbund)*
Dechaud, Georg
Deiglmeier, Elisabeth
Deike, Walter
Demmel, Auguste
Demockl, Ida
Dresel, Maximilian
Düntzel, Hans
Eckart, Paul
Ehrengut, Leopold
Engelbrecht, Otto
Feilitzsch, Franz (alleen *Kampfbund*)
Feldbauer, Hermann

Fiehler, Karl (erelid)
Frank, Michel Hans
Freudenberger, Lucie
Freyholt, Ella von
Fries, Valentin
Frühauf, Ludwig
Führer, Thesi
Fülle, Anton
Funk, Leonhard
Gaiser, Karl
Gathmann, Erna
Gathmann, Otto
Gaubatz, Georg
Gaubatz, Käthe
Gessel, Tilde
Geyer, Johann
Göppeler, Hans
Gräber, Georg
Grassinger, Hans (*Kampfbund*)
Griehl, Arthur
Gronbach, Adolf
Gutberlet, Wilhelm (alleen *Kampfbund*)
Häckel, Ernst
Halbritter, Ernst
Hammer, Johann
Hammermayer, Ernst
Hampel, Paul
Harrer, Karl
Hartmann, Fritz
Heiden, Adolf von
Heim, Gustav
Heimburg, Werner von
Herbst, Fritz
Herdegen, Johann
Hering, Elsa
Hering, Johannes
Hering, Therese
Hertel, Otto
Heß, Rudolf (*Kampfbund*)
Heuß, Theodor
Hollerith, Franz
Hollweg, Fritz
Hölzl, Hermann
Holzwarth, Willi
Holnstein, Graf von
Holnstein, Gräfin von
Horn, Adolf
Hühmann, Alwine
Jakobi, Karl
Imhof, Rudolf von
Jost, Heinrich
Kahl, Wilhelm
Kaindl, Georg
Kaiser, Johann
Karl, Laura
Karl, Maria
Kautzer, Eugen
Kerlen, Kurt
Keßler, Georg
Klein, Ernst
Kleinmann, Hugo
Klöck, Anton
Knauf, Friedrich
Knauf, Grete

Kneil, Elisabeth
Kneil, Julius
Krallinger, Johann
Kraus, Edgar (*Kamfbund*)
Kurz, Heinz (*Kampfbund*)
Lack, Josef
Laforce, Wilhelm
Lang, Karl
Lang, Michael
Langenegger, Lia
Legl, Georg
Lehmann, Julius
Leoprechting, Karl
Leoprechting, Mathilde
Liebermann von Sonnenberg
Lindau, Otto
Lippe, Kurt
Lob, Franz
Löffelholz, Freiherr von
Lützelburg, Ernst, Freiherr von
Malm, Bruno
Mars, Hans
März, Karl
Matthes, Karl
Matthiessen, Wilhelm
Mayer, Hugo
Mayer, Otto
Merz, Georg
Metz, Georg
Meusel, Arthur
Michaelis, Friedrich

Mikusch, Adelheid, Baronin von
Miller, Therese
Molz, Anni
Moschick, Paul
Moseldick, Paul
Müller, Franz
Müller, Hanns Georg
Müller, Karolina
Nagel, Paul
Nauhaus, Walter
Neumaier, Rosa
Ott, Johann (*Kampfbund*)
Parcus, Leo (alleen van de *Kampfbund*)
Pfeiffer, Karl
Pfister, Georg
Pöhner, Ernst
Polscher, Walter
Pongratz, Wolfgang (*Kampfbund*)
Purpus, Friedrich
Rauch, Max
Reichenbach, Leonhard
Reitzenstein, Freiherr von
Repp, Karl (*Kampfbund*)
Rexhäuser, Valentin
Riedl, Georg
Riedmayer, Johann
Riemann, Hans
Riemann-Bucherer, Gertrud
Ritzler, Konrad

Rohmeder, Wilhelm
Röhrer, Josef
Ruppert, Albin
Sailer, Georg
Sassiger, Georg
Schanze, Max
Scheppeler, Ernst
Scheuermann, Marie
Schlitt, Wilhelm
Schmidt, Hermann
Schmidt, Therese
Schneeberger, Ludwig
Schröder, Franz Josef
Schröder, Karl
Schulthes, Hans
Schwabe, Karl (alleen *Kampfbund*)
Schwaiger, Paula
Sedlmeier (*Kampfbund*)
Seeger, Georg
Seidlitz, Friedrich Wilhelm, Freiherr von (*Kampfbund*)
Seilnacht, Genofeva
Sesselmann, Max
Singer, Karl
Sommer. Luise
Söttl, Franz
Spießhofer, Albert
Stecher, Karl (alleen *Kampfbund*)
Steinle, Franz
Stoiber, Michael
Straub, Marie
Thurn und Taxis, Gustav Franz Maria, Prinz von
Ulsamer, Hubert
Utsch, Friedrich
Vopelius, Alwine
Vopelius, Ludwig
Walter, Ludwig
Waydelin, Paul
Weber, Ludwig
Welz, Eduard von
Welz, Laura von
Weinberg, Karl
Weinrich, Karl
Weinrich, Käthe
Westarp, Heila Gräfin von
Westermann, Hermann
Westerndorf, Anna
Westphal, Hans
Widmann
Weidemann (*Kampfbund*)
Wieser, Fritz
Wilde, Richard
Wittgenberg, Else, Freiin von
Wittgenberg, Wilhelm, Freiherr von
Wittmann, Kurt
Witzgall, Karl (*Kampfbund*)
Wolf, Johann
Woerner, Anton (alleen *Kampfbund*)
Wutschka, Adelgunde
Zahn, Georg

Zarnkl, Heinz
Zember, Bernhard
Zentsch, Walter
Zepperlin, Rudolf von
Zöllner, Betty
Zremer, Gustav

Guest of the Thule Society:

Dingfelder, Johannes
Drexler, Anton
Echart, Dietrich
Hitler, Adolf
Rosenberg, Alfred

Thurn und Taxis, Gustav Franz Maria, Prinz von (1888 - 1919). Member of the Thule Society in 1918. Was murdered as a hostage in the *Luitpold Gymnasium* by red guards on 30 April 1919.

Timm, Johannes (1866 - 1945), tailor, trade unionist and left-wing politician. Member of the *Sozialdemokratische Partei Deutschlands* (SPD). Member of the Bavarian Landdag from 1905 - 1933 and Minister of Justice in Kurt Eisner's cabinet from November 1918 to February 1919 (see there).

Toller, Ernst (1893 Samotschin, Poland - 1939 New York), writer and left-wing politician. Initially studied law in Grenoble. Signed up as a volunteer when World War I broke out, but returned from the front heavily wounded in 1916. Studies literature and political science in Heidelberg and Munich. There he gets to know

Thomas Mann, Rainer Maria Rilke and Kurt Eisner (see there). Becomes a member of the *Unabhängige Sozialdemokratische Partei Deutschlands* (USDP) and became temporary chairman of that party in 1919. During the Munich revolution, commander of the Red Army. After the defeat of the Raden Republic (see there), he is arrested and imprisoned from 1920 -1924. Writes several plays and publishes a collection of poems. Settles in Berlin after his release. After Hitler's rise to power, he defected to Switzerland. In 1933, his books, partly published by Querido in Amsterdam, are burned. In 1934, he went to England. On a tour of the US in 1939, he committed suicide. Well-known works include: *Hinkemann, Hoppla, wir leben!, Eine Jugend in Deutschland.*

Transrhenania, Student fraternity in Munich, whose members were mainly from Rheinland-Pflaz.

Unterleitner, Hans (1890 - 1971), banker, politician. Was married to a daughter of Kurt Eisner (see there) and was appointed minister of social affairs in his cabinet (1918/19). After Eisner's assassination, Unterleitner became a deputy in the Reichstag, initially for the *Unabhängige Sozialdemokratsiche Partei Deutschlands* (USPD), later for the *Sozialdemokratische Partei Deutschlands* (SPD). In 1933, he was arrested and taken to concentration camp Dacau, from which he managed to escape in 1936. Via Switzerland, he ended up in the US in 1939, where he died in 1971.

Utsch, Friedrich, captain b.d.

Utzendorfer, Left-wing politician and member of the College of Eleven, which formed the *Zentralrat* in the Bavarian Raden Republic from February to March 1919.

Trade unions, Organisations representing the interests of workers. In Germany in 1918, in addition to a number of small, four large trade unions (*Gewerkschaften*) existed, namely: *Freie Gewerkschaft* (Marxist) with about 4.75 million members, *Christliche Gewerkschaft* with about 1 million le- den, *Hirsch-Dunckersche Gewerkschaft* with about 0.6 million members, *Kommunistische- syndikalistische rote Gewerkschaft* with about 75,000 members.

Verständigungsfriede, As the submarine war of 1 February 1917 against England had failed, Matthias Erzberger (see there) made a proposal on 6 June 1917 to to reach peace by means of a settlement, which proposal was rejected in Great-German (and thus right-wing) circles, which hoped to annex large areas after the end of the war.

Vier Jahreszeiten, Hotel *Vier Jahreszeiten* in Munich's Maximilianstraße was opened in 1858. The hotel was already during World War I the centre of national socialist agitation of the *Alldeutscher Verband (*see there). Later, the leaders of the SS often joined here. Since 2007, the hotel has belonged to the Kempinski Group.

Flemings, Sebottendorff says the following about Flemings: 'Germanic Belgians, tribal kin to the Dutch. It is strange that the Dutch and the Flemish do not want to know anything about their Germanic ancestry.

They believe they are descended from the Batavians. Both Flemish and Dutch call Germans 'moffen'. This swear word comes from Blücher's Hussars, who wore Krauts. These Hussars retaliated because of Schill's death, which involved Dutch helpers in Stralsund and that is the reason for the hatred. The Flemish, together with the Walloons, separated from Holland in 1930 and formed the kingdom of Belgium.' (Gebhard Leberecht von Blücher (1742 - 1819) was a Prussian general who fought against Napoleon, among others - transl.)

Völkisch, Called a romanticised attitude to life, based on unconditional patriotism, blood relations, love for people and ancestors and his or her native soil. It also implies a life as nature intended, according to the rhythm of the seasons, a return to the ideal man, as the first man Adam was imagined before the Fall. This man was thought of exclusively as a white northerner, the Aryan, as elaborated in Guide von List's ariosofie (see there). In addition, the *Völkisch* movement, which emerged in Germany around 1890, had a great penchant for esotericism and mysticism. Later, racist elements came into play as well, and still a little later political ones, as part of the national-socialist ideology.

Vollnhals, Became chief of police in Munich after the fall of the Raden Republic (see there). Successor to communist chief of police Mairgünther.

Vorwärts, Organ of the *Sozialdemokratische Partei Deutschlands* (SPD). First appeared in 1876. Banned in

Germany in 1933 after Hitler's rise to power. First reappeared in Germany in 1948.

Wagnerbräu, Well-known hotel and brewery in Munich.

Walloons, Roman Belgians.

Walterspiel, Brothers. Owners of hotel *Vier Jahreszeiten* (see there). The Thule Society (see there) had rented the sports club in the hotel for the purpose of its meetings. The Walterspiel brothers were very supportive of the Thule Society.

Walvater, see at Wodan.

We, The trinity Odin (aka Wodan - see there), Willi, We arose from the first thing created. The trinity then created the world and the first people, Odin gave the spirit, the animating life force, Willi the mind and will, We the feeling.

Weber, Ludwig. Administrator of the Thule Society (see there).

Westarp, Heila countess von (1886 - 1919). Secretary of the Thule Society (see there). Was murdered as a hostage in the *Luitpold Gymnasium* by red guards on 30 April 1919.

Widl, Josef. Was sentenced to death for involvement in the murder of the hostages in the *Luitpold Gymnasium* on 30 April 1919.

Wiedemann, Lieutenant and member of the *Kampfbund* of Thule. Killed at Haar in 1919 as a member of the *Freikorps Chiemgau*.

Wieser, Fritz. Editor of the *Beobachter*.

Wilser, Ludwig (1850 - 1923), physician, anthropologist, race expert, member of the Alldeutscher Verband (see there). Performed skull measurements from 1886 to 1894 and studied the origins of peoples and races, especially the Germanic people. He published books and wrote in various magazines. According to Wilser, the Germanic people, originating from Scandinavia, were the strongest race and consequently called upon to rule the world. Criticism of this was drowned out by approval from *völkisch* circles. Wilser had a great influence on the ideology of the later National Socialists. A popular work of his is a.o. *Das Hakenkreuz nach Ursprung, Vorkommen und Bedeutung*.

Wittelsbach, Old Bavarian royal family dating back to the 10th century. The last king was Ludwig III (1913 - 1918), who had to flee abroad when revolution broke out in Bavaria in 1918 and Kurt Eisner (see there) proclaimed the *Freistate of Bayern*.

Wittgenberg, Wilhelm, Freiherr von. Sebottendorff must have been mistaken here. The author of the *Semi-Gotha*, the *Semi-Alliancen* and of the *Semi-Kürschner*, published by Philipp Stauff, was the radical anti-Semite Wilhelm Pickl von Witkenberg (1866 – 1922, suicide). Whether there existed another Wilhelm Freiherr von Wittgenberg besides him, who was a member of the Thule Society, or whether he was the same, cannot be determined.

Witzgall, Karl. Student and soldier in the First World War. Member of the Thule Society and the *Kampfbund*. Was killed in a car accident after 1920.

Wodan, (also: Odin, Walvater). Supreme god of the German gods in Germanic mythology.

Wolffbüro, Full name: *Wolffs Telegraphisches Bureau* (WTB). Press agency founded by Bernhard Wolff in Berlin in 1849. Nationalised by the Nazis in 1934.

Literature

Bärsch, C-E., *Die politische Religion des Nationalsozialismus. Die religiösen Dimensionen der NS- Ideologie in den Schrif- ten von Dietrich Eckart, Joseph Goebbels, Alfred Rosenberg und Adolf Hitler.* (Munich 2002)

Barth, C., *Über alles in der Welt-Esoterik und Leitkultur. Eine Einführung in die Kritik irrationaler Welterklärungen.* (Aschaffenburg 2006)

Blavatsky, H.P., *De sleutel tot theosophie.* (Den Haag)

Ben-Itto, H., *De protocollen van de wijzen van Sion. Anatomie van een vervalsing.* (Soesterberg 2000)

Bräuninger, W., *Hitlers Kontrahenten in der NSDAP 1921- 1945.* (Munich 2004)

Breuer, S., *Aesthetischer Fundamentalismus. Stefan George und der Deutsche Antimodernismus.* (Darmstadt 1995)

Daim, W., *Der Mann der Hitler die Ideen gab. Jörg Lanz von Liebenfels.* (Wien 1994)

Ein Kampf für Freiheit und Frieden. Ludendorff's Tannenberg bund 1925-1933. (Pähl 1997)

Flood, C.B., *Hitler, The Path to Power.* (Boston 1989)

Fritsch, Th., *Handbuch der Judenfrage.* (Leipzig 1933)

Fritsch, Th., *Der falsche Gott: Ursprung und Wesen des Judentums.* (Leipzig 1922)

Gilst, A. van, R. *Walther Darré. Minister and ideologue.* (Soesterberg 2013)

Goodrick-Clarke, N., *The Occult Roots of Nazism. Secret*

Aryan Cults and their Influence on Nazi Ideology. (London 1992)

Hägele, U./König, G.M., *Völkische Posen, volkskundliche Dokumente. Hans Retzlaffs Fotografien 1930 bis 1945.* (Marburg 1999)

Harskamp, J., *Kapitalisme en romantiek. Noord-zuid in de 19de eeuw.*

Heller, F.P./Maegerle, A., *Thule. Vom völkischen Okkultismus bis zur Neuen Rechten.* (Stuttgart 1995)

Hemleben, J., *Rudolf Steiner in Selbstzeugnissen und Bilddokumenten.* (Reinbek bei Hamburg 1963)

Herman, A., *Propheten des Niedergangs. Der Endzeitmythos im westlichen Denken.* (Berlin 1998)

Hieronimus, E. (hg.), *Lanz von Liebenfels. Eine Bibliographie. Topppenstedter Reihe 11.* (Toppenstedt 1991)

Irmer, T., *Das 'erste antisemitische Denkmal Deutschlands'. - Zur Geschichte eines Denkmals für Theodor Fritsch im kommunalen öffentlichen Raum Berlins 1935-1945. In: Gideon Botsch/Christoph Kopke, Lars Rensmann, Julius H. Schoeps (hg.), Politik des Hasses, Antisemitismus und ra- dikale Rechte in Europa.* Haskala, wissenschaftliche Abhandlungen Band 44. (Hildesheim, Zurich, New York 2010)

Jäckel, E., *Hitler's Weltanschauung.* (Stuttgart 1981) Ketelsen, U-K., *Völkisch-nationale und nationalsozialistische Literatur in Deutschland 1890-1945.* Sammlung Metzler band 142 (Stuttgart 1976).

Khersaw, I., *Hitler.* (London 2001)

Kinross, Lord, *Atatürk. The Rebirth of a Nation.* (London 1964)

Koch-Hillebrecht, M., *Hitler. Ein Sohn des Krieges. Fronterlebnis und Weltbild.* (Munich 2003)

Kopp, H., *Geschichte der Ludendorff Bewegung. Erster band 1925-1939* (1975)

Labrie, A., *Zuiverheid en decadentie. Over de grenzen van de burgerlijke cultuur in West-Europa.* (Amsterdam 2001)

Langer, W.C., *The Mind of Adolf Hitler. The Secret Wartime Report.* (New York/London 1972)

Locher, *Astrological Calendar.*

Luhrssen, D., *Hammer of the Gods. The Thule Soceity and the Birth of Nazism.* (Dulles 2012)

Mosse, G.L., *The Crisis of German Ideology. Intellectual Origins of the Third Reich.* (New York 1964)

Mund, R.J., *Jörg Lanz von Liebenfels und der Neue Templer Orden. Die Esoterik des Christentums.* (Stuttgart 1976) Münkler, H., *Die Deutschen und ihre Mythen* (Reinbek bei Hamburg 2009)

Opitz, R., *Faschismus und Neofaschismus.* (Bonn 1996)

Pierik, Perry., D*e geopolitiek van het Derde Rijk. De geestelijke wortels van de veroveringsveldtocht naar het oosten.* (Soesterberg 2012)

Poliakov, L., *De arische mythe. Over de bronnen van het racisme en de verschillende vormen van het nationalisme.* (Amsterdam 1971)

Prinz, M./ Zitelmann, R., (hg.), *National-Sozialismus und Modernisierung.* (Darmstadt 1991)

Rose, D., *Die Thule-Gesellschaft. Legende, Mythos, Wirklich- keit.* (Tübingen 2000)

Rupp, H., *Bevor Hitler kam. Rudolf von Sebottendorff und die Münchener Geheimgesellschaft 'Thule' zwischen 1919 und 1920.* Seminararbeit Universität Trier 1988.

Schild, H.W./Gregory, A., *Der Nordland Verlag. Eine Bibliographie. Toppenstedter Reihe 12.* (Toppenstedt 2005)

Schöfer, I., *Het nationaal-socialistische beeld van de geschiedenis der Nederlanden. Een historiograsche en bibliografische studie.* (Arnhem/Amsterdam)

Schreiber, G., *Hitler Interpretationen 1923-1983.* (Darmstadt 1984)

Steiner, R., *Theosophie. Einführung in übersinnliche Welterkenntnis und Menschenbestimmung.* (Stuttgart 1962)

Surén, H., *Mensch und Sonne. Aryan-Olympian Geist.* (Berlin 1936)

Taylor, C., *De malaise van de moderniteit.* (Kampen 1998)

Term, Jac. P. van, *Het ontstaan, streven en einddoel der vrijmetselarij.* (Hilversum 1928)

Viereck, P., Metapolitics. *The Roots of the Nazi Mind.* (New York 1961)

Vries, D. de, *Der Feldherr und der Führer. Het leven van Erich Ludendorff en zijn relatie met Adolf Hitler.* In: Perry Pierik/ Bert van Nieuwenhuizen (red.), *Elfde Bulletin Tweede Wereldoorlog.* (Soesterberg 2012)

Wichtl, Fr., *Weltfreimaurerei, Weltrevolution, Weltrepublik.* (Munich 1923)